# HED[illegible]'S CELTIC ADVENTURE



**by VALERIE WALKER**

**Illustrations by SUSAN WALDIE**

To Justen
Happy Adventuring
Valerie Walker

This book is dedicated to my grandchildren
Marissa, David, Landon, Zoe and Andrew

---

Special thanks to Gerry and Pat

Published by Valerie Walker-Booktime
PO Box 63083,
2604, Kensington Rd. N.W.
Calgary, AB, Canada, T2N 4S5

www.hedleythehedgehog.com



ISBN No. 0-9699587-2-2

**Canadian Cataloguing in Publication Data**

Walker, Valerie 1937-
Hedley's Celtic Adventure

ISBN 0-9699587-2-2

1.Hedgehogs – Juvenile fiction. I. Waldie, Susan (Gale), 1950- II. Kozak, Pat. III Title

PS8595.A5598H4 2001 jC813'.54 C00-911054-2
PZ7.WI538He 2001

First Printing 2001
Graphic Layout: Gerry Place / Printing: Friesen Printers

Printed and Bound in Canada

# CHAPTER ONE
# HEDLEY FINDS A TREASURE

Hedley the hedgehog and Marvin mouse were happy living on the farm in Somerset. They often talked of their long journey from their old home in Wales and the many adventures they had on the way.

"The blossoms were just coming out on the hawthorn hedge when we arrived," said Hedley. "Do you remember how concerned I was when Billy goat started eating the leaves? I thought I was going to lose my lovely new home."

"It does seem a long time ago, Hedley. I'm so glad I smuggled myself onto the cart. It was really rather brave of me."

Hedley nodded. "Adventuring is more fun with a friend. We did have some exciting times didn't we?

Getting lost, being found, escaping from a poacher and meeting the old hedgehog and the big grey rabbit."

"Hedley, do you think we shall have more adventures here in Somerset?"

"I certainly hope so, as long as they don't include poachers. Since we arrived, Marvin, I'm spending less time sleeping and more time exploring!  I now take lots of hog naps to keep up my strength! I think I'll wander over to the vegetable garden, my tummy is making grumbly noises, it's time for a snack."

"I'll join you," piped up Marvin. "I haven't looked in the compost for a few days. I might find something extra tasty."

The two friends left the hawthorn hedge and walked towards the carrot patch where Grandfather was busy weeding. It was this kindly old man and his ten-year-old grandson, James, who had brought Hedley and Marvin to Somerset.

"There you are, Hedley," said the old man. "I was just telling James and Robert that thanks to your wonderful appetite, there are very few slugs in the lettuce."

Hedley bristled with pleasure and proudly made his way down the rows of vegetables like a sentry on his rounds. He peeped under the leaves and hummed his favourite song. "Wibberly, wobberly, slickery sloo, slugs and worms, I'm looking for you."

"Yuck!" said Marvin. "You're spoiling my appetite. I prefer something that doesn't wriggle — like cheese, but I'll settle for whatever I can find in the compost." The little mouse scurried off, leaving his friend happily humming among the lettuce leaves.

Hedley moved to the brussels sprouts and sniffed among the leaves. While digging for earthworms, he saw something shiny poking out of the earth. "Mmm, that looks interesting. I wonder if it tastes good." He approached it cautiously, his little nose sniffing the newly turned earth.

"Doesn't smell tasty." He licked it. "Doesn't taste tasty." He tried biting it. "Ouch, that hurt. Well, it's no good for eating, but there may be something under it." He dug all around the strange object but found nothing. The 'thing' was round with a hole in the middle. Hedley pushed his nose into the hole for a good sniff.

He was so absorbed with his find, he didn't notice Marvin creep up beside him. "What have you found, Hedley? Doesn't look like your usual creepy crawly!"

Startled, Hedley jumped and stuck out his prickles. He saw the little mouse and began to answer but the words didn't come out right. "On't eep up o me," was all he could manage. Marvin stared in surprise.

"Why, Hedley, what's that on your nose? What did you say? I can't understand you. Would you mind repeating that please?"

"Nnnn, eee, ant," mumbled Hedley, running in circles around his astonished friend.

"Is this a new game? May I play?" asked Marvin, his voice squeaking with excitement. "Oh, I know, it's follow the leader. Hey, Hedley, where are you going? Wait for me."

Hedley had darted towards Grandfather, who was working his way along the cabbages. The old man looked up in surprise, then bent creakily to his knees.

"Well now, what have we here? Slow down little feller, let's see what you've found."

Hedley was very glad to see Grandfather and stood quite still while the old man gently eased the 'thing' off his nose.

While Hedley was licking his sore nose, Grandfather turned the shiny object in his gnarled, old hands.

"Well I'll be . . . Do you know what you've found here, Hedley? It's a ring. Looks like it's bronze. It has a design around it and there's an inscription inside. Hmm . . . can't read it with these glasses," he said while straightening up. “I’ll take it in to Jane. Thank you, Hedley. You’ve found a missing treasure.” He nodded absently to Hedley and murmuring to himself, went back to the house.

“Missing treasure! Did you hear that, Hedley?” squeaked Marvin, scampering up from behind a clump of earth. “You found the missing treasure, how clever you are. How did you do it? Did you know it was there? What’s treasure, Hedley?”

“It’s something to do with humans I expect. Though what good it is if you can’t eat it, I’m sure I don’t know. Come on, let’s go and ask Billy goat. He might know what treasure is.”

They found Billy in the pasture talking to Nanny and the kids. “Hello Hedley, Marvin, how nice to see you. I was just telling Nanny that the kids need to see a little more of the world. I thought I’d take them to the far pasture today. Would you like to join us? By the way, what happened to your nose? It looks a little swollen.”

“Yes, it is tender, that’s what I wanted to talk to you about, Billy.”

"You want to talk to me about your nose? Well, I don't think I can help you there, maybe . . ."

"No, no," interrupted Hedley, "not my nose — about how it got like this."

"Oh, did you have an accident? I hope the kids didn't kick you. They're rather careless the way they kick out their hooves."

"No, it wasn't the kids, Billy, and it wasn't really an accident. Well, I suppose it was in a way. I was sniffing around in the vegetable garden when I found a ring. Or, I suppose you could say, it found me."

"Found you?" asked Billy in surprise. "How could a ring find you? Just what sort of ring was it?"

"The old Grandfather said It was a bronze ring," said Hedley a trifle crossly. "And it got stuck on my nose."

"And he couldn't talk properly," added Marvin. "He just mumbled and looked so funny," said the mouse with a titter.

"Yes, well, the point is, Billy, Grandfather seemed very excited and said I had found a treasure. I don't know what a treasure is, and Marvin doesn't know what a treasure is, so we came to ask you!"

"Well, you came to the right place," said Billy. "I've found lots of treasures in my time. Why, I must have found hundreds of shiny bottle caps, not to mention all the lovely tin cans. They make a satisfying scrunching sound when I bite on them and . . . "

"Not that kind of treasure, Billy, I mean special treasure. Grandfather took it to Aunt Jane."

"Ah well, why didn't you say so. Humans do seem to lose things. I once found something round and shiny by the back door. I couldn't eat it, nearly broke a tooth! The young human came along and took it from me. He called it his 'pocket money'. He was so pleased, he gave me the rest of his ham sandwich."

"Well, what I found had a hole in it and Grandfather said it had something written on it."

“Yes,” added Marvin, “he said it was a ‘prescription’ or a ‘conscription’ or something like that.”

“I think the word was ‘inscription’, Marvin,” said Hedley. “Do you know what that is, Billy?”

“Can’t say I do,” said Billy thoughtfully. “But, I do remember Aunt Jane wearing a shiny thing on her finger. It was the time she was scolding me for eating the red socks off the clothes line. Quite cross she was too. Maybe it’s her treasure and she lost it in the vegetable patch.”

“Yes, I expect that’s what happened,” sighed Hedley.“Thank you, Billy, you’ve been a big help.”

“Your welcome, I’m sure, Hedley. Now, would you like to come to the far pasture with me and the kids?”

“Maybe tomorrow, Billy. I think I’ll just go back to the vegetable garden and have another look around.”

“I’ll come with you,” squeaked Marvin. “We might find more missing treasure.”

# CHAPTER TWO
# A TRIP TO THE FAR PASTURE

Hedley and Marvin hurried back to the vegetable garden. “I have a feeling this is our lucky day,” said Hedley. “Why don’t you look beside the gravel path, Marvin. I’ll go back to where I found the ring and dig deeper. Hmm, don’t smell anything here, maybe I’ll try farther along. No, nothing here either.” He moved on to the next row humming his little song, but the words didn’t seem quite right so he made up some more.

“Spickerly, sparkerly, chinkerly choo, missing treasure I’m looking for you.”

He was pleased with the new words and repeated them over to himself as he sniffed his way along the neat rows of vegetables.

A little robin was following Hedley, pecking at insects the little hedgehog had turned up. "I don't think Grandfather will be very happy with the mess you're making, Hedley, but I'm happy with the snacks I'm finding. Are you looking for something in particular?

"Treasure!" said Hedley. "Missing treasure. I have found a bronze ring already, I thought I might find something else."

"Jackdaw likes treasures," cheeped the robin. "He found something the other day, quite close to here."

"Oh," said Hedley, "what did he do with it?"

"He took it to the hollow tree. He has quite a collection. He's always bragging about them. Well, thanks for the treats, must be off."

"Please wait a minute, Robin. Can you tell me where to find this hollow tree?"

"It's in the far pasture," said the little red-breasted bird. "Beside the crooked stile, you can't miss it. Goodbye for now."

"The far pasture, that's where Billy is taking the kids. Maybe if I hurry, I can catch up to him."

Hedley shook himself, licked his nose and set off. "Come on, Marvin, Robin just told me where we might find more treasure."

"Oh good, another adventure. Where are we going now, Hedley?"

"We're off to the far pasture. We must hurry and catch up with Billy."

The two friends were quite out of breath when they finally found Billy and the kids and told them the exciting news.

"Ha, he's up to his old tricks again," said Billy. "He took one of Aunt Jane's silver coffee spoons and her silver thimble. Fortunately, Robert saw him fly off and followed him. Found them in a nest in the oak tree. Aunt Jane was so pleased to have them back, she gave Robert more 'pocket money'."

"Is the oak tree hollow?" asked Hedley.

"Yes indeed. It's right beside the stile."

"That's right!" said Hedley. "That's where Robin said it was. Can we go and look for the treasure?"

"We can," said Billy, "as long as the kids come too. I must keep an eye on them or they'll be up to some mischief or other. Come along then, this way."

"Where are we going, Uncle Billy?" asked the first kid.

"Are we there yet, Uncle Billy?" asked the second kid.

"We're going to find hidden treasure, Kid Number One and no, we're not there yet, Kid Number Two. Look, there's the stile. You run along, we'll catch up."

Hedley and Marvin ran ahead. "What's a stile, Hedley?" asked Marvin.

"It's sort of steps in the fence that humans climb over," answered Hedley.

"Well, we don't need to climb over it, we can squeeze under the fence."

"Yes, we can, Marvin, but Billy and the kids are too big. They'll have to stay on this side of the fence."

Billy joined the others at the fence. "That's the tree on the other side of the stile. If I remember rightly, Robert used to hide in it when it was bedtime."

"What a good hiding place," said Hedley.

"Come on, Hedley, what are we waiting for? Let's go!" squeaked Marvin. "Er, maybe you should go first."

Hedley squeezed under the fence, closely followed by Marvin. Billy and the kids watched enviously from the other side.

"Why can't we go, Uncle Billy? I bet I can climb that silly old fence," said Kid Number One, reaching up with his front hooves.

"Me too, I can do it, watch me, Uncle Billy." said Kid Number Two, scrambling after his brother.

"Ouch!" cried Kid Number One, as he tumbled backwards.

"Watch out!" cried Kid Number Two, as his brother fell on top of him.

While Billy was busy with the kids, Hedley and Marvin were creeping cautiously into the hollow tree.

"Hmm," said Hedley, sniffing among the sawdust.

"Hmm," he said again, sniffing among the leaves.

"What is it, Hedley? What do you smell? Is it safe?" asked Marvin timidly.

"Squirrels," said Hedley. "And birds."

"What kind of birds, Hedley? I hope there are no owls in this tree," said Marvin, twitching nervously.

"Owls are my enemies too. No, I don't think it smells like owls, probably it's the scent of Jackdaw that I'm picking up."

"Phew, that's a relief," sighed Marvin. "What do we do now, Hedley?"

"Dig."

"Dig? I'm not very good at digging. I'm better at climbing. Would you like me to climb up inside and look around, Hedley?"

"Good idea, Marvin. There may be little holes inside the bark, or an old nest. Keep your eyes open and call me if you see anything shiny."

Hedley went back to his search among the leaves and Marvin scampered up the inside of  the tree.

# CHAPTER THREE
# GRANDFATHER SOLVES A PUZZLE

Meanwhile, Grandfather had returned to the old farmhouse. "Jane, come and see what Hedley found in the garden," he called as he walked in the door. Aunt Jane, who was washing dishes, dried her hands on the kitchen towel.

"Don't tell me, let me guess. A big fat worm, an enormous slug or a giant earwig!" she laughed.

"Much better than that, Jane my dear. Look, he found a bronze ring. It has an inscription inside, but I can't make it out. Your eyes are younger than mine, can you see what it is?"

“A ring! Well bless my soul. Let me take a look. Hmm. It’s very faded, I’ll get the magnifying glass.”

Just then, James and his cousin Robert came into the kitchen and dumped their school books on the table. “Hello, what are you are looking at?” asked James, pushing back his tousled, blond hair.

“It’s an old bronze ring. It has an interesting design, probably Celtic. It has writing on the inside but It’s so faded I can’t make it out. Maybe you boys can.

“Where did you find it?” asked Robert, who looked like a brown-haired version of his cousin.

“Hedley found it in the vegetable garden,” said Grandfather. “I think that little fellow is part bloodhound, he’s always wandering around with his nose to the ground.”

“Good old Hedley,’ laughed James. He’s found some pirate’s treasure. Maybe there are pieces of eight and precious gems in the garden, too!”

Robert was peering closely at the ring. "James, look at this design, it looks like a picture in our history book."

The boys rummaged through their books until they found the one they were looking for. "Here it is," said James. "Celtic history." He hurriedly flipped through the pages. "There, on page five, it looks almost the same. See Grandfather?"

Grandfather put the ring on the page beside the drawing. "Yes indeed, the design is almost the same. Read what it says, James."

James cleared his throat. "It says it's an ancient Celtic design worn mainly by Druid healers and workers of magic!" His eyes widened with glee. "Magicians, wizards. Gosh, this is exciting, Robert. Let's go and see if Hedley has found anything else."

The boys ran to the vegetable garden, but there was no sign of Hedley. "Look you can see where he's been digging. Get the garden fork, Robert, I'll get the spade. Maybe we can turn up more treasure."

"Here's something," called Robert excitedly. He stooped down and picked up a brass button. "Hardly a treasure, it's off my school blazer. I expect Mum will be happy I've found it though. Are you having any luck, James?"

"No. Just a minute, I think I see something." James picked up a key. "Look, Robert, It's too small for a door key, it's more likely to fit a case or a china cabinet"

"Let me see, it might be from the desk drawer, Dad said he couldn't find it the other day. Could be, old Jackdaw took it. He's always hopping in the window and stealing things. Of course, why didn't I think of it before? We found a missing spoon in Jackdaw's nest. Come on, James, let's go over to the far pasture, that's where his nest is."

Meanwhile, Hedley and Marvin were busy at work. Marvin was searching the walls of the hollow tree while Hedley was snuffling around the roots.

"Ouch!" mumbled Hedley. "This is dangerous work. That's the second time I've bruised my nose. Hmm. There's a different smell just here. Let's see, yes, quite different, maybe if I scratch a little deeper — yes, there is something hard. Marvin, can you hear me? I need your help."

"I'm up here, Hedley. Have you found something? I'm coming down." Marvin scampered down the tree to join his friend. "What is it, Hedley, more treasure?" asked Marvin breathlessly.

"I don't know yet. Can you help me dig a hole, Marvin?"

"I'll do my best, " replied Marvin, "but remember, I have very small paws."

While they were busy digging, Billy bleated a warning to let them know James and Robert were on their way.

"Look, Robert, there's Billy and the kids standing by the stile. Hello, old Billy, what are you doing over here? Don't tell me you've caught Hedley's exploring bug!"

James gave Billy a pat then followed Robert to the stile.

"There's the old hollow tree I used to hide in, James. Let's go and have a look." They hopped over the stile and ran to the tree.

"Well look who's here," said Robert. "It's our favourite hedgehog. What are you up to now, Hedley?"

"Grandfather was right, Hedley. I think you are part bloodhound. Have you found something? By golly! Look, Robert, he has scratched away the earth. There may be something there. Give me a hand."

Hedley decided to get out of their way and search for Marvin, who on hearing the boys coming, had disappeared.

"Marvin, where are you?" called Hedley.

"Here I am, Hedley, is the coast clear? what's happening?"

"James and Robert are digging in the same spot we

were Marvin, do you want to come and see?"

"No thanks, I'll just wait among the tree roots. You can tell me what's happening."

Hedley heard a triumphant shout from the boys and ran over to see what all the fuss was about. "They're so excited, Marvin. They've found something. Now they're lifting it out of the ground."

Hedley was scratching himself in glee. "It looks like a wooden box. They're trying to open the lid but it's locked. Now they are talking about a key they found in the garden. Marvin, it seems we missed something." Hedley was running back and forth. "Oh, look, now they're putting the key into the lock!"

"Let me see, let me see," said Marvin as he scurried up to Hedley. "Does the key fit? Have they opened it yet? What's inside, Hedley?"

"They are brushing the dirt away from the lock, they've put the key in and . . . I can't wait any longer,

I'm going to get a closer look." He ran towards the boys. Marvin, forgetting his fear, followed.

As the boys struggled with the rusty lock, they were startled by a loud shriek. Hedley curled into a ball and Marvin hid in a rabbit hole.

Jackdaw landed on a branch just above the boys. He cawed loudly and puffed out his feathers.

"Look, Robert, old Jackdaw wants to get in on the treasure hunt. No you don't you scoundrel," scolded James. You've stolen too many treasures. Come on Robert, let's go back to the house. Grandfather and the others will be interested in seeing this!"

# CHAPTER FOUR
# JACKDAW ON THE WARPATH

Hedley peeked out from under his bristles. Jackdaw was sitting on a branch muttering to himself. The little hedgehog slowly unrolled and asked Jackdaw why he was so upset.

"They've gone off with my treasure!" screeched Jackdaw.

"Your treasure?" said Hedley in disbelief. "How can it be yours? Did you put it there?"

"No!" replied the bird, "but if it's shiny and bright it's mine!"

"Have you found many bright and shiny things?" asked Hedley innocently.

"Lots," said the wily old bird proudly.

"What do you do with them?"

"I hide the shiniest in my nest. The others I put . . . oh no you don't. You can't trick me into telling you where I hide my treasures. You might steal them from me."

"Why would I want them?" asked Hedley. "If you can't eat them, what good are they?"

"I like to look at them; they're my treasures. I like to see them sparkle in the sun."

"Is that all? You just like looking at them?"

"Of course," said Jackdaw, "they're pretty and they're mine!"

"But they're not yours, Jackdaw," said Hedley. "You have stolen things from Aunt Jane and Uncle Giles. They get very upset when you take their treasures."

"They're not all their treasures," said Jackdaw sulkily.

"What do you mean, not theirs. Who else's treasures have you stolen?"

"I haven't stolen anybody's treasures. I found them in the ground, in an old sack. Finders keepers!"

"Where did you hide them, Jackdaw? Can I see them? I like shiny things too," said Hedley.

"I hid them where you'll never find them," said Jackdaw smugly, "I'm very good at hiding things." The thieving bird flew to the top of the tree, turned his back on Hedley and started preening his feathers.

"I don't want to see your silly old treasures, Jackdaw. I'm going back to the farm. Goodbye." Hedley walked towards the stile. Marvin, who had been watching from his hiding place, followed.

"What do we do now, Hedley? Do you have a plan? What can I do?"

"Yes, Marvin. When we get to the stile, you go ahead and tell Billy to wait for us at the farm. I'm going to double back and watch from the bushes to see what Jackdaw does."

"Don't be long, Hedley, this is so exciting!" squeaked Marvin as he scampered off. Hedley followed a little way, then hid in the bushes and quietly made his way back to the hollow tree. Jackdaw, thinking they had gone, flew down to a lower branch at the back of the tree.

"Aha," muttered Hedley. "Just as I thought, that crafty bird is going to his hiding place." Jackdaw poked his beak into a hole and picked up a stone.

Hedley was straining to see what the stone looked like. "Oh, I wish Marvin were here, his eyes are better than mine."

"Looking for me?" squeaked the little mouse. Hedley jumped six inches off the ground.

"Marvin, stop creeping up on me like that!"

"Sorry if I startled you, Hedley. I thought I would come back and see if you needed me. What can I do?"

"You can tell me what Jackdaw has in his beak. The sun is glinting off something."

Marvin scrambled onto a rock to get a better view. "It's a big blue stone, very sparkly," he reported. "He's put it on the branch beside him. Now he's reaching for something else. It looks as if he has two more stones. Oops, he dropped one. He hasn't noticed. Now he's picking up the big blue one and he's flying away. Hedley, where's he going?"

"That smart old bird is probably looking for a new hiding place. He's still flying, can you see where he is now, Marvin, I can't see him anymore. Has he landed?"

"No," said Marvin, he's going to the forest. He's getting farther and farther away. Now he's just a dot in the sky."

We'll never find him now. Do you think you can find the stone he dropped?"

"Certainly, Hedley. There's nothing wrong with my eyesight. Come on." Marvin scurried to the bottom of the tree and rooted among the leaves. "Here it is!" he squeaked triumphantly. "I've found it, Hedley!"

"Good work, Marvin. Now I'm going to pick it up in my mouth and take it to Grandfather, so don't talk to me anymore as I don't want to drop it. Let's go."

Marvin marched proudly forward. "This is another fine adventure we're having, Hedley. Won't Grandfather be surprised? I wonder what's in the box? Just think, Hedley, we have found two treasures in one day. I was a big help wasn't I, Hedley? Oops, sorry, don't answer. I wonder if they have opened the box yet? What do you think is in there, Hedley? Never mind, we'll soon find out. We . . . yikes! It's Jackdaw. Hide, Hedley."

Marvin scooted down a hole and Hedley rolled into a tight little ball.

"You've stolen my treasure, where is it you prickly pest?" screeched Jackdaw. "I dropped one and it's not there, I know you have it, give it back to me." He tried poking Hedley with his beak, but he couldn't get past the spines. "Give it back I say!" he screamed, clawing at Hedley. "Ouch, you interfering bundle of bristles, always poking that twitchy little nose of yours into other people's business. Well, I can wait, I'll just sit up here in the tree and watch. The minute you unroll, I'll get it. You'll see!" Jackdaw flew up to a branch and stared at Hedley with beady eyes.

Marvin, horrified, watched from the safety of a hole. "Poor Hedley, he'll have to stay rolled up forever, what am I going to do? I know, I'll follow the rabbit warren to the farm. Maybe I can get Billy to come and scare that rascally Jackdaw away." With that, Marvin darted back down the hole.

# CHAPTER FIVE
# BILLY AND SHEP TO THE RESCUE

Marvin was quite out of breath when he reached the farm and was overjoyed to see Billy grazing close by. He crept forward until he was within a few feet of Billy's shaggy beard.

"Psst, Billy, it's me, Marvin," he squeaked. The goat jerked his head up in surprise and saw the little mouse peering at him from behind a clump of earth.

"Why, hello, Marvin. Where's Hedley? Did you find any other treasure in the hollow tree? James and Robert are very excited. They're in the house now with the other humans. You seem to be quite out of breath, Is something wrong?"

"It's Hedley," panted the little mouse. "He's curled up in a ball and Jackdaw is keeping watch."

"Keeping watch! Whatever for? Why would he want to watch Hedley curled up in a ball?"

"Because Hedley has the stone Jackdaw dropped from his beak," said Marvin.

"Why would Hedley want a stone, there are lots of them all around here," said Billy, shaking his shaggy head.

"Not just an ordinary stone, Billy, a treasure stone," said the little mouse, twitching his whiskers in frustration. "Hedley found a stone from the stolen treasure. We were on our way home when Jackdaw came screeching down on us. Oh, please, Billy, you must come and scare Jackdaw away."

"Why didn't you say so? Unfortunately, I can't get over the fence. Besides, that old bird isn't scared of me. The only thing Jackdaw is scared of is the sheep dog, Shep. Shep likes to chase him. Nearly caught him once. I don't think they like each other very much."

"Shep?" squeaked Marvin in alarm. "I'm scared of him, too, he likes to chase me. I don't think I want to ask him for help."

"I'll ask him," said Billy. "He and I are quite good pals. I'm sure he would be happy to teach old Jackdaw a lesson. Come on, let's find him."

"Er, I don't think I'll come with you, Billy. I'll go back by the rabbit warren and wait there for you."

"Right you are, Marvin. Ah, here comes Shep now, see you later."

Marvin had already disappeared into the rabbit hole. "I must hurry and see how Hedley is and let him know help is on the way," thought Marvin as he scurried along the twisting warren. "I hope he doesn't think I've deserted him." When he finally reached the end of the tunnel, he peeked out and whispered, "Hedley, it's me," then ducked back in as he caught Jackdaw's beady eye on him.

“Squark, another intruder. You meddling mouse, I suppose you’re after my treasure too. Well you can’t have it!” Jackdaw flew down and hopped towards the rabbit hole.

“Yikes!” squeaked Marvin, scurrying back to safety. Hedley, who was in a tight ball beside the rabbit warren, pushed with all his might, and rolled until he was blocking the hole.

“You puffed up pincushion, you think you’re so smart, just wait till I get you uncurled, I’ll . . .”

“Woof, woof.”

“Drat! Here comes that miserable dog. Well, I’ll be back!” Jackdaw screamed as he hastily flew to the safety of the tree.

Shep came bounding up and jumped at the tree, snarling and snapping his jaws. Hedley was too scared to uncurl so just rolled backwards into the rabbit hole. He rolled and rolled and rolled until he bumped into

a tree root. He waited for a moment then poked his nose out and sniffed around.

"Doesn't smell like fox, *sniff, sniff*. Doesn't smell like badger, *sniff, sniff*. Just smells like rabbit."

He slowly uncurled and dropped the stone. Blinking, he looked around and called out,

"Marvin, are you all right?"

"Gosh, Hedley, that was quite a trick. You rolled by me so fast I had to run to catch up with you. Billy was right, Jackdaw is as afraid of Shep as I am."

"I don't think he would harm us. He knows we're Billy's friends. Still, it doesn't hurt to be cautious. Let's get back to James and Robert." Hedley popped the stone back in his mouth and headed to the farm.

"Billy said the boys are very excited. What do you think is in the box, Hedley? Why do humans like treasure, Hedley? Do they like to look at shiny things just as Jackdaw does? What do they do with them,

Hedley. Why . . . oops, sorry, I forgot you can't answer me. That was very clever of you, Hedley, blocking the rabbit hole. Was it hard to roll like that? How did you do it? Oh, I forgot, I won't ask any more questions. Ouch! Why did you stop, Hedley?"

Hedley was sniffing the air. Something was not quite right. "It's not badger," he thought. "It's not fox." Then he saw a large black rabbit blocking his path.

"Halt, who goes there?" demanded the rabbit.

Hedley carefully put down the stone between his front paws. "It's Hedley hedgehog and Marvin mouse," he answered. "We have to get back to the farm with a treasure. Jackdaw is after us and this is the safest route. I hope you don't mind us using your warren."

"Hedley the hedgehog, yes, I've heard about you. My name is Blackie, I am the Leader of this area. My sentries reported a little mouse running back and forth. I see he is with you, Hedley. It is indeed, a pleasure to meet you," said the rabbit, nodding his head.

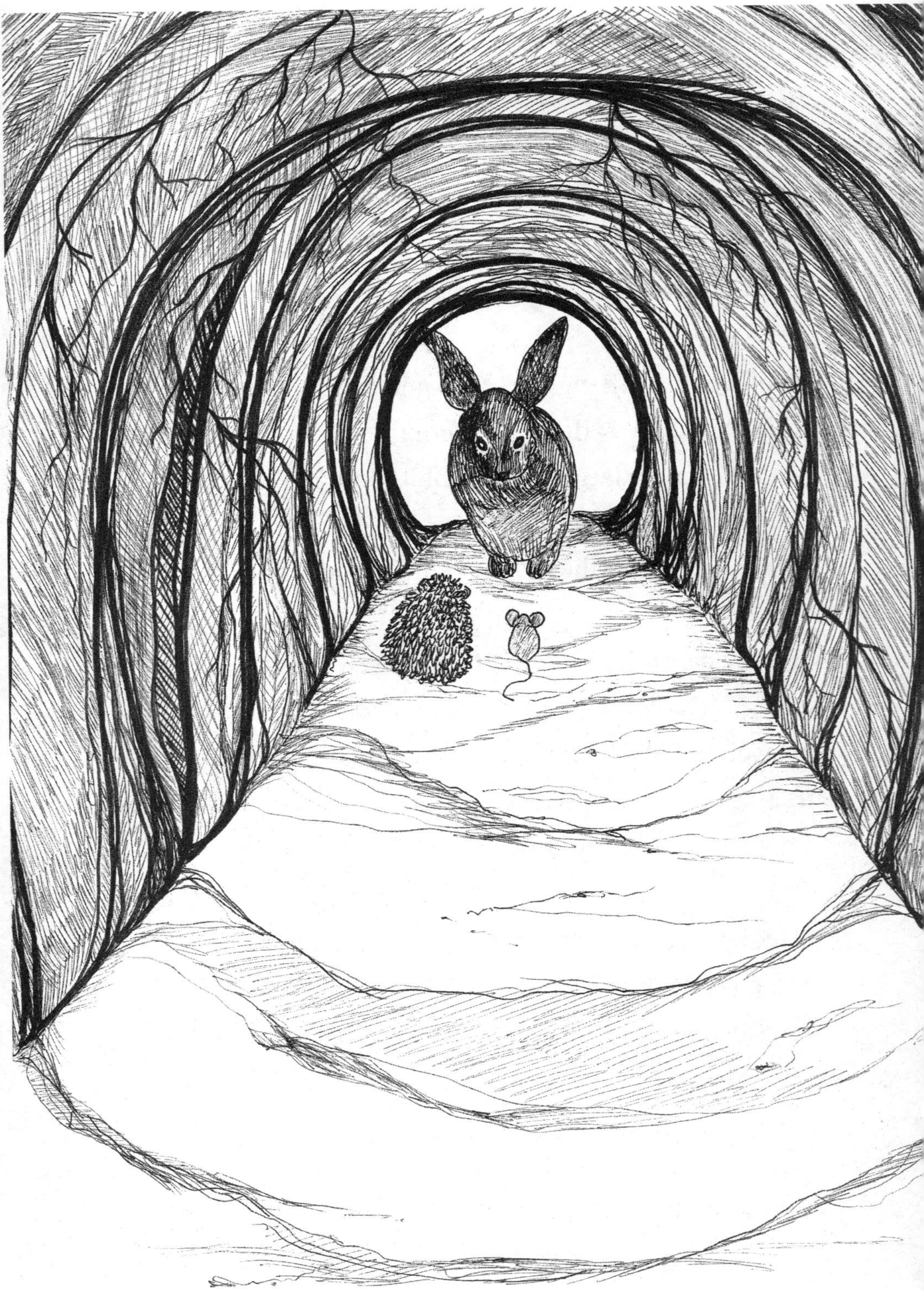

"You know my name," said Hedley in surprise. "It's a pleasure to meet you too, I'm sure, but . . ."

"You are the little hedgehog who saved young Chester from that nasty encounter with the poacher a few moons ago. And if I remember correctly, there was a mouse called Marvin who was also very helpful in the rescue. Would that mouse be you?" he asked, turning to look at Marvin, who was trying very hard to hide behind Hedley.

"You're quite right, Blackie, sir, how did you know about our adventure with Chester?"

"You forget how well we rabbits communicate, Hedley. Remember Conrad? You met him on your journey here. He is my Uncle, on my mother's side. We know all about you and your adventures. On behalf of my family, we welcome you and little Marvin to our home. You are most welcome to use our warren any time you wish. We are delighted you outwitted that old rascal, Jackdaw."

“My goodness, you are up to date on the latest news!” said Hedley. “It’s a pleasure to meet you, too, Blackie. How are Conrad and Chester? I often think of them and the hedgehog Elder.”

“They are quite well. In fact, they asked me to keep an eye out for you and to let you know that things have been terribly dull since you left.”

“Please give them our best regards,” said Hedley.

“I certainly will, but why don’t you do that yourself? The Elder and Conrad will be at our gathering. We meet midsummer’s eve by the big rock in the meadow by the stream. Do you know where that is, Hedley?”

“Yes, I do. Billy took me there when I first arrived. We would be delighted to join you, wouldn’t we, Marvin?”

“Er, yes,” squeaked Marvin, still unsure of this very large rabbit. “Delighted.”

With a nod of his head, Blackie hopped away and was lost in the darkness.

"What do you think of that, Marvin? We have been invited to meet the Somerset family. I didn't know Chester and Conrad were related, did you?"

"No, but rabbits do have very large families, Hedley."

"I'm so glad to hear Chester is safe. Imagine the Elder and Conrad saying they miss us. It will be wonderful to see them again. Well, we mustn't waste any more time. Let's get moving. I'm going to pick up the stone again, so no more chatting until we get back to the farm. All right, Marvin?"

"Understood, Hedley," squeaked Marvin as they set off down the tunnel to the farm — and the treasure.

# CHAPTER SIX
# MYSTERY AND MAGIC

James and Robert were telling Grandfather, Aunt Jane and Uncle Giles how they had found the box.

"We found this key in the garden, said James. "It fits the lock . . . "

"But we can't make it turn," Robert said excitedly.

Grandfather took the box in his large, brown hands and studied it. He then peered at the key. "Judging from the design on the key and the oak box, I would guess they are Celtic. Just like the ring."

"That young hedgehog has quite a remarkable sense of smell," said Uncle Giles. "It seems he has a knack for finding things. I wonder if he can find the key to my desk? It's been missing for weeks."

Grandfather carefully oiled the lock and handed the key to Robert. "Since you and James found this box, perhaps you should open it." The family crowded around the table.

"I'll put the key in, and you can turn it," said Robert . The key slipped in easily. Holding his breath, James reached forward and put his fingers firmly on the key — it turned in the lock with a loud click. They all stared in surprise at the contents.

"It isn't treasure," said James disappointedly. "There are no jewels, or gold, just bunches of old, dried weeds!"

"They're not weeds, James," said Grandfather. "I rather think they're herbs. The Druids, the priests of the Celts, were quite knowledgeable in their use of herbs for medicine."

"And magic!" added Robert.

"Possibly," said Grandfather. "Ordinary folk were a

little scared of the Druids. They knew they were healers and wise men but didn't understand their methods. They thought the Druids healed by magic. You've found a real treasure. The special herbs of the Druid healers is the equivalent of a first aid kit."

"You mean like medicine men in Indian tribes of the Wild West?" asked James.

"Something like that," said the old man thoughtfully. "I don't think we should touch the herbs. This box should be taken to the museum at Glastonbury." The others nodded in agreement. Grandfather closed the lid and locked the box.

"We must put this in a safe place until we can go to the museum and . . ."

The old man's words were drowned out by loud barking and bleating at the back door. Robert rushed to open the door and was almost bowled over by the sheep dog.

"What's the fuss old feller?" asked Robert as he stroked the dog's head.

"Where's Hedley?" James asked with concern. He looked around and was surprised to see Hedley curled in a tight ball beside the step. "Hush, Shep, you are scaring Hedley. Sit!"

Shep sat, his tongue lolling out. Billy, hopping from hoof to hoof, stood next to him. Hedley opened his eyes and looked around. "Hmm that dog has finally stopped barking. Well, I suppose it's safe, James is here." Hedley uncurled, hurried up to James and dropped the stone at his feet.

"What have you found now, Hedley?" James picked up the stone and wiped it on his shirt.

"Look, Hedley has found a piece of old, red glass."

"Let me see, James," said Grandfather. "Hmm. Not glass, James; it looks very much like a ruby. I wonder who it belongs to."

"Gosh, a real ruby!" said James excitedly. "I bet old Jackdaw had it hidden and Hedley found it. When Robert and I dug up the box, Jackdaw made such a fuss, he probably has other things hidden there."

"I think we should all explore that tree," said Uncle Giles. "Jackdaw may have stolen things from the neighbours. I'll get the step ladder, it's time we got to the bottom of this!"

Grandfather agreed. "There's more to this than meets the eye. Jane, dear, please put the box and key in the cupboard under the stairs. Be sure to lock it securely. We have something of great value here."

"What about the ruby, Grandfather?" asked James.

"It's safely buttoned in my waistcoat pocket, James. Maybe we should take Hedley to the tree with us. His sense of smell will be a great help."

"Good idea. Come on, Hedley." To James' surprise, Hedley had already scurried off. Shep bounded after him. "Heel boy," James called. " I don't want you scaring poor Hedley again. Gosh! Look how fast he can move. I didn't know hedgehogs could run like that, did you, Grandfather?"

"They certainly can move if they have to. Look, he's

going down a rabbit hole. Maybe Hedley has a short cut," said Grandfather with a laugh.

"Wait for me, Hedley," squeaked Marvin as he scampered out from under a clump of clover.

"What are we going to do now? What was in the box? Did James like the pretty stone you found?"

"We're going back to the hollow tree, Marvin. I don't know what was in the box, something like weeds I heard James say. Grandfather seems to think it's important, and yes, Marvin, James liked the pretty stone. They're going to see if they can find more of Jackdaw's treasures. Maybe you can help."

"Er, I don't think so, Hedley. I'll just watch from a safe place."

"We're just coming to the end of the tunnel. I'll sniff around to make sure it's safe. You can stay in here if you want." Hedley poked his nose out and took a big sniff. "Oh, oh, Jackdaw is around somewhere, I can smell bird. Can you see him Marvin?"

The quaking mouse crept to the opening and peeked out. “Yes, he’s up in the tree. Oops, I think he’s seen us. Get back in the hole!”

Jackdaw swooped down shrieking, “You two interfering busy bodies again? Where’s my treasure? What have you done with it? I’ll get you for this!” The angry bird hopped up to the rabbit hole and thrust in his beak.

“Yikes, he’s coming after us. Let’s get out of here,” squeaked Marvin as he scampered down the hole. Hedley had already curled into a ball. Jackdaw was so cross he was pushing his head farther and farther into the burrow.

“Come back, you miserable little mouse and you, you, needle nosed, sniffing bundle of spines, come back!”

A loud bark stopped Jackdaw’s scolding. “Drat, that stupid, sheep dog is back,” screamed Jackdaw in alarm. He just made it to the lowest branch of the tree before Shep came nipping at his tail feathers.

“Good old Shep. Here boy, heel,” called Robert. Shep

gave one last jump at the branch, then sat, growling softly, his eyes still on the wily bird.

"Phew, that Jackdaw was getting too close for comfort." said Hedley "Thank goodness Shep scared him off. I'm going out, Marvin. You watch and then follow me. I need you as lookout. My sense of smell is good but my eyesight isn't as good as yours."

"Well, all right, Hedley," said Marvin bravely. "Since you really need me and since this is such an exciting adventure, I'll help you."

Hedley and Marvin crept forward and settled under a bush and watched Uncle Giles put the stepladder against the tree.

"Old Jackdaw doesn't like that one bit. He's flapping around and screeching. Aha, now he's flying away, can you see him, Marvin?"

"Yes, Hedley, he's going in the same direction as before. It's a long way, I don't think I can go that far, it's deep in the forest," said Marvin nervously.

"We'll worry about that later," said Hedley. "Uncle Giles is up the ladder now, tell me what you can see. Has he found anything?"

"Yes, He's taking a large handkerchief from his pocket and is putting something into it — he's tying it up and putting it back in his pocket — Now he's coming back down. Oh, Hedley, this is so exciting."

"I'm going to see what they have found, Marvin. You can stay under the bush if you like. Keep your eyes peeled for Jackdaw. "

Hedley got to the ladder just as Uncle Giles stepped down. "Well lads, old Jackdaw has quite a haul. Look at this." The farmer spread the handkerchief on the ground. They gazed in amazement at the assortment of treasures.

"Gosh, are they jewels?" James gasped.

"Do you think they're pirate's treasure, Dad?" asked Robert.

"I don't know, son," said his dad pulling a dirt-stained bag from his pocket. “But they must have been in this old sack when that crafty bird found them. They’ve been buried for a long time, the sacking is pretty rotten.”

“Well, there’s only one thing to do now,” said Grandfather, struggling stiffly to his feet. “We shall have to take it to police constable Thompson in the village. They may have been stolen, although I rather think that whoever owned them has long departed this earth.” The old man looked thoughtful as he brushed the dirt from his old, patched trousers. “I wonder if they are linked to the box of herbs?”

“You mean they may not be pirate’s treasure after all?” said Robert. I was hoping we might have found some pieces of eight.”

“Ah, lad, anything is possible. Let’s take everything to the police station and then inform the museum. I have a hunch there may be more clues that will lead us to the original owners of these treasures. But for now, we had better put these with the wooden box.”

“You can come out now, Marvin. They’re all going

back to the house. They don't know about Jackdaw's other hiding place. I think it's time we did more investigating. It will soon be time for the Rabbit Gathering by the big rock. We'll tell Blackie and his friends what we've found. I'm sure they'll help us find Jackdaw's new hiding place. Come on, we'll go back by the burrows. That's the safest way to travel while that screeching bird is on the warpath."

# Chapter Seven
# The Meeting of the Clan

Hedley woke from his hog-nap under the hawthorn hedge. He stretched, scratched and shook his bristles. "Marvin, wake up. It's time for us to go the clan meeting," he said, sniffing around the vegetable garden. "Where are you, Marvin? This is no time for games. It's full moon and the air smells exciting."

"Exciting? How can the air smell exciting?" asked Marvin, creeping out from under the parsley.

"Oh, there you are. Well, it's tingly and sharp, I don't know, it's just different. Something is in the wind, I know it. Come along, let's hurry to the big rock and the gathering." Hedley bustled down the path, his spines bristling with expectation.

"Hey, wait for me, Hedley. Slow down," Marvin called as Hedley disappeared down a rabbit hole.

"Just follow me, Blackie will meet us at the end of this tunnel and lead us the rest of the way. Look, there he is just ahead." Hedley stopped so suddenly, Marvin almost ran into him.

"Good evening, Hedley, Marvin," said Blackie. "You are right on time. My sentries tell me you have been very busy discovering human treasure! And what's this about a medicine box?"

Hedley quickly told Blackie about the mysterious box. "Hmm, this all sounds very interesting, Hedley. We'll see what we can do to help. Now we must hurry, the ceremony is about to begin. Follow me please." Blackie hopped out of the warren and into the clear night. He stopped just long enough to make sure Hedley and Marvin were following, then loped ahead through the bushes and trees. An owl hooted overhead and Marvin stopped in his tracks.

"Don't worry, Marvin, on this special night, no harm will come to you from owl or badger. Tonight, we all gather as friends." Marvin, still trembling, followed Hedley and Blackie.

The moon was shining brightly on the big rock, clearly showing the strange markings carved on its face. Forming a semi-circle around the rock was the largest gathering of rabbits Hedley had ever seen. Hedley and Marvin stayed at the edge while Blackie hopped into the circle. He was joined by a large grey rabbit and an elderly hedgehog.

"Look, Marvin,"said Hedley, excitedly. "There's our friend, Conrad?"

"I see him," replied Marvin. "And isn't that the Elder?"

"I do believe it is. Hush they are about to speak." Hedley and Marvin edged closer. Blackie hopped forward, thumped his hind leg for silence, then began his speech.

"Good evening friends and welcome. Tonight, we are gathered to celebrate Midsummer's eve. You all know our honoured guests from Gloucester, The Hedgehog Elder and Conrad, leader of the Gloucester clan. We also have two very special guests who are joining us for the first time. They are Hedley hedgehog and Marvin mouse. Come forward please, Hedley and Marvin."

Marvin was rooted to the spot. "Come on, Marvin, this is no time to lose your nerve. Remember, we're not afraid of anything, especially when we're among friends."

Hedley moved forward and Marvin gathered up all his courage and followed closely behind. A loud thumping noise surrounded them as the clan welcomed the pair.

"Hedley and Marvin have travelled all the way from Wales to make their home here in Somerset," said Blackie. "As you know, they were both very helpful in rescuing the young rabbit, Chester, from a poacher's pot. Now, they need our help." He paused and looked around. "It seems Jackdaw has become a rebel and is greedy for human possessions. Now, we don't usually meddle in human affairs, but the old Grandfather believes these 'treasures' Jackdaw is hiding have something to do with the ancient Druids."

There was a rustling all around the circle at the mention of the ancient Druids. Blackie hopped back as Conrad, his nose twitching wildly, came forward to speak.

"As you all know, *twitch, twitch*, the Druids were able to communicate with animals. The humans of today have forgotten how. The old Grandfather who came with Hedley is a wise and gentle man. He has an understanding of the animals. The Elder, Conrad and I think it is important, *twitch, twitch*, that we help in any way we can."

The rabbits stirred nervously at the mention of humans.

"Hedley and Marvin were very clever in leading the humans to an old Druid medicine box that has been buried for centuries, *twitch, twitch.* The old man knows the importance of this box and may even know who it belonged to."

Again, there was a rustling around the gathering.

"Jackdaw stole some precious jewels, *twitch, twitch,* but moved them when Hedley and Marvin discovered the hiding place. We must help find the missing jewels. Because tonight is midsummer's eve, it is the perfect time for us to search. As you know, *twitch, twitch*, all animals on this special night are sworn to a truce — none of us shall be prey tonight. Jackdaw, however, is an outlaw and will do all he can to stop us from finding the treasure. Go now, and Blackie will give you your instructions."

"Phew, that was exciting, Hedley. You were right about something happening. I didn't know about the Druids, did you, Hedley? Just who are they anyway? Do you think Grandfather knows who owns the treasure?"

A gruff voice interrupted Marvin's stream of questions. "Hello there my young friends, it is indeed a pleasure to meet with you again. You seem to be in the middle of another adventure, Hedley. How do you do it?" The friends turned to see the Elder. The moon came from behind a cloud and lit up the old hedgehog's face.

"Why, Elder, sir, it is a pleasure to see you again, isn't it, Marvin?" The little mouse was trying very hard to keep his tail from trembling.

"Yes, it is," said Marvin, bobbing his head up and down. "A pleasure."

"No need to fear me, young Marvin. As I once heard you say, my bark is worse than my bite! Well, I must say, you have caused quite a stir here tonight, Hedley. What's all this about treasure and just what do you know about the Druids?"

"Er, well, nothing actually, Elder, sir."

"Then, it's time you did. Come on, we can talk while we search. Conrad is leading our team. Off we go."

Hedley and Marvin followed the old hedgehog towards the distant forest. They were joined by Conrad and several other rabbits.

"Good to see you both again," said Conrad warmly, "It seems, *twitch, twitch*, wherever you are, Hedley,

adventure is sure to follow — or should that be — wherever adventure is, Hedley is sure to follow? Hmm, never mind. Now, Marvin, *twitch, twitch*, I believe you were the last one to see Jackdaw. Just tell us which direction he flew and we will be on our way." He nudged the little mouse gently and said kindly, "You had better stay beside me. Hedley and the Elder can bring up the rear. Off we go."

While the little group headed towards the forest, Hedley told the Elder all that had happened since he found the ring.

"So, the humans say it was Celtic," said the Elder. "And the Grandfather thinks it was a medicine box. Hmm, very interesting. You see, Hedley, we are very near the ancient city of Glastonbury. Long, long ago, a very special Druid, a healer and wizard, came to Glastonbury with a young boy. Some say the boy was his pupil, others say he was a prince. The legend goes that they spent some time in these woods."

"But, Elder sir," said Hedley, " how do you know all this?" asked Hedley.

"Ah, that is quite a story, Hedley. My ancestors lived in these parts, as did Conrad's. They passed the story down from generation to generation. Every midsummer's eve, Conrad and I come back here to keep the legend alive. You see, Hedley, we hope that some day, other humans like the Druid wizard will come and speak with us again. Now, enough chattering; let's catch up with the others, it looks as if Conrad has something to say."

# CHAPTER EIGHT
# THE CLAN HATCHES A PLAN

They all gathered around and waited for Conrad to communicate. He appeared to be listening to something. His eyes were closed but his whiskers were twitching wildly. They heard a faint thumping in the distance.

"That's it! *twitch, twitch*. My sentries have spotted a large nest that looks like Jackdaws', *twitch, twitch*. Now we must be very quiet and get a little closer. With a bit of luck, Jackdaw will be sleeping. The squirrels have gone up the tree to investigate. Let's go."

Hedley and the Elder followed closely behind Conrad and Marvin. The little mouse looked very brave and proud of himself. They all stopped at the bottom of a tall oak tree. A little red squirrel came scampering up to Conrad. "Jackdaw is sleeping in the branches. His nest is full of shiny things. Owl is keeping watch," chattered the squirrel.

At the mention of owl, Marvin started trembling.

"Now, now, Marvin, keep your whiskers up," said Conrad reassuringly. "Remember, Owl is our friend tonight."

"Yes, Elder, sir," said Marvin, bravely. I'll try to remember that."

Conrad and Elder had a brief conference, then Conrad gave the orders.

"Marvin, I want you to go up the tree to the first knothole. It's right below the nest and you will have a good view of what is happening. Squirrel-the-red, I want you and your team to start emptying the nest. Just throw everything down, we'll look after the rest. Mole, are you close by?"

"I'm right here, Conrad, sir."

"Have you dug a deep hole beneath the nest?"

"Yes indeed, I covered it with branches in case Jackdaw got suspicious."

"Good work, Mole, now let's pull them away, and as soon as the squirrels throw the treasure down, I want everyone to push the jewels into the hole. Right, here they come." Like a shower of coloured hailstones, the gems tumbled to the ground, landing with a soft thud at the foot of the tree.

Hedley, the Elder and the rabbits were busy pushing the shiny treasures into the hole when they heard Jackdaw's angry protest.

"No! no! You can't take my treasure." He lunged at the squirrels, who scurried down the tree to get away from his jabbing beak. "No, no you miserable rabbits, you shan't take my treasure either." He swooped down at the little rabbits, darting from one to another, scattering them in all directions. "And you, you spiny spying little meddler, you're certainly not going to get my treasure."

He darted at Hedley, who not only curled into a ball, but rolled into the hole.

"Curses! You pilfering prickle ball. Give me back my treasure!" screamed the angry bird and attacked Hedley with his beak. The Elder lowered his head, stuck out his spines and charged at Jackdaw.

"Ouch, ow, stay away from me you bristly busybody, ouch, ow."

Owl flew down from the tree and gripped Jackdaw with his sharp talons, so he couldn't fly away.

"No, no, it's not fair, it's midsummer's eve, you can't hurt me, it's not fair."

"I'm not going to hurt you, Jackdaw, just keep you from hurting anyone else. You have been behaving very badly and Conrad has something to say to you."

"Yes, indeed," said Conrad, twitching his whiskers. "You are hereby banished from this forest. Owl and his friends will escort you to the next county, and woe betide you if you come back here again."

"Consider yourself getting off lightly," said the Elder, who was still glowering.

Jackdaw scowled and muttered, "You haven't seen the last of me. I'll be back one day, just you see."

Four barn owls flew silently through the woods carrying strawberry netting they had taken from the vegetable garden. They dropped it over Jackdaw, who struggled helplessly. Then, each taking a corner of the net, they lifted the screeching bird and flew away into the moonlit sky.

Hedley climbed out of the hole and the Elder hurried to his side. "Good work, Hedley, that was using your head, rolling onto the treasure. I hope you are unharmed."

"Yes, thank you, Elder, no harm done. Do you think Jackdaw will come back?"

"Oh, he'll be back, but not for a long time. And when he does, we will be ready for him," said the stately old hedgehog. "Now, let's look at the treasure. Hmm. quite a collection. The problem is — just how do we lead the humans to the jewels?"

"I think I can help you there, Elder. Old Shep the sheep dog, seems to be able to get the humans to follow him anywhere. I'm sure he can lead them here."

"Hmm, well, let's cover the hole and leave a sentry keeping watch. We'll go back to the farm and talk to Shep tonight. Being midsummer's eve, he won't misbehave. He is bound to do as we ask."

Conrad hopped up to the Elder and together they thanked all the animals for their help. "That was a good night's work," said the old hedgehog proudly. "Your rabbits did a fine job, Conrad, and that was quite a trick the barn owls pulled — strawberry netting — splendid idea! Just shows how much we can get done when we all pull together. That old bird sure looked surprised when I charged him. Made me feel like a young 'un again! "

Chattering excitedly, Hedley, Marvin, Conrad and the Elder, made their way back to the farm. Shep heard them coming and waited quietly as the procession of animals came towards him.

“Shep, do you know who I am?”

“Yes, Elder sir, you are a leader of the Midsummer Gathering.”

“Quite right. We have a very important task for you. Hedley tells me you have a special way of getting humans to do things. We need you to lead them to the treasure Jackdaw hid in the forest. Do you think you could do that? We have left a good trail, which I’m sure you can follow.”

Shep sniffed the ground, then moved around the little group sniffing gently at each one. Marvin almost collapsed with fear but bravely stood his ground.

“Yes, Elder, I have the scent, but I’ll have to wait till morning. Humans don’t like to be disturbed at night.”

“So I understand. Never mind, morning is soon enough. We have left one of Blackie’s rabbits guarding the hole where the treasure is hidden. Be sure not to chase him, he’ll probably be nervous when he sees you. Just remember, this is a very important task; don’t let us down.”

“No, Elder, I won’t let you down. I shall make sure the humans follow me to the treasure,” said the dog earnestly.

“Good, then we shall be on our way. Hedley, will you and Marvin walk with us back to the pasture?” Marvin stayed close to Hedley’s side and looked nervously over his shoulder to make sure Shep was not following. He was relieved to see the old dog had settled down for a sleep.

“Where are you going now, Elder?” asked Hedley.

Conrad and I have a meeting with Blackie; then we must head back to Gloucester. When you have led the humans to the treasure, the Grandfather will know what to do. He’s a very wise man and will make sure these treasures are safe. If you have any problems, just talk to Blackie."

Hedley thanked the Elder for his help in finding the jewels. "We couldn't have done it without you and Blackie."

"The clan was happy to help you, Hedley. By finding the jewels and the medicine box, you have also helped us. If the old Grandfather takes them to Glastonbury, he may learn more about the old ways. Take care, young Hedley, see you next year at the gathering."

The Elder turned and slowly walked away. Conrad, still bursting with energy, hopped up to Hedley. "It was a pleasure seeing you both again," he said. "Goodbye and good luck." With a final twitch of his whiskers, he bounded off to join the Elder.

"Gosh, Hedley, that was a really big adventure, the biggest we've had yet. How are you going to get James and Grandfather to go with Shep?"

"Don't worry about Shep, he'll do his job. I don't think you need be afraid of him anymore."

"That's easy for you to say, Hedley, you have prickles and you're bigger than I am. What if you're not around and he forgets his promise?"

"He won't, but if you're still nervous, you can stay out of his way and I'll talk to him alone."

"No, I'll come with you. I can always run and hide if he scares me. When are we going, Hedley?"

"There's time for a nap before the sun comes up, we have a busy day ahead of us."

# CHAPTER NINE
# SHEP LEADS THE WAY

Hedley woke with a start as the cock started to crow. He unrolled and stretched, then sniffed in the straw where Marvin was sleeping. "Wake up. It's time to go." Marvin opened his eyes, nodded and sleepily crawled from his cosy bed. They made their way through the dew covered vegetables. Hedley stopped to drink some sparkling water trapped in a leaf. When they reached the farmyard, Shep was waiting for them.

"Good morning, Shep," said Hedley.

"Good morning, Hedley. Is that Marvin hiding behind you? It's all right, Marvin, I won't chase you. I made a promise to Elder. The Grandfather will be out soon. I'll get him to follow us. Wait, here he comes now."

Grandfather came out of the house with food for Shep and was surprised to see the dog lying with Hedley and the mouse. “Well, I’ll be . . . Hedley, you seem to have charmed old Shep. Imagine the three of you becoming friends. Must have something to do with midsummer’s eve. Well, I’m sure Shep won’t mind you sharing some of his breakfast.”

Shep ignored his breakfast and ran back and forth between Grandfather and the forest barking loudly.

“What’s up old feller, what’s the fuss? Where do you want me to go? Hold on a minute, I’ll get James and Robert. If there is something you want to show me, then they’ll want to come along.” Grandfather put down the dish then went back in the house to call the boys.

“You certainly seem to have a way with humans, Shep,” said Hedley. Your plan is working, isn’t it, Marvin?”

Marvin was eyeing Shep’s dish hungrily.

"It's all right, Marvin, you can share. You too, Hedley," said Shep. I think we need a little breakfast to get us on our way."

When the boys came out into the yard they were surprised to see Hedley and the mouse sharing Shep's food. "Look, Grandfather, Shep has made friends with Hedley and that little mouse. I thought Hedley was afraid of Shep."

"Looks as if they have settled their differences," said Grandfather. Shep looked up as the humans came out and ran from one to the other, whining and barking.

"Shep wants us to follow him, Grandfather, Hedley too. They must have found something. Let's go."

Satisfied that the humans had understood, Shep sniffed around for a while then started following the trail into the forest. Hedley and Marvin popped into the rabbit warren.

"There goes Hedley down the rabbit hole again, Grandfather. You were right, he must have a shortcut.

Come on, Shep, maybe you'll lead us to more treasure!"

Hedley and Marvin reached the forest first and met the tired rabbit sentry, who was dozing off.

"Morning, Hedley, Marvin. Quiet night, no intruders. I hear that old dog. Be on my way now. You can look after it from here." The rabbit took off down the rabbit hole as Shep came into view.

"Look, Grandfather, Hedley beat us. He's standing beside a pile of branches. Maybe there's something hidden there."

Grandfather and the boys knelt down and pulled away the branches, then reached into the hole and scooped up several handfuls of coloured stones. They looked at the gems in amazement. "More treasure! How did Shep know it was here?" asked James.

"Who dug this hole in the ground?" asked Robert.

“Why is Shep so friendly with Hedley and the mouse?” laughed James.

“Sounds like a midsummer mystery to me,” laughed Grandfather.

“More like midsummer magic,” murmured James as he gazed at the stones. “They don’t look very much like precious gems, they are rough and not very shiny.”

“That’s because they haven’t been cut,” said Grandfather. “They need to be cut and polished before they look their best. Jackdaw must have moved them here from his old hiding place. I wonder where he is, there’s no sign of him today. Maybe he has given up and is looking for treasure somewhere else. Here, put them in my handkerchief and tie it up. I think we had better see the police constable, then go to Glastonbury. But first, let’s get some breakfast.”

After breakfast, Grandfather hitched the old horse to the wagon. With all the treasures carefully stored in a box, the threesome set off for town. Their first stop was the police station to see constable Thompson, who couldn't believe his eyes when they gave him the jewels.

"By gum, I do believe those are the jewels that were mysteriously stolen from the museum some fifty years ago. I was just a lad at the time, about your age young Robert. My schoolmates and I must have dug around half the county looking for them. How did you lads come by them?"

While the boys were telling their story, the policeman looked puzzled. "What I don't understand," he said, scratching his chin, "is how they got to be in a freshly dug hole under a tree."

"Yes, well that is a bit of a puzzler," said Grandfather. "But the important thing is that they have been found."

"Quite right, sir, and I'd appreciate it if you would leave them with me. However, if you want to take the wooden box to the museum I would be most appreciative. The box isn't on my list of missing property."

"Thank you. I will. Now boys, let's get on our way to Glastonbury, it's a good hour's journey."

By the time they pulled into Glastonbury, it was lunch time. "I think we might as well stop for a bite to eat, the museum doesn't open until 1:30."

"Good idea, I'm starved," said James. "Me too," said Robert. Can we go to the tea shop in the High Street? They have the best treacle tart."

"Why not?" said Grandfather. "I think you boys deserve a treat after all this treasure hunting. Treacle tart is my favourite as well."

They left Ned and the cart beside the water trough and crossed the street to the tea shop. Grandfather settled into a window seat so he could watch Ned.

After the waitress had taken their order, Grandfather straightened his glasses and asked, "So what do you boys know about midsummer's eve?"

"Not much," said James. "We did a play in school but

it was all about fairy kings and queens. What's so special about it, Grandfather?"

"Well, lad, when I was a boy, my Grandmother told me that it was a magical time when all the animals met together as friends. The fox and the hound, the mouse and the owl, the badger and the hedgehog, all met without fear of being prey. Now I thought it was a fairy story, but after seeing Hedley, Shep and the little mouse together, I'm not so sure."

"Magic!" sighed James, "That's how Hedley and his friends knew the treasure was there."

"I'd like to know where Jackdaw is," said Robert. "He seems to have disappeared."

"If all the animals were friends, they wouldn't hurt him," said James.

Grandfather nodded. "He may have decided to fly to another part of the forest. Perhaps he'd had enough of Shep and Hedley spoiling his plans. Anyway, eat up, we have an appointment with the curator."

# CHAPTER TEN
# THE CURATOR AT GLASTONBURY

When Grandfather and the boys reached the museum they found the curator in his office. He was a tall, thin man with a shiny egg-shaped head ringed with wispy, white hair. He ushered them in and introduced himself as Horace Watson.

After introducing himself and the boys, Grandfather gave the box to the curator and explained how it was found.

Mr. Watson took the box and placed it on the desk in front of him. "Extraordinary! You found this box under a hollow tree after finding the ring and key in the garden? The ring is indeed Celtic in design, as is the carving on the box. To think such a treasure has been lying there all these years. The wood is oak, of course, the sacred tree of the Druids."

He placed the key in the lock and turned it. He opened the lid and drew in his breath. "My word, this is a treasure. These are dried herbs, probably medicinal, and most certainly they must have belonged to a Druid healer. We shall have to send them to be examined by experts, but I think it safe to say what you have found is of great importance to the museum."

"You were right, Grandfather," said Robert proudly.

"And to think it's all thanks to Hedley for digging in the garden," said James with pride. Grandfather was about to caution James from saying any more, when the curator spoke again.

"Hedley, is he another of your friends?" asked the curator.

James looked at Grandfather then tried to explain. "Hedley is a hedgehog who loves to explore. He was digging in the garden and turned up the ring but it got

stuck on his nose. That's how Grandfather found it."

"You say, the hedgehog found this ring?" said the curator looking confused. "How about the key? Did the hedgehog find that, too?"

The boys took it in turns to explain the whole story and when they had finished, the curator was scratching his shiny head in confusion. "This hedgehog, Hedley I believe you call him, seems remarkably clever," he said in wonder. "Just when did all this happen?"

"It was midsummer's eve." said Robert.

"Midsummer's eve," said the curator thoughtfully. "That might explain it. There are several stories about the wonders of that special night. It has been said that the animals all meet as friends with no fear of being preyed upon."

Grandfather nodded his agreement. "I was just telling James and Robert the same story. It was told to me by my Grandmother."

The curator leaned forward on his desk "It is also said that the animals used to be able to communicate with the Druids. But of course," he added looking directly at Grandfather. "We have no proof of that."

"As you say," said Grandfather. "We have no proof. But this is a very magical part of Somerset."

After a pause, the curator sat back in his chair, smiling. "Your story is quite remarkable, I do thank you for bringing this wonderful treasure to me. I can assure you, it will be examined most carefully and I shall call on you, if I may, to inform you of what we find."

"That would be most kind," said Grandfather. "Now I think we have taken enough of your time and we should be getting home."

The curator walked with them to the door. "I do hope you all come back to see our exhibits. I think you would find them of great interest — especially those concerning the legendary King Arthur and, of course, Merlin. These treasures just may have a connection —

with the legend, I mean."

"Yes," said Grandfather. "I rather thought they might."

"We shall just have to wait until our experts have had a chance to date them." The Curator smiled and shook Grandfather's hand. "I would be delighted to see you again, I think we have a good deal in common. Thank you for coming, I will visit you as soon as we get the results of the examination. Goodbye for now."

When Grandfather and the boys were back outside, they looked at one another. "Just imagine," said James, "Mr. Watson knows the stories of midsummer's eve."

"And they have exhibits about King Arthur. Do you think the box does have something to do with Merlin, Grandfather?" asked Robert.

"Who knows for sure, lad," said Grandfather.

"Some of those stories about Merlin and Arthur could be true. If the box can be linked to the legends, maybe it will prove they really did exist."

"I wonder if that's what the curator is thinking?" said Robert .

"Perhaps," said the old man quietly. "I think we shall learn a good deal more after Mr. Watson's visit."

"It looks like we are going to have an interesting summer," said James. "Let's go home and see if Hedley has turned up any more treasures."

Ned was happy to see them and neighed loudly as they climbed onto the wagon. Grandfather took up the reins and led the cart back onto the road. "Yes indeed, it should be very interesting. Something tells me Hedley will be having more exciting adventures."

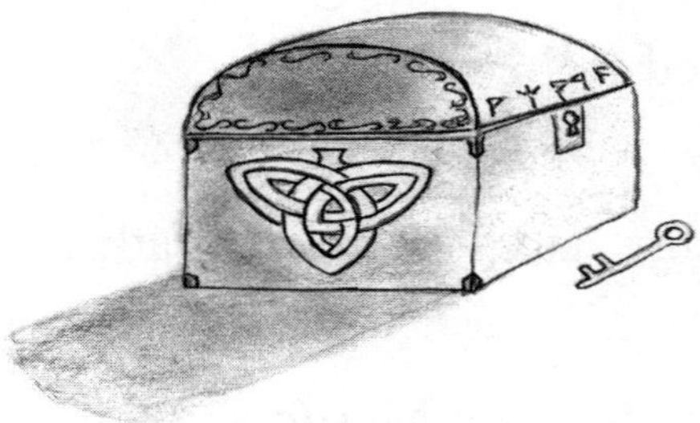

Book 2 of
The Mech Trilogy

# MECH
## Worlds Away

KEN DEEPROSE

Cover Design: Jason Deeprose/Ken Deeprose



ISBN
978-1-7780920-1-5 (Hardcover)
978-1-7780920-0-8 (Paperback)
978-1-7780920-2-2 (eBook)

1. JUVENILE FICTION, SCIENCE FICTION

To Martelle

For your love, support and patience.

# 1

*How could they leave him behind like that?*

Todd watched as his friends paddled around a bend in the river, slowly disappearing from view. Based on the current plan, he wouldn't see them again for at least three days.

"Aaaaaaaaaaaw!" he shouted at the sky with all the power he could muster, the desperate call echoing off the canyon walls. Looking down, he spotted a small rock and kicked it as hard as he could, sending it skittering into the river. That failed to make him feel any better, so he kicked another one.

Even the sheer beauty of his surroundings did nothing to lighten his mood. He stood on a gravel clearing by the bank of the river on a glorious sunlit day. The brilliant blue sky above was framed by towering red rock walls that dominated the view in every direction. Soothing sounds of passing water joined the shriek of a hawk as it floated on a breeze in search of prey.

Todd and three of his friends were in the midst of a five-day kayak trip on the Colorado River, where it passed along the southern edge of the Grand Canyon. This wasn't the simple stretch the tourists travelled. No, there were real challenges on this section, so he'd been looking forward to the trip for weeks.

And now it was over. He looked to his kayak, a large hole in the hull staring back at him like a giant evil eye, taunting him to get back on the water. And was that really such a bad idea? Sitting around here, waiting for his friends to come back, would be the most boring thing he'd ever done.

Todd wasn't built for boring. Three days alone, with nothing to do but watch the river float by, would be agonizing. His friends had left him with enough food to keep him alive for a few days, but what was the point? Given a choice between boredom and starvation, he wasn't entirely sure which one he'd pick.

*No! There had to be a better way.*

He walked over to his damaged kayak, and the broken paddle leaning against it, trying his best to see things in a more optimistic light. The hole wasn't *that* big, and a paddle snapped in half was only a few pieces of duct tape away from being fully functional. His friends had declared both items unsalvageable, but maybe the thought of repairing them wasn't so far-fetched after all.

It certainly wasn't the worst idea he'd ever had. Why, only two hours ago, he had carried his kayak to the top of a small waterfall and attempted a daring drop into the churning rock-lined pool below. That idea had been much worse.

Granted, it was the reason he now found himself stranded miles from civilization with no way of getting home. But still... he did manage to live through that one. The possibility of getting the boat back on the water was looking more reasonable with each passing minute.

Two hours later, Todd stood back to admire his handiwork. It wasn't great. The hull repair could have used a few more layers of tape, but he'd used up most of it strapping a driftwood stick along the shaft of his paddle to add some much-needed strength. It was certainly good enough to survive a leisurely cruise across a serene lake, but during the spring run-off, this piece of river was an extremely aggressive environment.

The question was... should he go for it? His stepmom generally used words like reckless and impulsive when describing her son, but

Todd preferred the terms adventurous and courageous. He'd come this far. Turning back now made no sense at all. Besides, his friends were getting further away every moment he spent standing around, so the time had come to stop thinking and start moving.

He gathered together all his supplies, then stuffed everything into a watertight hold in the back of his kayak. The added weight would make the boat less manoeuvrable, but he couldn't afford to leave anything behind in case he was unable to catch up with his friends before nightfall.

As soon as loading was complete, he donned his lifejacket and helmet, before dragging the craft to the edge of the water. After sitting down in the cockpit, he took his time securing the neoprene skirt to the outer rim, so water couldn't get inside the boat. Once settled, he pushed away from the bank and began drifting with the current. Starting with a couple of tentative strokes to make sure the repairs would hold, he soon found a strong rhythm and began paddling forcefully in pursuit of his friends.

An hour into the trip, things were progressing well. His feet were dry, which meant the tape covering the hole was still in place. The paddle was in one piece, but it was flexing a little more than he would have liked. All in all, he couldn't have asked for things to be going any better. But he knew well an important decision lay ahead, as a challenging set of rapids was coming up shortly. They would be Class IV at this time of year, maybe even Class V. That made them difficult under ideal conditions, and even worse if the health of your boat was compromised. It came down to being smart versus being bold.

The speed of the water picked up as the rapids drew closer. Todd dreaded the thought of portaging around them. He'd lose an hour in the effort, effectively ending any chance he had of catching his friends before dusk. As his pace increased and the sound of the rushing water intensified, he realized if he didn't act soon, the river would decide for him.

"For once in my life, I'll do the smart thing," he said, before plunging the paddle deep into the water to steer back towards the bank.

*Snap!*

Without warning, the paddle blew apart in his hands, with one half spinning away, lost to the current. Down to half a paddle, getting to shore was no longer an option. He turned back to the centre of the flow, getting into the best possible position to run the rapids.

Controlling the boat soon became impossible. Todd flailed helplessly as the power of the raging water grabbed the kayak and plunged it into the heart of the rapids. A shuddering impact with a submerged rock tore the tape away from the hole in the hull, allowing surging water to flood the cockpit.

The next rock flipped the kayak over, trapping Todd underwater, unable to breathe. He was a skilled kayaker, quite capable of rolling his boat back to an upright position, but not without the leverage of a full-length paddle, and certainly not with a boat full of water. His choices were now limited to bailing out or drowning.

Reaching out through the bubbling water, he tugged on the release loop of the skirt and pulled it free from the boat. He popped to the surface and immediately drew in a huge breath to fill his burning lungs. Unfortunately, his relief was short-lived. Once again, the churning water plunged him into the murky depths. The violence of the water made it difficult to establish up from down. He lost track of the kayak and was now completely at the mercy of the river.

On those rare occasions his head rose above the surface, he sucked in air and called out, even knowing no one was there to hear him. A powerful surge sent him crashing headfirst into a rock, splitting his helmet with a resounding crack.

Suddenly, everything went quiet, peaceful. He was still tumbling through the water, but somehow felt detached from it, like it was happening to someone else. A question formed in his mind.

*Is this what dying feels like?*

He no longer had any awareness of his surroundings. His lungs cried out for air, but he had no idea if he was underwater or on the surface. Sensing a terrifying shadow looming over him, he felt himself rising into the sky, causing another question to take hold in his mind.

*Am I on my way to heaven?*

As darkness overtook him on his paralyzing descent into unconsciousness, one final, and somewhat unusual, question popped into his head.

*Was that a giant?*

⚙ ⚙ ⚙

*Whoomp!*

Air exploded from Orin's lungs as a sudden landing found him flat on his back. Looking up, all he could see were stars. He found this strange. It wasn't nighttime. In fact, he wasn't even outside. Then, as he lay there trying to figure it all out, Juna's lovely face drifted into view. Her long brown hair was pulled into a ponytail that fell past her face, and her brilliant green eyes echoed the smile on her lips.

"You OK?"

"I think I might have actually broken something this time."

"Oh, stop your whining," she said, extending her hand to help him up. "You're the one who wanted princess lessons."

Combat training had become a part of his daily routine over the last several months, but Orin didn't know if he would ever get used to being tossed around like a rag doll. His fighting skills were getting better, though. Apparently, when he first started, he fought worse than Pom in a pillow suit, whatever that meant. Now his battles with Juna could last as long as a full minute before he found himself flying through the air and landing with a thud.

But it was all good. Orin had always been more about brains than brawn. Besides, spending time with Juna was nice, even if it meant slamming into the ground occasionally.

Now that he was vertical again, he felt much better. He probably had the wind knocked out of him. Not necessarily eager to get back to the action, he paused for a moment to stretch the kinks from his body and survey his surroundings.

He was standing on a large padded mat in the middle of a small cave. A dozen light bulbs lined the domed ceiling, revealing rock walls layered with ribbons of red and orange.

It was called the training room, and it made up only a tiny fraction of the enormous network of caves he and his friends were now calling home. Their stay here was meant to be temporary. Fleeing a battle with an evil emperor and his army of Mech clones had left them with no other option than to find a new planet to live on for a while. So, here they were for who knew how long. He was probably a year older than he was when they first arrived, but it was tough to keep track of that sort of thing when you were orbiting the wrong sun.

The planet on which they now resided was called Earth. It seemed like a boring name for such an interesting place. It was inhabited by billions of people, or humans, as they liked to call themselves, but that didn't matter much to the little group living in this cave. Their plan was to hide out here until the time was right to return to their home planet of Cambria, then pack up and leave without anyone ever knowing they were here. Maybe there were billions of people living on this planet, but if things went according to plan, they'd never meet a single one of them.

A gentle tap on the shoulder brought him back from his daydreams.

"Hey, you still with me?" Juna asked, a touch of concern in her voice.

"Yeah, I'm good. Just lost in thought, I guess. But I think I've had enough pummelling for one day. Why don't we pick it up again tomorrow?"

"Sounds good." She gave him a gentle squeeze on the shoulder. "I'm going for a quick shower. I'll see you for dinner."

Orin watched as she ducked away through the small passage leading to the rest of the cave. Without question, the best part of his new life here on Earth was how much time he got to spend with Juna. They weren't a couple or anything, but they had become such good friends, and did almost everything together. Sometimes he could hardly believe it. The emperor's youngest daughter, an actual princess, was now his best friend.

Well, maybe not his best friend. He still considered Gigahertz to be his best friend, but he was a thirty-foot tall, fifteen-ton Mech. So, as wonderful as their friendship was, a flesh-and-blood friend certainly had its advantages. Anyway, Gig wasn't around as much as he used to be. There was less for the Mechs to do over here than there was back home, so they spent a lot of their time in wait state, trying not to burn through too many fuel cells.

Orin picked up his towel and dabbed a little moisture off his face. He didn't feel like he needed a shower. It seemed throwing someone around worked up more of a sweat than being thrown did. He walked back across the mat, flipped off the lights, then zipped through the entryway to make his way to the central cavern.

After rounding the corner into the enormous space, Orin was, as always, awed by his first glimpse of the Gate. The huge metal ring, sitting upright on its edge, was the amazing device that had brought them to this strange new world. Able to open a portal through space, the machine was so large it almost made this immense cave seem small. He glanced over to the Tech Station parked to the right of the spectacular structure, and noticed Diara, her short blond hair bobbing to a tune only she could hear. When she spotted him, her frantic wave signalled him to join her.

"Hey Orin, I found a new satellite today. Do you want to help break the encryption on it?"

"Absolutely! I wonder what we'll find this time."

When they first arrived on this planet, one of the group's favourite things to do was spend the evening outside, staring up at the beautiful night sky. They noticed some stars were unexpectedly moving, and soon concluded that a network of man-made objects circled the globe. With so many science geeks around, the desire to figure out what they were doing up there was overwhelming.

Antennas, detectors and scanners were built, and soon hundreds of the satellites had been located. Some rotated at the same speed as the planet, so you didn't even notice them moving in the night sky. These turned out to be communications devices of some sort, constantly bombarding the world with data. Naturally, the team set out to determine what it was they were trying to say.

Professor Umbra and Professor Oletta, Cambria's two most accomplished scientists, spent hours analyzing the data stream, experimenting with different decoding algorithms and eventually cracked the code. What they discovered was the single craziest thing any of them had ever seen.

It was called television. At first, none of what they were seeing made sense. Cambria certainly had nothing like it. There were images in constant motion, with people doing peculiar things and speaking in a language they didn't understand.

There were hundreds of channels, each of them showing something completely different. Some featured people talking all day, while others showed teams playing ball sports with huge crowds watching and cheering. One channel might show nothing but non-stop battles and explosions, while another, only cute furry animals wandering through a forest. It took them a while to figure out that not everything they were seeing was actually happening. Some of it was completely made up—just people pretending to be in the stories being shown.

It was baffling. What was the purpose of it? Could this much effort and technology possibly be dedicated to providing nothing more than entertainment?

In the early days after the discovery, the most useful channels were ones featuring colourful puppets and talking animals, obviously designed as educational tools for children. Everyone in the group, particularly the younger members of the team, would spend hours watching on the Tech Station monitors, trying to master the language they now knew as English. Nobody did it thinking they may run into a human someday. They only wanted to understand all the amazing things being shown on the other channels.

Before long, everyone in the group could understand most of what was being said, and some were even speaking it quite well. Skeet and Pom were the best, holding conversations that sounded much like the people on TV.

General Zatari, in his role as leader of their group, encouraged everyone to learn English. One of his guiding principles was to hope for the best, but plan for the worst. He didn't expect they would ever meet a human, but if it happened, knowing the language could be extremely useful.

As Orin and Diara crunched through the data, looking for the key that would unlock it, Professor Umbra came up and peered over their shoulders.

"I hope you're not wasting your time with those television signals again," he scoffed. "That stuff is going to rot your brains. As if we haven't found enough channels already. What's the next one going to be about? Paint drying?"

"We never know until it's decoded, Dad. It might be something useful this time."

His father often complained about how much time people wasted watching TV, but he was always the first one there on movie night.

"Shouldn't you be working on that Disruptor of yours?" his father added. "Now *that* would be something useful."

There wasn't much the group had to do on this planet, but their one job was important. The emperor of Cambria, who was also Juna's father, had a Gate of his own, and an army of Mech clones he was using in an attempt to conquer a planet called Mara. Whenever he tried, the team here would detect it, fire up their own Gate and send four of their Mechs to repel the invasion. The attacks had become quite rare lately, but they always needed to be ready.

Orin was currently working on an invention called a Disruptor. Someday, he hoped it could eliminate the need for any more battles by preventing their enemy from opening a portal in the first place. Thinking about it now, he decided completing that project offered a much more productive use of his time.

"Hey Diara, Dad's right. I should be working on something else. I'll catch you later."

Orin made his way to the maintenance shop at the furthest end of the cave. When he arrived, Dorel, Annu and Taz, the "Wrenches" in their group, and the three largest people he had ever known, were putting the final touches on one of the two new Mechs they had built since coming to Earth.

"Hey guys, how is Gecko doing?"

"Really good," Dorel replied. "He's powered down now, but I think he's going to be a lot of fun. It's strange working on a Mech this small."

"Yeah, the General wanted to have something the same size as an Earth vehicle, just in case we need to leave the cave for some reason," Orin said. "You know what he says: hope for the best…"

"Plan for the worst," they all finished in unison.

Gecko was a Bio, so he looked more like a vehicle than a traditional two-legged walking Mech. With four large rubber tires and coloured bright green, he looked like the small Earth animal for which he was named.

"I can't wait to meet him," Orin said as he wandered over to his workbench. "But right now, I've got work to do."

As he sat down, Orin looked at the pile of electronic components and jumble of wires that made up his Disruptor prototype. A Gate sent out strands of inter-dimensional energy that eventually knit themselves together to form a portal through space. In theory, his Disruptor could be placed at the destination point, and tie the strands into knots before a portal could form.

If Orin got this device working, they could protect the Marans without the Mechs ever having to fight the clones again. It could end up being a lifesaving breakthrough.

Just as he was getting started, an excited voice drew his attention to the entrance of the shop. It sounded like Skeet. Despite being the youngest and fittest member of the team, he was obviously winded from what must have been a long sprint from the other end of the cave. He bent over, dropping his hands to his knees to catch his breath.

"Everybody, come quick!" he finally managed. "Vortex found a human and he brought it here!"

# 2

*So, that's what they look like up close.*

Juna watched as Vortex laid the dripping human body on the big table tucked in a back corner of the central cavern. At first she thought he might be dead, looking limp and scarred with a bluish tinge, but she noticed his chest rising and falling with each shallow breath he took.

His body had been battered, torn clothes revealing an array of dark bruises all along his arms and legs. He appeared young, maybe a year older than her, with a lean athletic body rippling with powerful muscles. Wavy blonde hair framed a pleasant face with a broad nose and square jaw.

"What should we do with him?" Pom asked as she stepped over to join the group by the table.

Nobody on their team had any medical training, and certainly no one who knew the first thing about fixing an injured human.

"We should probably keep him warm so he doesn't go into shock," Professor Oletta suggested. "I'll go get some blankets."

Juna ran her eyes up and down the length of the damaged body. Since seeing the first images on television, it was apparent humans and Cambrians were similar in appearance. The upper ridge of the human ear was a little smooth and boring, but other than that, the two species appeared essentially identical.

The professors had endless discussions about how this might explain the origins of life in the universe, but everyone else considered it a fortunate coincidence.

Juna looked up to see the General pacing the length of the cavern, his muscular body, perfect posture and forceful strides carrying him with an ever-present air of authority. He was not at all happy about the presence of the cave's newest occupant and wasn't shy about letting everyone know it. His trip across the cave brought him back to the group standing by the table.

"No one can know we're here," he repeated for what must have been the tenth time. "We have to get it out of here before it wakes up."

"It's not an it," Juna snapped. "It's a him, and he's hurt, so we need to take care of him."

The General rolled his eyes, let out a heavy sigh and continued his journey back to the far side of the chamber.

Juna agreed the human's presence created a major complication in their lives, but he was here now, so they'd have to deal with it.

"OK, let's get him bundled up," Professor Oletta said as she arrived with the blankets. "Here, get this pillow tucked under his head."

Juna and Pom helped the professor, or Aeva as they were calling her now, get the human wrapped up. As they were finishing, Orin, Skeet and the Wrenches came running up to join them.

"Wow! An actual human!" Skeet exclaimed as he arrived at the table. "I didn't think we'd ever meet one."

"Well, you certainly won't be meeting this one," the General jumped in, having completed his latest lap of the cave. "Getting it out of here before it wakes up is now our highest priority."

Juna shot him a disapproving scowl.

"Oh, I'm sorry. Getting *him* out of here is now our highest priority."

Juna's temper flared. "And where is it you propose we take him? He needs our help."

"No," the General said, "he needs help from someone who knows how to care for an injured human. That is not us. We must get him to a medical facility where they'll know what to do. How to do that without revealing ourselves will be the trick."

Juna knew he was right. It seemed wrong not to do everything they could to care for the boy, but somewhere safe, with people who knew what to do, was the best place for him right now.

"Look Juna," the General continued. "I'm not trying to be cruel, and I do want what's best for this young man, but we all have to think about how much trouble we'll be in if someone finds us here. Think about all those movies you've been watching—the ones where aliens are discovered on this planet. Does that ever end well?"

"So, what do you propose we do?" She put her hands on her hips and sent him another scowl.

The General wisely chose not to answer.

"Dorel, how close is that new Bio Mech to being ready?" he asked instead.

"Gecko?" Dorel seemed surprised to be involved in the conversation. "He still needs work, but if we push it, he could be running first thing tomorrow."

"Do we have a way to get him out of the canyon?"

"We can strap him to a couple of Atomics," Dorel replied. "If they max out their thrusters, they can drag him up to the rim. We found a nice flat spot near the top. He can drive out from there."

"OK, that's good." The General looked relieved to have a plan. "For now, let's get the human someplace a little quieter and more secluded. If he does come to, I don't want the Gate to be the first thing he sees."

"We can put him in my room," Juna offered.

"Do that," the General agreed. "But whatever you do, don't wake him up."

Juna had Taz gently lift the human off the table, then led them to her room. She flipped on the light, revealing a small space tucked against the red rock wall of the cave. A tiny bed, a bedside table and a box for her clothes were the only items occupying the cramped space. Taz carefully set the limp body down on her bed, then zipped off to join the other Wrenches to finish up the remaining work on Gecko.

Looking down on the damaged alien, Juna wondered if leaving him to rest was all they could be doing for him right now. It seemed a little research might be required, so she turned off the light, slipped quietly out of the room, and started back towards the central cavern.

Halfway there, she saw Orin walking towards her. She couldn't help but notice how much he'd changed in his time here on Earth. He was taller now, and their daily workouts had definitely removed the skinny label from him. His dark brown hair was longer, framing a gentle face and those beautiful, deep brown eyes. Not that she paid attention to that sort of thing.

"How's he doing?" Orin asked as he reached her.

"Still unconscious."

"That'll keep the General's blood pressure down for a bit. He certainly wouldn't be happy seeing a human roaming around the cave. Where did he come from, anyway?"

"Vortex was down by the river filling his water tank when he heard yelling. A couple of seconds later, a body floated by next to a small boat, so he scooped them up and brought them here."

"I hope he's going to be OK. It sounds like Vortex might have saved his life."

"I think he did," Juna agreed. "He may be a hero, but he's upset right now. With the General so angry, he thinks he made a mistake by bringing him here."

The Professor always said Mechs weren't capable of feeling emotions, but Juna didn't believe it for a second. She grew up with

Helion as one of her closest friends and cared about him as much as anyone else in her life. All the hours they spent together told her that he felt the same way about her. Orin had grown up with Gigahertz as his best friend, and she knew his views on Mech emotional capabilities matched her own.

"Maybe I'll go wake Gig," Orin offered. "Vortex thinks of him as a big brother, so I'm sure he'd appreciate a chance to talk."

"That's a great idea. Thanks," she said as she turned to continue her trip to the central cavern. "I'm going to check the internet to see if there's something else we can do to help the human."

When the science geeks in their group found all those satellites orbiting the planet, and figured out a way to talk to them, cracking the code on television was their first major accomplishment. Juna enjoyed a good movie as much as the next person, but for her, the greatest discovery floating around up there came the day they discovered the internet.

It was amazing! Simply typing in a question would instantly provide thousands of places to find the answer.

Juna spent hours on it every day, learning everything she could about this spectacular planet. It was such a fascinating place. There were billions of people living in hundreds of countries, with too many races, religions, languages and cultures to count. Cambria had none of those things. On her home planet, there were three distinct classes of people—Elites, commoners and hods—but everyone lived in the same country, spoke the same language, and looked basically the same as everyone else.

Juna's time spent learning about all aspects of life on Earth was more than idle curiosity. Life on Cambria wasn't fair, and she wanted to fix it. Hods were little more than slaves, doing all the horrible jobs no one else wanted to do. In contrast, the Elites sat around all day having everything done for them. It simply wasn't right.

Fortunately, she had found other people who felt the same way. The team here on Earth, as well as a group back on Cambria called the Underground, were all committed to changing things for the better. It was important to everyone, but for Juna it took on a special meaning. For generations, *her* family had been the cause of the shameful situation on their planet. Her father was only the latest in a long line of evil Emperor Volaras. The hours she spent studying Earth's history were all in hopes of finding some way to create a society that could work for everybody.

As Juna entered the central cavern and passed by the Gate, her heart sunk noticing Helion standing next to it. There were always four Mechs in wait state stationed next to the Gate, with all their weapons attached. They were the four that would be called to battle the next time her father attacked Mara. She always worried when her friend stood in that position.

Shaking off images of Helion being blown to bits, she made her way past the Tech Station over to the computer they'd set up specifically for accessing the internet. Shortly after realizing how useful it could be, they opened a portal to Lano's warehouse on Cambria to collect the parts needed to build a computer, then brought them back here to assemble. It was a good thing they did. If she had to bug Diara and Pom at the Tech Station every time she accessed the internet, they would have thrown her out of the cave long ago. She sat down in the familiar chair and logged on.

Just as she was getting started, Pom walked over from the Tech Station, knelt down, and gave her a hug. Pom was Juna's dearest friend. They'd been together since they were toddlers. In a way, she was the reason Juna was so passionate about improving the world they lived in. Pom was a hod, so technically, their friendship was forbidden. Making a life where they were allowed to be friends had been Juna's driving force for as long as she could remember.

"So, my dear princess, what is it you're trying to learn today?" Pom teased. "How best to fix the world again?"

"I believe I have mentioned my disdain for the word 'princess' on several occasions, so I would appreciate you refraining from ever using it again," Juna said, trying her best to sound offended. "And, if you must know, it's something different this time. I'm checking medical sites to see if there's more we can do to help the human."

"He is cute, isn't he?"

"What did I say about him being cute? It's not because he's cute. It's simply the right thing to do."

"So, you do think he's cute."

"Whatever."

"I'll leave you to it then," she said as she rose to leave, directing a wink and a mischievous smile Juna's way. "Some of us have a job to do. We all can't sit around and dream of saving Earth boys."

Juna rolled her eyes as she watched her friend walk away. Of all the people in their group, it was likely Pom whose life had changed the most over the last two years. She'd gone from being a princess's personal servant, roaming the halls of the royal palace, to a highly trained Tech, supporting a team of giant fighting robots on the other side of the galaxy. Juna knew Pom was happier in her new role and looked forward to a time when all hods could expect more from their lives.

Juna shook herself from her daydream and began typing queries, trying to learn what might be wrong with their human visitor. After an hour of searching, she still wasn't sure she'd correctly diagnosed the problem. Her best guess was he had fallen into something called a coma. If that was true, moving him to a medical facility as soon as possible was crucial. Being hooked up to a supply of food and water was critical to keeping him alive.

One piece of information she found particularly intriguing was that talking to someone in a coma may be helpful in the healing process. It was unlikely the patient would understand what was being said, but the sound of a friendly voice might be beneficial to their recovery.

"It's worth a try," she said to herself as she logged off and stood to leave. "Let's go talk to an earthling."

Sitting beside him, staring at his peaceful face, she found herself unsure what to say. Speaking English would limit her options. With all the time she spent on the internet, her reading and writing in English were excellent. Hours of watching movies had fine-tuned her listening skills, but she'd never actually spoken it before.

"Hello. My name is Juna," she began hesitantly. "I am a princess. No! Why would I say that? I hate to be a princess. This is hard."

Frustrated, she took a deep breath to gather her thoughts and started again. "I live here with my friends, but we not come from here. We hide from my father. He is the emperor, but is not nice."

The afternoon passed quickly, as she told him about her life. When she didn't show up for dinner, Orin brought her a plate of food, leaving her to continue her tale. She told the human about her absent mother and Jakol, her horrible brother. Then she mentioned her sister Lacee and how sweet she was, but that they weren't very close. Next came Pom and Orin, how she met Skeet while stealing a car, and Taz while breaking Pom out of prison. She told him about sneaking through the rafters to spy on her father, and about the Mechs defeating the Marans in the war before discovering they were actually Cambrians that had survived the failed Starchaser mission.

It amazed Juna how easy this guy was to talk to. Maybe conversations were simpler when you weren't being interrupted by the other person all the time. When she was done with her own history, she started in on her early impressions of Earth.

"It is nice planet and I like movies, but you do strange things. You kiss each other... *on the mouth*! That is gross! Annu and Dorel did it for joke. We made a laugh, but I think they like it."

Juna glanced at the clock she kept on her bedside table and realized she'd been talking for hours. Her one-man audience was still in a coma, but she hoped it had helped a bit. She stood tall, turned off the light, and slipped silently out of her room. Upon reaching the central cavern, she stepped behind the Tech Station and rested her hands on Pom's shoulders.

"Hey, can I bunk with you tonight? My bed is full of human."

"Sure, my pleasure," Pom replied with a smile. "And how's your new roommate doing?"

"No change. I guess my life story isn't as stimulating as I thought."

"That's a good thing. The General is still pacing like a caged animal. If that human wakes up, it might push him over the edge."

Juna looked up to watch the General's endless journey from one side of the cave to the other.

"I'll go see if I can calm him down," she said, turning to leave. "Catch ya' later."

"How is it... *he* doing?" the General asked as soon as she arrived.

"Asleep and still breathing. I think he'll be fine until morning."

"That's good news," he replied with a sigh of relief. "Listen Juna, I think we should cancel our trip to Cambria tomorrow with all this going on."

Juna and the General made periodic trips back home to help build support for The Underground. The General knew that victory over the emperor would be impossible until most Cambrians felt motivated to change things. He thought Juna's popularity there might be helpful.

"Sure, no problem—we'll do it another time. And don't worry, General. Everything will be fine." She gave his arm a reassuring squeeze.

Leaving him to continue his relentless pacing, Juna walked through the central cavern and, when no one was looking, ducked down a narrow passage outside the entrance. It tightened further as she moved along it, eventually requiring her to start climbing. Soon, she was thirty feet above the floor, and squeezing through a small vent that took her outside the cave. It was an exit no one else knew about, a spot where she could be alone to think.

*Her new quiet place.*

Perched on a small ledge, she stared at the sky and drew in a glorious breath of fresh air. The moon was out, a half circle of light joined in the night sky by a few wispy clouds and a billion stars. The moon was so tiny here. Back home, they had two moons that dominated the sky when they were overhead, but here, the lone moon cycled from a slim crescent to a small circle. It was pretty in its own way, but seeing it always made her homesick.

As she sat there, enjoying the solitude, she heard a faint buzzing. It took her a moment to realize it was the alarms ringing back in the cave. It surprised her. She hadn't heard them in weeks, and never from out here. Scampering back through the vent, she flew down the rock walls as fast as her legs could carry her.

By the time she reached the central cavern, the alarms were silent. The Gate was already powered down and the four Mechs that were stationed there earlier were gone, no doubt on the surface of Mara, fighting four of the emperor's clones. She sprinted to the Tech Station, joining Orin to watch the battle unfold.

"So, my dad's at it again, is he?"

"Yup. Whenever we think we'll never hear from him again, he..."

Orin stopped abruptly mid-sentence. He had turned to face her, but his gaze had drifted over her shoulder, and a look of disbelief swept across his face. She spun to see what had distracted him, releasing a gasp at the unexpected sight. The human stood there, wrapped in a blanket, staring at them.

"Who the heck are you guys?" he asked.

# 3

The question seemed simple enough, but nobody knew quite how to respond. Not only was an explanation tough to work out, but no one in the group had ever tested their English skills on an actual human before. Orin was grateful when Skeet stepped up, so he didn't have to.

"We are nice people," Skeet replied mechanically, looking somewhat unsure if he'd answered the question correctly.

"Nice people, huh?" the human shot back. "Then why did you steal my clothes and leave me alone in a dark room?"

Skeet looked back at the group and shrugged, his eyes pleading for help in coming up with a reasonable answer.

"You were in the water," Orin jumped in. "We did the rescue on you."

The human gave Orin a puzzled look. "OK," he finally replied. "I guess that makes sense. The last thing I remember is running the rapids and everything going sideways. So, thank you for... doing the rescue on me. Maybe you are nice people, after all." He paused, appearing to mull over the situation. "So, why didn't you take me to a hospital?"

*Argh!*

Why did this human keep asking such difficult questions? Orin's mind churned, trying to think of some possible reason not to take an injured person to a hospital.

"We could not find one," Skeet blurted out. He looked over to Orin, his eyes questioning whether he'd come up with something good.

Orin shrugged. He had no idea.

"That doesn't make any sense," the human said. "In fact, none of this makes sense. What are you guys doing here, anyway? Making a movie?"

And with that one question, Orin felt the weight of the world lifted from his shoulders. Since the moment this conversation began, he'd been racking his brain, trying to think of a rational explanation, and the human came up with it for him.

"Yes!" he replied with far too much enthusiasm. "We are making a movie."

"Cool. I've always wanted to be in one. Do you have any parts open? Even being an extra would be fine with me."

*That's just great. He's back to being difficult.*

Now Orin had to come up with some part the human could play in a nonexistent movie. As he was thinking of a way to get out of this one, he felt a hand settle on his shoulder, and heard the General whisper in his ear.

"Orin, there is a battle on Mara going on right now. You have to get the human out of here. Try getting it back to Juna's room."

"Hey, who's that?" the human asked. "Is that the director?"

"Yes," Orin replied. "He is the director. He says for us to take you away for the movie to be made."

"Sure. Tell him I'm here if he needs me."

As Orin began walking, he signalled Skeet and Taz to join him. He wanted Skeet there because his English was so good, and he thought Taz might be useful should the human decide to make a break for it.

Taz had stayed in the background until now, so it was the first chance for the human to get a good look at him.

"Whoa, you are one huge dude," he said, obviously intimidated by Taz's stature. "Are you a wrestler or something?"

“I do not know what this is.” Taz appeared to be confused. “Is it good to be a wrestler or something?”

The human stared at him, looking unsure what to say. “You people are strange,” he finally managed, as he followed the group out of the central cavern. “I’ve heard actors are weird, but you guys are off the charts.”

Orin glanced at Skeet, wondering if he understood what that meant. The blank stare returned, told him he did not.

“We are not actors,” Skeet surprisingly volunteered. “We use the cameras.”

“What’s with the fake ears, then?” the human asked. “Even the director was wearing them.”

“Yes, he was.” Orin realized he didn’t answer the question, but hoped the human wouldn’t notice. “Here we are,” he said as they arrived at the door to Juna’s room. “You should rest more.”

“Actually, I’m alright. My body feels like it’s been pounded with a sledgehammer, but my head feels fine. If someone would give me a ride home, I’ll get out of your hair,” he said, stepping into the room.

“You are not in my hair,” Skeet replied. “But we have no car today. Tomorrow, we will have a car.”

The human returned a confused look. “Why do you guys talk so funny? That’s a strange accent. Are you from Australia?”

“Yes, we are from Australia,” Skeet agreed.

“From down under, eh mate?”

The group exchanged glances, but no one knew what to say. In the end, they didn’t bother trying. Orin hoped changing the subject might help.

“My name is Orin. What is your name?”

“Todd.”

Orin managed to stifle his reaction, but both Skeet and Taz burst out with an awkward laugh.

"What's so funny about Todd?"

After a moment to collect his thoughts, Orin responded. "In our language, that word means a different thing. It does not make a good name."

"I thought you were from Australia. Don't they speak English in Australia?"

"Yes. Yes, they do," Orin confirmed, once again failing to answer the question, but pretending he did.

"OK, this is getting a little strange for me," Todd said. "I'd really like to get out of here now."

Just as he made a step for the exit, there was a gentle knock at the door and Juna stepped inside.

"Hello. I hope you are good," she said, carefully pronouncing each word. "My name is Juna."

"Todd."

Juna's mouth dropped open, looking more offended than she'd ever been, but she had no idea how to respond.

"His name is Todd," Orin explained, hoping to clear things up.

"Yeah, I know. I have a funny name," Todd said, stepping towards Juna with his hand extended. "I'm pleased to meet you. Wow, you sure are pretty. Are you the lead actress?"

Juna's look changed from offended to confused, but she still had no idea what to say.

"We told Todd about the movie we are making here in this cave," Skeet explained, adding a wink he hoped Todd wouldn't see.

"Yes!" Juna exclaimed, obviously relieved to finally understand what was going on. "We are making a movie!"

Todd stood there, still wrapped in his blanket, looking from one person to the next. He finally settled on Orin.

"Listen, I appreciate you guys pulling me out of the river, but I have to say, this is freaking me out a bit. As nice as it would be to help with your movie, I think I want to go home. Why don't we go talk to the director?" He made another move towards the door.

Taz stepped into his path, blocking the way.

"What is *that*?" Todd exclaimed, pointing to the wall at the back of the room. As everyone turned to look, he slipped past Taz and out the door, sprinting for the other end of the cave.

Orin chided himself for being so foolish. He'd seen enough movies to know how sneaky humans could be. Dashing out the door, he gave chase, with Skeet, Taz and Juna right on his heels. Todd had a big lead, reaching the central cavern well ahead of them. Orin noticed him stop at the entrance, his eyes focusing straight ahead as his jaw dropped open.

When Orin caught up, he gazed into the central cavern to see what had captured Todd's attention. There, stepping through the Gate, was Carnage, followed closely by Geiger, Helion and Vortex, all returning from what appeared to be a successful battle on Mara. Todd turned to face Orin, grabbed onto one of his ears, and gave it a mighty tug.

"Ouch!" Orin howled. "What did you do that for?" Unfortunately, he'd spoken Cambrian for all of it.

"I knew it!" Todd proclaimed triumphantly. "Those ears aren't fake. You guys are aliens!"

Orin was too stunned to speak, so Skeet jumped in.

"No. We are not aliens. We are from Australia."

"I hate to tell you this Martian boy, but they don't have giant glowy rings with robot monsters coming out of them in Australia."

By this time, both the General and the Professor had arrived to join the conversation. "I'm afraid the jig is up," the General said to Orin, not even trying to use English. "We'd better tell him the truth and hope he can keep a secret."

"What did he say?" Todd demanded, obviously beginning to

panic. "You guys aren't going to melt my brain, are you?"

"What an odd question," Orin said, not able to hide his confusion. "We will not melt your brain. Let us tell you who we are and why we are here."

For the next hour, Todd sat at the big table with all eleven of the Cambrians, listening to the story of how they came to be hiding out in a secluded cave in Earth's Grand Canyon. He learned about their plan to bring the Marans home and gain freedom for the hods. He heard about their discovery of the satellites, learning English by watching TV and everyone's love of movies.

Todd appeared to become more comfortable with the idea of aliens on his planet with each passing moment. At one point, he interrupted Skeet's retelling of the prison break story, to say it all sounded strangely familiar. When he said this, Orin noticed Juna squirming awkwardly in her seat and looking a little guilty, but he didn't know why. By the end, Todd had totally embraced the idea of sitting in a cave with a bunch of aliens. In fact, he seemed quite excited about it.

"This is so cool. I'm probably the first person on Earth to meet someone from another planet. I wonder if they'll build a statue of me some day."

"No. No. No," the General insisted, still making no attempt to speak English. "We must remain hidden. I'm afraid the young man will have to stay with us until we're ready to leave."

"What?" Orin demanded, also choosing to speak Cambrian. "Are you kidding? We can't keep him here. That would be kidnapping."

"Have you got a better idea? We can start looking for a new planet right away, but we can't let him go until we're off this world."

"What if he promises not to tell anyone?"

"We can't take the chance. How could we possibly trust him?"

"Hey guys," Todd interrupted. "Why do I get the feeling you're talking about me? I'm getting a little spooked here. You're not rethinking the whole brain melting thing, are you?"

"He wants to keep you here," Juna chimed in. "Until we leave."

"What!" Todd burst out in horror. "You can't keep me prisoner. If my friends don't find me when they come back, everyone will think I'm dead."

"They'll send out search parties," Orin told the General calmly. "Either way, they're going to find us."

"Alright Orin, we can take him home if you can figure out a way to do it that won't expose our presence here."

"What did he say?" Todd pleaded. "What are you guys going to do to me?"

"You do not worry," Orin assured him, switching back to English. "He is scared you will tell about us. If you can keep us secret, we will take you home."

"Sure. Sure, no problem. I won't tell a soul. In fact, I can help you guys. Why don't I go home to tell my friends they don't have to save me? Then I'll come right back here, so you won't have to worry about me blabbing."

"How do we know you will come back?" Orin asked.

"Somebody can stay with me the whole time. I think Juna would be the perfect choice." He flashed her a smile.

Orin directed a questioning look at the General and received a subtle nod in reply.

"OK, that is good. We will make a plan."

They would need Gecko, so waiting until morning was the only option. It was already late in the evening, but everyone was completely wired, so Orin and Juna took Todd for a quick tour of the cave. When they reached the back entrance, he was overjoyed to see his kayak sitting there.

"Awesome! I've got a change of clothes in here," he said as he rummaged around in the small hold at the back of the boat, retrieving a large watertight bag. "My wallet and cell phone are in here too."

"I am pleased you have your things," Orin said, watching Todd pull on a new shirt. "Why do you want to help us?"

"Because it's an adventure, man." Todd gave him an enthusiastic slap on the back. "I get to hang out with a bunch of space people! This is going to be a blast!"

"Yes, we will have a blast with you," Orin agreed. "But first, we sleep. Tomorrow we will start to adventure."

They escorted Todd back to Juna's room and wished him good night. Juna headed for Pom's room while Orin walked quietly to his own. Slipping into his bed, he lay staring at the ceiling, too excited to sleep. Tomorrow, he would join Todd and Juna on a trip to a real Earth city. Part of him was terrified, but the truth was, he could hardly wait to get started. He finally drifted off, dreaming of visiting a world that, until now, he'd only seen in the movies.

Early the next morning, the entire group assembled at the back entrance to the cave. When they'd first arrived here, the only access was a small opening facing the river, not large enough for even the smallest Mech to fit through.

The General wasn't happy with the Mechs' only means of exiting being through the Gate, so he had them excavate a new access. In theory, the new opening increased the odds of their hidden location being discovered, but the General felt its secluded location, tucked inside an existing crevasse, meant the chance of anyone stumbling upon it was essentially zero.

As soon as Todd passed through the tunnel, his eyes drifted to Gecko.

"Whoa! Why do you have a monster truck that looks like a lizard?"

"I am not a monster or a truck," Gecko replied, noticeably insulted.

Diara and Pom had created a translation program and loaded it into every Mech, so they could now speak perfect English. This made Orin more than a little jealous. It didn't seem fair that the Mechs could pick it up so easily. He'd spent countless hours trying to master the language, and still wasn't any good at it.

"That is so awesome. Sorry, dude. I didn't realize you were one of those Mech things," Todd said. "But, are you sure fluorescent green is the way to go? I thought you guys were trying to hide."

"Perhaps you are right," Gecko agreed as his colour drifted from bright green to a dusty red until he was almost a perfect match for the surrounding rock. "Is that better?"

"Too cool," Todd said, shaking his head as he climbed through Gecko's access hatch. Juna followed right behind him. As Orin approached the ladder, the Professor stepped in and gave him a hug.

"You be careful, son. I'm sorry the General and I aren't able to help, but not speaking the language is limiting our usefulness here. I'm afraid the youngsters in the group will be called upon to do more than their share while we're on this planet."

"No problem, Dad. I think we're ready. And I promise to be careful."

Orin noticed Gigahertz crouched in front of Gecko, so he went over to check. Heavy chains were being connected from Gecko's front tow hooks to Fallout and Isotope, the two Atomic Mechs who would drag him out of the canyon. Because the Atomics used a levitation technology to move, they hovered over the ground rather than touching it. The two massive machines would assist with Gecko's exit by towing him up the vertical rock walls leading to the rim.

"Hey Gig, do you think those chains will hold?"

"Orin, I would hardly allow this process to continue if I were not certain every component could perform its function."

"Thanks, big guy. I wouldn't expect anything less. You hold down the fort while I'm gone, and I'll tell you all about life in an Earth city when I get back."

"I do not know which fort you speak of, nor do I understand why it would need to be held down, but I will look forward to hearing about your journey when you return. And Orin... please keep your head down."

Orin smiled up at his mechanical friend, realizing that was the same request he made of Gig the day before he went to war with the Marans.

"You know I will."

Orin offered a few words of encouragement to Fallout and Isotope, then walked back to climb aboard Gecko. The space inside his hold was significantly smaller than in the other Bio Mechs, but it was fine for today's mission. Todd and Juna were strapped into two of the three cushioned seats lined up in a row facing Gecko's front window. Orin took his spot in the seat on the right and began buckling up his own harness.

As soon as they were settled, Gecko fired up his engine and followed Fallout and Isotope towards the face of the cliff. The Atomics rose as Gecko's tires bit, churning to drag him up the wall until he was pointing straight up. Orin was pushed back in his seat, staring through the window at the soaring red rock wall and the sky beyond. A knot formed in his stomach, only now realizing how terrifying this trip would be.

He felt a little better when Juna's hand reached out and grabbed his, but an unexpected pang of jealousy hit when he noticed her other hand clasped in Todd's. That feeling disappeared immediately when

Gecko hit the accelerator, and they began flying up the side of the canyon.

The General wanted their trip up the rock face to be as quick as possible. Gecko was camouflaged nicely, but the shiny white bodies of the Atomics would be visible from miles away. All three passengers screamed for the entire thirty seconds of their bumpy sprint to the rim. When they reached the top, there was a jarring thud before finding themselves horizontal again.

"Woo hoo!" Todd bellowed. "That was amazing! Let's do it again!"

Orin and Juna looked at each other in disbelief, shocked anyone would want to do something like that again. They had emerged into a small clearing surrounded by a tangled thicket of leafless bushes. Fallout and Isotope disconnected their chains and slipped over the edge for their return trip to the bottom, while Gecko skilfully crawled over a series of large boulders. Soon he was clear of the canyon, sitting on the loose gravel surrounding its perimeter.

Their destination was Todd's hometown: a city called Flagstaff, Arizona, located roughly fifty miles due south of their hideout in the canyon.

Gecko revved his engine and spun his tires on the loose rock surface to get their journey underway. After a quick two-mile drive across sandy terrain, they hit a paved road.

"This is Highway 64," Todd told them. "Go west until we hit the 89. That'll take us south, right into Flagstaff."

"Diara has downloaded a mapping application into my central processor," Gecko reported. "I have the route plotted and auto-drive engaged. We shall be there in less than one hour."

There were no other vehicles on the road for as far as Orin could see. The surrounding view reminded him of the high desert back on Cambria, but somehow even flatter and more desolate. Small tufts of grass and weeds dotted the landscape, but there was nothing more than a foot high between them and the horizon in every direction. He settled into his seat, readying himself for the trip ahead, when a wailing sound sent a chill down his spine.

He glanced at Juna, whose panicked look likely mirrored his own. They'd both seen enough movies to know the sound of a police siren when they heard one.

# 4

"Don't worry, I've got this," Todd assured them. "Just don't let him get a good look at you. And whatever you do, don't say anything." He tapped on Gecko's dashboard. "That goes for you, too. If this guy says you're a truck... you're a truck."

Juna's heart pounded in her chest. She couldn't imagine getting off to a worse start. Not being discovered was their number one priority, yet here they were, ten minutes into the trip and already stopped by the police. This sort of thing happened to her all the time back home, but here it was different. As an underage driver with a need for speed, she'd been pulled over dozens of times. But on Cambria, she was the emperor's youngest daughter. The worst penalty she'd ever received there was a harsh stare and a gentle warning. This had the potential to be so much worse.

"Good morning, officer," Todd said cheerily as the policeman appeared at Gecko's side window. "Is there something I can do for you?"

"Licence and registration."

"Here is my driver's license," Todd said, fishing a small card from his wallet and passing it through the window. "But I'm afraid there could be a slight problem with the registration."

The officer reached up to grab the card. "I thought there might be," he said with some humour in his voice. "What with this vehicle having no license plate and all. In fact, I couldn't help but notice a few other things missing: brake lights, turn signals, bumpers. Stuff like that."

"And you would be correct in questioning the street-legal status of this vehicle," Todd replied agreeably. "You see, this truck really is built more for off-roading—something I shouldn't be driving on this lovely highway of yours. That was definitely a mistake on my part."

"Yes, it was Todd. Do you have a particularly good reason for making that mistake?"

"Well, my friends here are from out of town. I wanted them to experience the beauty of our local surroundings, so I took them for a ride in the desert. We were all getting bounced around pretty good, so I thought it might be nice to take a break by driving on a smooth surface for a while."

The officer seemed unmoved by Todd's explanation. "It appears your license has been issued quite recently," he said. "Young drivers must learn to become good drivers. Tell me, Todd, what have you learned today?"

"When I go off-roading, I should stay off the road."

"That is correct," the officer confirmed, passing the license back. "Just a warning today, son. That is one goofy looking truck you've got there. Fortunately for you, seeing it has put me in a good mood."

Juna let out a sigh as the officer walked away, relieved to have this ordeal behind her. She couldn't believe Todd had talked his way out of that one.

"A good job you did," she told him. "I am glad we got in no trouble."

"Yeah, I was sweating the whole time. We got lucky. He could've been a real jerk about it."

"But what did he mean by goofy looking?" Gecko protested. "I am an extremely attractive machine, if I do say so myself."

"You're awesome, Geck," Todd chuckled. "But let's get you off this highway. Head straight south through the desert. We'll figure out what to do when we get closer to the city."

The ride was rough. The terrain appeared flat from a distance, but when you were barrelling over it in a speed-obsessed Mech, every bump felt like a mountain. Juna could hardly wait for the trip to be over. As they wound their way southward, the desert landscape soon turned to a sparse forest set among rocky cliffs. After travelling along winding trails and a series of gravel roads, they finally reached the edge of the city.

When they caught their first glimpse of it, Juna had to admit to being a bit disappointed. The movies they watched took place in cities like New York, Los Angeles and Tokyo. Flagstaff was not like those at all. There were no gleaming glass towers soaring high into the sky. No stacked freeways or massive bridges. It was an endless expanse of houses, shops, and nondescript buildings tucked into a small valley.

"I want to swing by the observatory first," Todd said. "Lots of tourists go there, so we should find something to hide those ears of yours."

"What is an observatory?" Juna asked.

"It's a place with a big telescope. Hey, I bet they look at your star sometimes."

"We look at stars often," Juna said wistfully. "But I don't know which is ours."

"That's kinda sad... Hey, wait! Geck, turn here!"

Gecko pulled out of the forest and jumped a curb into a large parking lot. Todd had him come to a stop near a wheeled cart, where a vendor was selling colourful clothing and small trinkets.

"Let me out here," Todd said. "I'll be right back."

Juna was leery about letting him out by himself, still not trusting he wouldn't make a break for freedom at his first opportunity. As he stepped out of Gecko's hold, she positioned herself near the hatch, ready to give chase should one be required. She watched him walk over to the cart, select a couple of hats from a rack, and hand the vendor some money.

Climbing back into Gecko's hold, Todd handed each of them a hat. Hers was a brilliant pink that said "Star Girl," while Orin's was red with a cartoon image of a scowling bird.

"Here, put these on. And make sure you get the tops of your ears tucked inside."

As they slipped on their new hats, Todd instructed Gecko to drive out of the parking lot and proceed down a winding hill.

"There's a park at the bottom. We can leave Gecko there and walk to my place."

"Leave Gecko? I don't want to get left."

"Do you want to get pulled over by the cops again? That won't go nearly as well in the city as it did on the highway."

"Alright," Gecko sulked, "but don't be gone too long."

After arriving at the lot, the rumbling Mech pulled into a quiet corner in the back. Juna leapt out as soon as his hatch opened, happy to be on solid ground again. Todd followed, then led the group through a nearby playground, and across the street into an adjacent residential area.

"I live one block over," Todd said.

"Will a person be there?" Juna asked. "You *cannot* tell about us."

"My stepmom will, but don't worry about her. She never listens to a word I say."

A sense of wonder swept through Juna as they walked, her eyes darting from one thing to the next. The houses were bigger than they were back home, and most had a smaller house next to it to hold a car. They were brightly painted and surrounded by gardens, overgrown with towering trees and some of the most beautiful flowers she'd ever seen. When they reached a blue house with a white fence, Todd turned up the driveway, skipped up the stairs, and swung the door open.

"Hey Mom, I'm home," he yelled, signalling Orin and Juna to join him. "I brought some new friends with me."

As she stepped into the house, Juna inhaled the glorious scent of freshly baked bread. She stood in a small, tidy kitchen with the morning sun streaming through the windows.

"That's nice, dear," a woman's voice came from down the hall.

"They're from out of town. Like *way* out."

Juna scowled at him and elbowed him in the ribs, but received only a wily grin in return.

"It's OK. She's always busy with the twins," he whispered. "She doesn't pay attention to anything I say." Then he called down the hallway. "I'm going to be helping them, so I'll be gone for a few days. If they take me to their planet, it might be longer."

"That's nice, dear. You have fun."

Both Juna *and* Orin gave him a smack for that one, but he laughed it off.

"I'll pick up a few things and we can go," he told them. "My room's down here."

He led them along a narrow hallway and into a small room that looked like it had been ransacked by thieves. The bed was piled high with a knot of blankets and pillows. Clothing and comic books were strewn over everything, and an unpleasant odour filled the air. The walls were decorated with posters of motorcycles flying through the air and people jumping from cliffs.

Juna looked at Orin, who was making a funny face and holding his nose. She giggled in return as they watched Todd pick up random pieces of clothing off the floor and stuff them into a small green duffel bag.

"All done," he reported after thirty second's work. "Let's roll."

As she and Orin stepped out of the house, a thundering sound overhead drew their eyes skyward. Of course, they'd seen airplanes on TV before, but this was the first time either of them had seen one in person. Juna stared at it, wondering how anyone could be daring enough to ride in such a machine. But when she looked at Orin, she saw his brain was spinning, no doubt plotting how he might build one.

"My car's not running right now," Todd said, pointing to a rusty yellow compact with no tires. "I'll borrow the minivan and we can head for downtown."

At Todd's insistence, Juna slid into the passenger seat, while Orin climbed into the back. Once out of Todd's neighbourhood, they encountered wider streets with heavier traffic. Juna was much more comfortable driving a car than she was as a passenger, cringing with each vehicle that passed. When they neared the first traffic light, she wondered why Todd wasn't slowing. To her right, she saw a vehicle approaching on the cross-street, yet Todd made no move towards the brake. Panicking, she slammed her hands on the dashboard and screamed "STOP!" as she closed her eyes and braced for impact.

When she realized they'd survived the ordeal, she opened her eyes to see Todd, giving her a curious look, as he cruised through the intersection under a green light.

"I guess green means 'go' on this planet," she said sheepishly. "Never mind."

The trip carried them past a beautiful brick railway station and into an expansive area littered with dozens of shops. Seeing the mind-boggling selection and recalling all the commercials she'd watched on TV, Juna realized how much time and effort humans put into buying things.

The van rolled to a stop in one of the few empty spots in the sprawling lot.

"I need to stop at work to let them know I'll be gone for a while."

"What is your work?" Juna asked.

"I flip burgers." When he saw his new friends had no idea what he was talking about, he elaborated. "I work at a restaurant making hamburgers."

"Ah yes, hamburgers. We have seen these on TV, but do not know what they are."

"They're great and I'm starving. Why don't I buy you guys lunch?"

After exiting the car, Todd led them towards a colourful building made almost entirely of windows. Juna noticed an unappealing smell getting stronger with every step. When Todd opened the door and ushered them in, the stench was unbearable.

"So, what can I get you?"

"What is a hamburger made from?" Juna asked, already fearing the answer.

"Well, it's a ground beef patty with some toppings that you stick it in a bun."

"And what is ground beef?"

"It's meat… from a cow. They grind it up, shape it into a circle and char it over a flame."

"From a cow?" Juna asked tentatively. "A cow is a large, slow animal. So, it is made from the flesh of an animal?"

"Yes."

"You eat the flesh of an animal?"

"Well, we cook it first."

"You eat the charred flesh of an animal?"

"Yes, we do. So, what can I get you?"

"Nothing," Juna replied.

"Nothing," echoed Orin.

"OK, suit yourself. You guys wait here while I talk to my boss and grab something for myself."

"We will wait outside," she told him, glancing out the window and pointing. "Way over there. By that tree."

"Sounds good. I'll see you there in a few minutes."

"Can you believe that?" Juna exclaimed as she and Orin sprinted across the parking lot to get as far away from the smell as they could. "They *eat* animals."

"Who would even think to try that? I certainly won't be sampling any Earth food while we're here."

"Me neither. Who knows *what* else they might try?"

They sat down on a bench under the tree to await Todd's return. As he approached, Juna saw him finish off the last of his hamburger before tossing the wrapper into a nearby trash can. He spoke into a small rectangular device held close to his ear. When he joined them, he said goodbye to the machine and placed it in his pocket. It must have been one of those cell phones she'd heard so much about.

"Good news. I told my friend's brother I don't need rescuing," Todd told them. "But if you guys don't mind, I'd like to do a little shopping while I'm here. If I can pick up a few things, I should get the kayak..."

Juna didn't hear the rest of it. Something else had caught her attention.

"It is good. I be right back," she mumbled before darting across the parking lot. She stopped in front of a vehicle that looked unlike anything else she'd seen here. It was built low to the ground and had an open cockpit with side-by-side seats. There were two wheels in the front and one in the back. It was a tri-racer! Just like hers back home. It was even red! Memories of cruising the streets of Volara flooded her mind. As she stood and stared at it, she could almost feel the wind whipping through her hair. She circled the machine, inspecting every square inch.

"Do you mind?"

Juna's attention snapped back to Earth. The tri-racer's owner approached from behind and pulled on his helmet.

"No. Sorry," she said, turning to make her way back to the tree. When she got there, neither Orin nor Todd were anywhere to be seen. Looking around, she spotted a familiar figure with a red hat staring into the window of a nearby shop with the word "Arcade" printed on it. She walked over and tapped Orin on the shoulder.

"Hey, where's Todd?" she asked, comfortably switching back to Cambrian.

"I don't know. I thought he was with you."

"What do you mean, with me? You two were talking."

"Yeah, he was saying something about fixing his boat when I spotted this place. I sort of wandered off."

Juna wasn't in a position to get angry. She'd done the exact same thing. "So, what should we do?"

"Wait here, I guess."

A half hour later, they were still waiting, getting more and more nervous with each passing second.

"Do you think he took off?" Juna asked.

"Why would he do that?"

"I don't know. So he could turn us in to get rich and famous. He seemed pretty excited about that statue."

"Why would he wait until now? He's had lots of chances to ditch us before this."

"We're miles from Gecko right now. Maybe he wanted to get us lost and alone. I have no idea where we are right now. Do you?"

"Not really. What should we do?"

Juna had to think about that one. What could they do?

She stood to pace, refusing to sit there waiting for something bad to happen.

"Go find the car," she suggested. "Do you remember what it

looked like?"

"Sort of. He called it a minivan, but all their cars look the same to me. I think it was white. Or maybe silver."

"Search the lot. Look for that green duffel bag of his. He left it on the back seat. When you find it, come get me. I'll wander around and see if I can find him."

"I don't think we should split up. How will I find you?"

"You brought your scanner, right?" she asked, tapping the necklace he'd made for her.

"Oh yeah, that'll work," he said, surveying the daunting expanse of vehicles. "I'll track you down after I find the car. Be careful."

"I will, you too," she said, lightly squeezing his shoulder and dashing off across the parking lot.

Juna was not optimistic about finding Todd. If his intention was to abandon them, he'd be long gone by now. Still, it felt better to be up and moving. A sense of helplessness took hold, an unpleasant reminder of that terrible day she roamed the streets of Volara, trying to find The Depot. She fought off an urge to panic.

And then, in an instant, despair turned to delight. Against all odds, through a churning sea of mouth-kissing, flesh-eating aliens, she spotted a familiar face.

There was Todd, emerging from a nearby store and starting off at a jog in the opposite direction.

*Was he trying to get away?*

Juna resolved right then to thwart any attempt at escape. She set off after him.

Weaving through a throng of pedestrians, she soon found herself directly behind him. She grabbed his shoulder, jerking it towards her and twisting him around to face her. As he spun, his expression went from shock, to recognition, and finally settled on confusion. The bag he was carrying flew from his grip as she snagged his flailing arm, yanked it behind his back and slammed him face first into the side of a building.

"Ouch! Juna, what did you do that for?"

"To stop you from getting away."

"Getting away? What are you talking about? I'm shopping. You were supposed to wait by the tree. I told you I'd be about an hour."

"I did not hear that part," she said, releasing her grip on his arm. "I am sorry to hurt you."

"That's OK. I'm pretty sure nothing's broken. Wow, are you ever strong," he said, rubbing his aching wrist. "Where's Orin?"

"He looks for the car. He will find us here."

"How's he going to do that?"

Juna pulled the metal bauble from beneath her blouse and showed it to Todd. "He made me this. His scan will find it."

"He made you a tracking device? That's a little creepy, don't you think?"

"That is what I said!" she beamed. "But it is because he cares about me. It has saved my life once. I like it very much."

"OK, if you say so. Let's wait at that table over there," he said, pointing to a nearby seating area. "Can I get you a soda?"

"What is a soda?"

"Something you drink. It's really good."

"Does it have meat in it?"

"No, it doesn't have meat in it," he replied with a chuckle. "I'll go grab us a couple."

Juna loved the soda. It was sweet and had little bubbles that tickled her nose when she drank it. They were sitting at a round metal table with built-in seats and a bright green umbrella overhead.

"So, are you and Orin an item?"

"I do not know what that is," she said, taking a sip from her soda. "If it is boyfriend, then no. I can never have one of those."

"Never? Why not?"

"That is something for normal life. I cannot have one. My family is bad. For many years, they are the boss and made life hard for people. I must spend my life to fix that. It is my..." She paused and smiled. "I cannot find the English word."

"What's your word?"

"Owangatuu."

"That's a pretty word. I think ours would be something like duty or obligation. It's great you want to help everyone, but you need to enjoy your life too. Maybe you can do all that and still have a normal life."

"I will hope that to be."

"You really are something," he said. "Gorgeous. Strong. Smart. Noble. You are truly amazing."

At that moment, a shadow fell over the table. They both looked up to see Orin standing over them.

"Todd, it is good to again see you," he said with obvious relief. "I am happy you did not leave us."

"Leave you? Are you kidding? I'm with you guys all the way to the end," he replied as he stood up to go. "Let's get moving. We've got a world to save."

# 5

"What is that blue square of water?"

Orin, Juna and Todd were in the minivan, on their way back to Todd's place. Something out in front of one of the motels had caught Orin's eye.

"It's a swimming pool."

"What is it for?"

"It's for swimming. You know, flailing your arms and kicking so you can move through the water." Todd moved an arm in a circle to demonstrate.

"On Cambria, we have animals that swim, but why would people do it?"

"Because it's fun, and it helps cool you down on a hot day."

"I guess that makes sense," Orin replied, not sure he believed it.

Being cooled down did sound nice, though. Apparently, it wasn't even summer yet, but he'd never felt heat like this. Flagstaff was a *very* hot place, and being trapped in this car only made it worse. As the sweat dripped down his face, he sat quietly in the back, hoping the drive would be over soon. A few minutes later, they passed a familiar house and turned into Todd's driveway.

"Would you mind bringing my duffel bag?" Todd asked. "There are a couple more things I want to grab while we're here."

Orin watched Todd remove the license plate from his rusty old car and throw it into a cardboard box filled with spare parts.

"With this stuff, your Wrenches should get Gecko looking street-legal. At least sort of."

Orin thought it unlikely Gecko would ever need to drive on the street again, but it never hurt to be prepared. Todd grabbed the box and the three of them began the walk back to Gecko's parking spot. When they got there, several people were milling around, taking pictures with him. Everyone commented how cool he was and asked where he came from. Todd politely dodged the questions as they climbed aboard for the return trip to the cave.

"Did you see all those people wanting to take my picture?" Gecko gloated. "I told you I was an extremely attractive machine."

"Just tell me you didn't talk to anyone," Orin begged.

"Orin. I'm insulted you would suggest such a thing. I'm a professional."

"Sorry Geck. I'll never even think something like that again," he laughed. "Let's go home."

They retraced their steps for the trip back, avoiding major roads along the way. Gecko kept Diara updated, so when they arrived at the hidden clearing on the edge of the rim, Skeet, Isotope and Fallout were there to greet them.

"So, what's an Earth city like?" Skeet demanded as soon as the group emerged from Gecko's hold. "Is it the same as in the movies?"

"Not really," Orin replied. "We didn't see a single explosion." He nodded towards Isotope and Fallout. "What's with the Atomics?"

Both were wrapped from top to bottom with a rough brown cloth and had dried branches sticking out all over. They looked like gigantic dead bushes.

"The General almost had a heart attack when he saw them hauling Gecko up that cliff. He asked me and Taz to camouflage them. Pretty good, huh?"

"What are you guys saying?" Todd interrupted. "Nothing about me, I hope."

"I am sorry," Skeet said. "Sometimes I forget to use English. I will do better."

"No problem. I appreciate it, though." He gave the disguised Mechs a curious glance. "So, how do we get back down?"

"The General wants Gecko to stay hidden up here in case we need him again. Isotope and Fallout will take the rest of us down."

"I guess it's wait state for me then," Gecko said as he nestled into some bushes and changed his colour to blend in. "Call me if you need me."

Orin joined Skeet by Isotope, while Todd and Juna wandered over to Fallout. The massive machines extended their powerful arms so they could clutch their passengers tightly to their bodies. Orin felt another unexpected jolt of jealousy when he saw Juna cozied up with Todd.

"The General wants the Mechs to spend as little time as possible out in the open, so this is going to be fast," Skeet warned them.

"Let it rip, Iz."

Instantly, Orin was in freefall, plunging down the side of the cliff faster than he thought possible. His stomach tried to leap from his body as the wind whistled by with so much force, he worried his skin might get peeled off. Just when he thought it couldn't get any worse, they started to slow, compressing his body so hard he feared his bones would snap. The whole trip lasted only a few seconds, but it felt like a lifetime.

"That was awesome!" Todd yelled after freeing himself from Fallout's grip. "I think that might be the coolest thing I've ever done."

Orin couldn't believe Todd's enthusiasm. A glance at Juna's pained expression told him her feelings on the subject were identical to his own.

"Let's go check in with the General," Skeet said. "He wants to hear all about the mission."

Orin briefed the team about the trip to Flagstaff. It impressed the General that everything had worked out so well, and he praised those on the mission for some quick thinking along the way.

"Please thank Todd for me," he told Orin, rising from his chair to shake the young human's hand. "He's a man of his word, and I admire that."

Todd smiled as he received the compliment and returned the handshake.

"Our situation has changed," the General continued. "We've now interacted with the people of Earth in ways we never expected. Diara and Pom, your daily duties now include a review of all local news sources. Pay attention to reports of strange sightings near the canyon or unusual rumours hinting at our presence here."

He looked at Orin and Juna with a flicker of pride in his eyes. "Well done, everyone. But if you'll excuse me, I must return to my other meeting."

With that, the professors stood and joined the General as he departed the cavern. Dorel and Annu left too, heading towards the maintenance shop. That meant only the younger members of the team remained.

Orin turned to Skeet. "What's this other meeting about?"

"A couple of people from the Underground have been here since you left. They've been locked away with the General all day. We have no idea what they're up to."

"I don't think it's going well," Pom added. "Anytime someone leaves the room, they look really stressed."

"We should speak English," Juna chimed in, speaking in English. "Todd will think we talk about him."

"That is a good idea," Orin agreed. "Sorry, Todd."

"That's OK, I don't mind. But if you do speak English, I can give you some tips that might help you get better at it."

True to his word, Todd embraced the challenge of helping everyone with their English, and it was certainly paying off. Even better, he suggested the movie for the night, and it was one of the best they'd ever seen. Orin was worried when none of the adults showed up, but everyone else brought pillows and blankets and enjoyed a wonderful evening.

Orin tried to keep his jealousy in check, but was finding it difficult. Back in Flagstaff, Todd came right out and said how amazing he thought Juna was. Orin thought that too. He simply didn't go around saying it all the time. He liked Todd, but his constant flirting with Juna was hard to watch. As he drifted off to sleep that night, he resolved not to let it bug him so much.

The next morning, Orin was dismayed to see Todd would be joining in on the daily training session. He was a little taller than Orin and had way more muscles, so it was fun to watch Juna toss him around as easily as she did with him.

"How can you possibly be that strong?" Todd asked after yet another hard landing.

"Gravity here is bigger," Juna replied. "So, if I work the same, my muscles do more. And it is not only strong. It is...," she stopped, unable to find the word.

"Technique?" Todd offered.

"Yes!" Juna agreed, pointing at him. "Technique is more important than strong."

"I'll try to remember that the next time I find myself flying through the air." He stood and dusted himself off. "But I've had enough humiliation for one day. Let's go for lunch."

As they exited the training room, Clank approached from the far end of the corridor. The Mechs spent most of their time in wait state here on Earth, but took turns waking up so they could move around to keep their joints lubricated.

Orin wasn't aware it was Clank's turn to be out and about. Otherwise, he would have given Todd a heads up. Clank was definitely the quirkiest of the Mechs, so Orin was curious to see how this first encounter would go.

"Is that the human?" Clank bellowed, stomping over and stooping, so his face hovered only inches above Todd's.

"Are we going to keep it?"

Todd cowered, terrified of the hulking machine looming over him. "What did he say? Is he going to hurt me?"

"Where are your manners, Clank?" Orin scolded. "Diara installed an English translation program in your central processor. You should always use it when Todd is around."

"Many apologies, human," Clank said, now speaking perfect English. "I did not intend to scare you in any way."

"Don't worry about it, dude. But you have to tone it down a bit. By the way, my name is Todd."

"Oh, dear. That is unfortunate."

"So I've been told."

"Despite your horrible name, I will still be your friend. I wish to ask you many questions about this wonderful planet."

"Like what?"

"I have watched movies from Earth. Why are there so many explosions here?"

And with that, Todd and Clank became fast friends. Chatting constantly as they walked, Clank asked one question after another, while Todd patiently answered each one.

When the group reached the central cavern, Diara was there to meet them.

"Get everybody together. The General wants a meeting."

"I think I'll pass," Todd said, continuing to walk along with Clank. "I never understand a word you guys are saying anyway."

Ten minutes later, the entire group, including two people from Cambria Orin didn't know, assembled around the big table.

"Our sources inside the royal palace tell us the emperor is increasingly concerned about the existence of the Underground," the General began. "He's planning to turn the city upside down to find our secret base."

The team exchanged nervous glances. Everyone knew if the hidden basement under Lano's warehouse was discovered, their mission here was doomed.

"We've waited long enough to make our move against the emperor," the General continued. "We'll spend some time collecting intelligence and getting ready. Then it will be our turn to attack him for a change."

Orin had been waiting for this announcement for months. Now that it was here, he was far less excited by the prospect than he expected to be.

The General stood at the whiteboard, making notes as he spoke. "Step one: find out how the people are feeling. Skeet, you know the city better than anyone. I'm sending you to Volara to learn all you can and find people who will join us should it come down to a fight."

"You can count on me, sir."

"Step two: try to get the Marans onboard. Juna, you'll go to Mara. Only a quick trip to say hello and introduce ourselves. We need to know if they're willing to help. As a member of the royal family, we believe you're best suited for this mission. Take a Mech with you for protection."

"OK, I'll take Helion."

"Not Helion," the Professor interrupted. "He is a Solar. Mara orbits a red dwarf star. His solar panels will be useless there."

"I'm only there for a short visit. He can run on batteries," Juna said. "I'm taking Helion. He'll do the best job of protecting me because he loves me."

The Professor rolled his eyes and scoffed, but knew better than to continue the argument. It was already lost.

The General chuckled at the exchange, then wrote "Taking Helion" on the whiteboard. "Step three," he continued. "Finish up our outstanding projects. Orin, I know you're making progress on that Disruptor of yours. Get it working. It could be a valuable tool."

"I'll do my best, sir."

"And Dorel, what's the status of that sneaky Mech you're building?"

"His name is Quark, sir. He's a small Atomic with some useful stealth features. We'll be powering him up for final testing today."

"Good, keep me posted." The General set down his marker and surveyed the room. "You all have your orders. Let's get to work."

Orin joined the rest of the youngsters in crowding around Juna.

"You're going to Mara!" Pom exclaimed, as she pulled Juna into a hug. "Alone! Are you scared?"

"Maybe a little. I'll have Helion with me, so I should be OK."

"No one's ever talked to a Maran before. Well, other than your father," Orin said. "They might be angry with us. We did blow up their factory a couple of years ago."

"I'll tell them my father made us do that. If I explain we're trying to bring them home, I think they'll forgive us."

"You're probably right, Princess," Skeet jumped in. "Would you mind helping me with something before you go?"

Skeet was the only person who could get away with calling Juna "Princess" without getting a smack on the head. Juna had come to think of him as a little brother.

"What do you want, Squirt?"

"I want tips for collecting information on Cambria. I know you're pretty good at it."

"Most of what I learned, I picked up sitting in the rafters above my father's office. On the streets, you'll do better than I ever could."

"Yeah, you're probably right," he joked. "I'm gonna miss you guys while I'm gone. Well, some of you at least," he added, making a funny face at Juna as he walked away.

"I should get going too," Orin said. "I need to be there for Quark's final testing, and I still have to get that Disruptor working." He was about to leave, but turned back to Juna. "I know you'll do great, but please be careful. I wish I was going with you."

"I wish you were too," she said, showing him her brightest smile. "I'll tell you all about it when I get back."

A thundering clunk drew their attention to the Gate, the hypnotic swirling pattern announcing a portal would soon be open. They rushed to the Tech Station to investigate.

"The General wants to get started right away," Diara told them. "A portal to Lano's will be here in a minute."

Orin always enjoyed stepping through the portal onto the familiar tiled floor of their secret hideout under Lano's warehouse. Earth was nice, but something about being on your home world felt right. Whenever the portal opened, most of their group would step across, even if it was only for a few minutes to say hello or get caught up on the latest gossip.

The most excited person making the trip today was Todd. Unfortunately, no one had warned the people on Cambria about his name, so there were more than a few shocked looks during introductions. To his credit, Todd didn't allow it to dampen his spirits.

"I'm the first human to ever set foot on another planet," he proclaimed proudly. "Too bad I'm in a warehouse that looks exactly the same as the ones back home."

Orin stood back to watch as everyone congratulated him on the accomplishment. Except for the General, of course. He simply glared—a little reminder to Todd that he wasn't allowed to tell anyone.

It was a brief stay on Cambria. Supplies were restocked and the Underground members that had been on Earth were left behind. Also remaining on this side was Skeet, now starting out on his mission for the General.

"You be careful," Orin warned. "There might be more security than you're used to."

"Stop worrying, Orin. No one is sneakier than me. I won't get caught."

Orin knew he was right, but that didn't mean he wasn't concerned for his young friend's safety. They shared a high-five before Orin joined the rest of the team back through the portal for the return trip to Earth.

Two hours later, Orin sat stewing at his workbench, no closer to solving his Disruptor problem than he was when he started. A heavy slap on the back jarred him from his thoughts.

"How do you guys stay cooped up like this all day?" Todd asked. "We gotta get some fresh air. Let's get the gang together for a hike in the canyon."

Orin wasn't thrilled by the idea, but agreed breathing a little outside air might help clear his head. Todd claimed they'd never meet a soul in this part of the canyon, but Orin insisted Gigahertz stay near the back entrance and engage his sensors at maximum sweep.

When Gig gave them the all clear, Todd and Juna led the way, moving upstream along the massive boulders lining the edge of the river. Orin was right behind them, followed closely by Pom and Diara.

Even though he wasn't eager to come, Orin had to admit the hike was a good idea. It was a glorious day, the sun high in a crystal blue sky. The roaring sound of the rushing water and the cool moist air seemed to energize him, draining away the stress of the day.

Up ahead, he saw Todd leap across an open gap between the rocks, landing nimbly on the other side. Juna followed gracefully behind him.

"There's an easier route down there," Todd yelled, pointing to a row of rocks further from the river's edge.

Pom and Diara, leisurely strolling hand-in-hand, gratefully acknowledged the safer path and started off in that direction. Orin, however, was having none of it. Refusing to appear weak, he launched himself over the gap, unfortunately coming up a little bit short.

His foot struck the side of the rock and before he knew it, he was sliding down the embankment and plunging into the churning water below. For the first time in his life, Orin found himself swimming. The water was like ice. He realized immediately how effective this activity would be at cooling you down on a hot day, but he was failing to see anything fun about it. He remembered Todd's description of swimming as flailing your arms and kicking, so he tried doing that.

Those efforts had little effect. His clothes now seemed to weigh as much as he did, constricting his movements as they clung tight to his body. Breathing was impossible, with his head constantly dipping below the surface. Tumbling through the rapids, he was terrified by the power the water held over him. He struggled to take in enough air. Up was down. Down was up. He squeezed his eyes shut, fighting off a wave of panic that would seal his fate. A sudden surge popped his head above the surface. He drew in a breath, hoping it wouldn't be his last.

The relentless flow whirled him about like a top until he

slammed something hard and rose into the air. Before he even realized what had happened, he found himself sitting in the palm of Gig's enormous hand, coughing uncontrollably and dripping into the raging river below.

His friends came running to make sure he was alright, but all he wanted was to get away. It was the most embarrassing moment of his entire life.

Hours later, he was back at his workbench, accomplishing nothing other than feeling sorry for himself. And worst of all, he hadn't even gone to see Juna off for her trip to Mara.

All this because he couldn't do something her muscly new Earth friend had managed so easily.

He felt terrible. The person he cared most about in the world was off on a dangerous mission, and he'd missed his chance to wish her well because he was acting like a child. What a fool. He couldn't wait for her return, so he could tell her how sorry he was.

# 6

*Another dreary day on Mara.*

Kalen zipped up his jacket, bracing for the icy blast that would hit the moment he opened the door. The walk would be short, but he activated the thermapads in his jacket and boots anyway. His gear was still a little big for him, so some extra heat would be nice to fill up the empty space. Besides, there was no sense suffering if you didn't need to.

He slipped down his goggles before leaving the warmth of the Hub, pushing the door open and stepping out onto the frozen ground to begin his daily walk to work. The wind wasn't *too* strong today, so he didn't need to lean into it to remain upright. Unfortunately, it was blowing directly at him, so ice pellets peppered his goggles making it difficult to see.

Not that there was much out there anyway. It was mid-morning, but the faint pink light offered by the sun had little to illuminate in this barren valley. Only distant sparks from buildbots, putting the finishing touches on the latest factory addition, pierced the haze.

After five minutes of trudging through the gloom, his destination came into view—a small cube-shaped building with no windows and a big red "1" painted on the side. It sat near the edge of the valley, dwarfed by the rock walls forming its perimeter. This was the building where Kalen had spent one half of every single day for the past year.

*Outpost 1.* He had no idea why they called it that. It wasn't like there was an Outpost 2 anywhere on the planet.

Making his way to the west side of the building, he stepped up to the door, engaged his ultrakey and slipped inside.

"Good morning, Kalen," Feldon said, already securely fastened into his outerwear. "Nothing happened last night." With that, he flung the door open and began his cold march back to the Hub.

"Thanks, Feldon," Kalen said, long after his co-worker had left the building.

It was essentially the same conversation they'd had every morning since Feldon started working here last month. He didn't judge the young man's attitude. Much like the six previous people to work the late shift this year, Feldon hated the job and would likely only do it until something better came along.

Kalen, on the other hand, loved working here. He couldn't imagine a better job. It was his intention to stay in the position for as long as they'd have him. Mara was a planet built upon the relentless pursuit of science and mathematics. Those were the skills hammered into kids from the moment they were born. The people who excelled in these pursuits, which was basically everyone, sought out positions where they could apply their abilities to designing and building wondrous tools for the future.

Kalen was *not* one of those people. He hated math and science, finding it all an incredible bore. Enjoying the creations that sprung from the minds of these brilliant people was something he fully embraced. He simply had no desire to dream them up himself.

Kalen tugged off his coat and settled in for a long day's work. He sat down at a sleek metal desk, then checked the logbook for new entries. As he'd already guessed from Feldon's cryptic update, there were none. After checking the detector's status, he jotted a couple of numbers on a form and readied himself for the only other activity this post required of him.

*Waiting.*

His job was a simple one. Somehow, Mara had become the focal point for some strange interplanetary conflict. Periodically, a space portal of some kind would begin to form on the rim of the valley, straight up the cliffs from Outpost 1. Moments later, another would begin the same process right next to it. For some reason, the second one would open first, four enormous robots would step through and wait for the other to finish.

That's when the fighting would start. Missiles would fly back and forth until the four that showed up first emerged victorious. They would then return to wherever it was they came from, and the giant portal structures would disappear.

Local experts surmised one group was attacking Mara, with the other appearing to defend. The Maran people often lacked creativity when it came to naming things, so the two groups were called "The Good Guys" and "The Bad Guys."

Kalen's job was to call his boss on the radio when a fight was underway, record any relevant details about the battle, then call his boss again when it was over. To help him gather information, he had two modified cannonbots at his disposal, which he could operate remotely. All their weaponry had been removed and replaced with camera equipment. In keeping with Maran tradition, the units had been given the unimaginative name of camerabots.

Kalen would position them off to the side of the portal-making structures and record all the activity from the beginning of the encounter to the end.

And that was it. The rest of the time was his to do with as he pleased. There'd been times in the past when the battles occurred quite frequently, sometimes four or five happening one right after another. Now, they had become quite rare. There'd been one a couple of nights ago on Feldon's shift, but Kalen hadn't reported one in weeks.

So, how was a young man to spend all this free time? Well, he loved to draw, so he spent much of his time doing that. The subject of his art was always the same. He gazed around the room and admired dozens of depictions of the target of his obsession. His life's passion was history. More specifically, the history of the ship that had brought his people to this forsaken planet 143 years ago.

*The Starchaser.*

Kalen knew more about the Starchaser mission than anyone else on the planet. The Marans were a forward-thinking society, so no one had ever taken the time to record the short, but rich history of the Maran people. He meant to change that. Pouring over pages of logs and listening to hours of audio files was how he liked to spend his days. He recorded each new piece of information in his own personal archives, creating a detailed history of every person who existed, and every event that occurred, between the launch of the Starchaser and the present day.

He used a database to store everything, but also kept written ledgers, schedules, and photo albums in three large file cabinets in the back storage room. His pride and joy was an extensive timeline charting the entire history of the Maran people that currently wrapped around three walls of the main office area in Outpost 1.

His historical records also included artifacts from the ship itself. The Starchaser's final resting place was only a two-hour walk from his current position, so he'd been there often. With no days off from work, he would plan his trips carefully, and hope for weather that wasn't too brutal. He would set off directly from work and walk as quickly as he could, leaving as much time as possible to roam the halls of the massive vessel. When it got late, he would choose a crewman's bunk to get a couple of hours' sleep, then walk directly back to work, exhausted but fulfilled.

Sometimes, his best friend Grigo would join him. Grigo was a technical geek of the highest order, so they would take batteries with them and power up long-dormant computer systems to recover logs and data Kalen could add to his archives. His goal was to set up a museum one day, a concept the mayor himself endorsed.

It was impossible to study Maran history without developing an overwhelming curiosity about Cambria. Their home world had rejected their return on three separate occasions. They also sent an armed robotic force here two years ago to destroy a factory, and were somehow involved in the ongoing portal battles being fought on the valley's rim.

In addition to recording their history, Kalen hoped his efforts to understand the past might someday contribute to a future where the Maran people *could* return to their ancestral home. It was a lofty dream, but one he always held close.

Kalen rose from the desk to get a large sheet of paper to begin his next drawing of the Starchaser. There was a pivotal event early in the mission, when an explosion in Environmental Pod 7C caused a tragic loss of life, and he wanted to capture the moment on paper.

Just as he sat down to begin, the detector chimed. The process of opening a portal caused a distortion in space, so their scientists had developed a device to detect it. Its pleasant ding was now telling him a portal would open soon. He activated the camerabots to prepare for the imminent battle.

A quick check of the detector's input gauges had him scratching his head. The portals for each side of the conflict emitted different frequency signatures. For some reason, The Good Guys were starting a portal first. He'd never seen that before.

A minute later, it opened, allowing a single robot to step through, followed closely by a lone individual. The figure was wrapped in what appeared to be a blanket, protection clearly insufficient for Mara's cruel environment.

Kalen zoomed in with the camera to get a better look. It was a girl, probably no older than he was. She was pretty and had a determined look on her face. Pulling the blanket up over her head, she started moving towards the rim of the valley.

"Well, this day just got a little more interesting," he said to himself as he reached over and grabbed the radio.

*Wow!*

Even with all the warnings, Juna was shocked by how horrible this place was. The sun was a giant pink orb in the sky, but it gave off little light, and certainly no heat. The wind whipped past, pelting her with tiny rocks that stung her face when they hit. She shivered at the thought of spending more than a few minutes out here. Wrapped in a blanket and wearing three layers of clothing, still wasn't enough to repel the bitter cold. She yanked the blanket over her head, then signalled Helion to follow as she moved to the edge of the valley to begin the long descent into the settlement below.

Her first steps were awkward. Wearing too much clothing and wrapped in a bulky blanket didn't help, but it was more than that. Something was wrong with the gravity. When she first walked on Earth, she felt heavy and sluggish. Here, it was the exact opposite. Her steps felt light, like there wasn't enough force holding her foot on the ground. It took her a few tentative steps to get a feel for it before she could even start to walk normally. She hoped it would get easier soon. The portal would return in four short hours, so she didn't want to waste the whole time learning how to walk.

Upon reaching the rim, she got her first look at the land the Marans called home. It wasn't much. There was one large building that appeared to be a factory, likely a replacement for the one they'd destroyed on their last visit. There were a couple of smaller structures and a large area completely covered with what looked like signs, but the visibility was so bad she couldn't make out exactly what they were. Nobody knew how many Marans lived on this planet, but it certainly didn't seem capable of supporting that many of them.

Standing up here wouldn't teach her anything, so she started down the rocky slope to the valley floor below. Beginning slowly, she picked up her pace as she went, realizing freezing to death was the likely outcome if she stayed out here too long. By the time she reached the bottom, she was shivering and tired, wanting nothing more than to find shelter from the relentless wind and biting cold. Not wanting to scare anyone with their unexpected arrival, she had Helion use his loudspeaker to continually broadcast the message: "We come in peace."

She scanned the area, trying to figure out what her ultimate destination should be. There was a tiny building to her right with a big red "1" painted on the side, but it seemed too small to be of any importance. She decided to make her way to the factory. Smoke was billowing out of several stacks on the roof, so at least they had heat. As she set out, movement to her left captured her attention. A lone figure appeared, dressed in rugged winter clothing, walking towards her from the far side of the compound.

"We come in peace," she said to him when he arrived.

"So your big friend keeps saying," he responded curtly. "It's easy to talk of peace while you're standing next to a weapon that big."

"Who, him?" she said, turning back to Helion and signalling him to stop his broadcast. "He's completely harmless." She added a knowing smile. "At least he is as long as I tell him to be."

"What do you want?"

"I want to talk. My friends and I wish to help you come home."

The stranger stared into her eyes, saying nothing, obviously unsure whether or not he could trust her.

"Soon would be good," she added. "I'm really cold."

At that, the man smiled. "Sure, follow me. But your friend stays outside."

As they walked, Helion spoke to Juna through the radio clipped to her ear.

"I dislike the idea of you being alone."

"I'll be fine," she replied, drawing a curious stare from her Maran escort. "We'll leave the radio channel open so you can hear everything that's going on. If something goes wrong, come in and get me."

With that, the man stopped and turned to face her, no doubt concerned about the only half of the conversation he was hearing.

Juna smiled back at him. "He's very protective. You'd best play nice."

The man shook his head and continued on his way. They were heading for a tiny shack near the area covered in those strange looking signs. As they got closer, Juna realized it was a vast expanse of solar panels. Seeing them made her feel much better. The Professor must have been wrong—Helion would be just fine over here.

Her companion pulled a tiny gizmo from his pocket and pushed it into a notch in the door. It swung open and Juna dashed in ahead of him, desperate to escape the cold. As soon as she stepped inside, she tore off the blanket and began stomping her feet to get some blood flowing.

"You can call me Wentz. I'm the Security Chief here." He pointed to her overstuffed outfit. "It's warm now. You can leave some of your clothes up here if you'd like."

"Thank you, Mister Wentz. I'm Juna," she replied, stripping down to a pair of black pants and a simple orange sweater. "That feels much better."

Juna soon realized the small enclosure they were in was an

access point to an underground complex of some kind. The space contained only the upper landing for two side-by-side staircases. Mister Wentz pointed in their direction, inviting her to descend. As she drew nearer, she noticed they were unlike any stairs she had ever seen. Exceptionally steep, they had an unusually large gap between each step.

After mounting the top one, she pondered the best method of getting to the next. Before she had time to consider her options, however, the entire assembly began gliding downwards. This was nice. It appeared the stairs would do all the work for her.

She descended through a short, dark tunnel, seeing a patch of light ahead and hearing the familiar sound of people in motion. When she passed out of the tunnel and into the light, the unexpected sight took her breath away. It was, without a doubt, the most spectacular place she had ever seen.

The walls were alive with moving images of familiar scenes from back on Cambria. Looking up, she saw the beautiful amber of the Cambrian sky, with images of drifting clouds that seemed so real, she thought she could reach out and touch them. The scent of flowers filled the air, though she saw none close by.

Below her, hundreds of people moved along automatic sidewalks, past beautiful parks filled with elaborate sculptures of trees and animals. Small flying drones whizzed about, narrowly avoiding collisions as they carried packages from place to place. The sights, sounds and smells were almost too much to take in, the contrast with the world outside, simply mind-boggling.

At the bottom of the stairs, a tall man with black hair and deep brown eyes was waiting for her. He wore a tasteful blue robe and a welcoming smile. Behind him stood dozens of onlookers. Every eye was focused on her.

"Greetings. I am Mayor Cartona. What brings you to our

humble home?"

"I've come to talk about the future—a future where the Maran people are free to return to the land of their ancestors."

"And why would they send such a young girl with a message so vital?"

"My name is Juna Volara."

The mayor could not hide his shock at the news. Some of those behind him even gasped.

"I do not represent the royal family. I, and those that fight with me, want to see an end to the emperor's reign and the creation of a new Cambria. We want all people to be treated fairly, and those that were outcast, to be welcomed home."

The mayor studied her for a moment, his expression giving away nothing. Then he broke into a beaming smile.

"Let's talk," he offered, turning and signalling her to follow. "Shall I call you Princess?"

"Please don't. Juna is fine," she said, her head pivoting, trying to take it all in. "This place is amazing."

"Thank you. We call it the Hub and have worked hard to make it this way. When the colony was first established, our ancestors declared one half of our resources be spent making life here comfortable, and the other half on trying to get home."

"You certainly got your money's worth from the half that built this."

"Indeed. And I would argue the end has not yet been written on the other half."

Juna wiped sweat from her hands, staring up to track the throngs of people keeping pace as they moved further into the complex. When the mayor reached its centre, he motioned her to stop.

"Please, sit."

Juna sat down on a long, curved bench with soft green cushions, and watched the mayor sit on one like it directly across from her. A look up revealed several levels stacked above her, the railings lined with people jostling to get a better view of the action.

"We're going to meet here?" Juna asked.

"Of course. I have all my meetings in the open. I wouldn't want people thinking I'm keeping secrets from them, now would I?"

"That's basically the opposite of how my father does it."

"Remember Juna, I am not an emperor here. I am the mayor. If these people decide I'm not doing a good job, they'll vote me out and find someone better." He cast his gaze across the crowd.

"Now Juna, tell us your story."

And so she did. Starting at the beginning, she recounted what the three Maran wars were like from their perspective, and how the true origins of the Maran people were still not known by the citizens of Cambria. She told them about the Gate, and the regrets they had in coming to Mara to destroy their factory. Then she revealed the emperor had built his own Gate and an army of clones, whose sole purpose was the conquest of Mara.

The people were riveted when told about the Great Mech Heist and the subsequent escape to Earth, so they could continue to defend Mara from there. The mayor was obviously engrossed in the story, nearly brought to tears when learning the hods were still not free after all these years. When it was over, he looked deep into her eyes.

"The people of Mara owe you our thanks," he said, reaching out to take her hands. "We pledge our support in your efforts to build a more just society on Cambria."

"Thank you, Mayor Cartona. I shall take that message back to our people. Do you mind if I ask a few questions? There's so much I wish to know about the Starchaser and how you came to be here."

"I never look to the past," he confessed. "But there is a young man here, about your age, who could answer your questions. I will make sure you two meet the next time you come."

"Thank you," she said, looking up to acknowledge the expanse of spectators staring down from above. "I'm already looking forward to my next visit."

With that, the entire facility erupted in a chorus of cheers. Juna rose and waved at the admiring crowd, her beaming smile returned by every face she saw. She was so happy she'd come.

It couldn't possibly have gone any better.

# 7

Still at his workbench, Orin glowered at his half-built Disruptor. The device stared back, mocking his lack of progress. His full attention would be required to get it working, and he didn't have that to give right now. Until he apologized to Juna, he feared his productivity would be limited. Shuffling parts and tools around the bench's surface, he hoped for inspiration that would likely never come.

"Hey Orin, get over here. We're firing up Quark."

Dorel's call was a much-needed distraction. Orin had created one of Quark's coolest features, and couldn't wait to see if it worked. When he crossed the shop to join in on the testing, he noticed both professors had come to watch as well.

"Hi Dad. Hi Aeva. Big day, huh?"

"That it is, son. Powering up a new Mech for the first time has always been my favourite part of the job."

"Yeah, mine too." He noticed Annu struggling with a stubborn connector, so he scooted over to help.

"Just like that first day with Spanner," she said, showing him a nervous smile. "It never gets easier."

Together, they completed the last connection and sent Dorel a thumbs-up. He crossed his fingers and hit the master switch.

Quark was the tiniest Mech ever built, being only a foot taller than Dorel. All white with a black faceplate, his modern look and soft curves were typical of all the Atomics. He looked much like Fallout, only a quarter the size. When the power came on, two bright red eyes lit behind his faceplate.

"Oh my," he said, his glowing eyes surveying the room. "I am afraid I do not know who any of you are. I am not entirely sure who I am either."

"That's alright," the Professor assured him. "You're among friends. In time, we'll figure it out together."

"And I'm here to teach you everything you need to know," Clank added from the back of the room.

Orin shook his head. That was the last thing they needed. Quark's primary function was stealth. Teaching him to blurt out every single thing that popped into his head seemed the wrong way to go. They'd have to get Clank back into wait state as soon as possible.

"That's a fine offer, Clank," the Professor said, lifting an eyebrow as he stifled a laugh. "But, perhaps for now, we'll run Quark through our standard initialization routines." Then he signalled Taz to go find Clank somewhere else to be.

Quark's basic functions were soon up and running, so they began introducing him to the team. Most of the Mechs were in wait state, but Gig was there to guide him through every step of the process. It was something he'd done for each new Mech since he himself was powered up almost twenty years ago.

Quark was a wonderful addition to the team. Quick with a joke, his sharp wit reminded Orin of Taz. Often, when his dad created a new artificial intelligence, he would use the brain scan of an actual person as a baseline. Orin had learned some time ago that Gig's AI was based on a scan of the General. Now he found himself wondering if the same thing might have been done with Quark and Taz. He hoped so. Despite his imposing size, there weren't many people more fun to be around than Taz.

The room was buzzing when it came time to test Quark's most advanced stealth feature. Orin once built an invisibility blanket that could make something vanish before your eyes. He had now installed the same optics technology over the entire surface of Quark's skin, allowing him to disappear too.

Anticipation for the test sent Orin's stomach rumbling. He drew in a calming breath as Dorel flipped the switch.

The effect was amazing. One moment, a small Atomic Mech hovered in the middle of the shop, and the next, a slightly distorted view of the far wall replaced him. Orin knew in advance it wouldn't be perfect. The system worked by matching Quark's surface to the background someone would see, based on the position from which they viewed him. This worked fine if only one person was present. In a room full of people, however, there was no way to simultaneously create the view from each person's perspective. The final effect looked a little fuzzy.

"OK Quark, pretend I'm the only one looking at you right now," Orin said.

The result brought a smile to his face. It *was* perfect. Quark had simply disappeared. Everyone lined up behind Orin to get a better look.

"Well done, my boy," the Professor said as he peered over Orin's shoulder. "Truly a gold star invention!"

The next test was to confirm that stealth mode worked while Quark was in motion. A game of hide-and-seek was arranged, with Taz playing the role of seeker.

Quark hovered in the middle of the room. Taz, of nearly equal size, stood next to him, eyes focused on his quarry. In the blink of an eye, Quark vanished and was on the move, while Taz desperately tried to keep track of him. Dorel had activated Quark's noise dampeners, so his movements were completely silent. After a minute of playing, Taz threw up his arms in frustration.

"I have no idea where he is," he confessed. "I'd swear he wasn't in the room at all."

"Perhaps you should get fitted for eyeglasses," Quark teased as he reappeared in front of Taz, not more than ten feet away.

Everyone in the room laughed at that, no one more loudly than Taz. Orin couldn't stop grinning while the team took turns slapping him on the back and tousling his hair. It was one of the proudest moments of his life as a young inventor. He found himself thinking of Juna, wishing she was here to share it with him.

"Congratulations Orin, you should be proud." He turned to see Aeva had joined him. "Also, I've been pondering your Disruptor problem. Perhaps introducing a feedback loop into the quantum stasis coupler would prove helpful."

Professor Oletta had designed the Gate and knew more about inter-dimensional energy strands than anyone. As progress on his project slowed, he'd asked for her advice to get things back on track. He considered her suggestion, seeing immediately how it might help.

"Thanks, Aeva," he said, already dashing for his workbench. "I think you might be onto something!"

Buoyed by the success of Quark's testing and new ideas spawned by Aeva's advice, Orin set to work on his Disruptor with an energy he hadn't felt in weeks. In less than an hour, he'd integrated a feedback loop into his design, and run a series of diagnostics on the new version. Excited by the results, he packed it up and made his way to the central cavern.

When he got there, he was pleased to see Spanner was one of the four Mechs lined up for the next trip through the Gate. Spanner was the first Mech ever built and still one of the wisest and most dependable. He couldn't think of a better choice to run the first test of his latest design.

A gentle rap on his foot brought the mighty machine out of his slumber.

"Ah Orin, is there something I can do for you?"

"Hey Spanner, I wanted you to help test my latest Disruptor prototype. Can I show you how it works?"

"It would be my pleasure."

In only a few minutes, Orin had run through the instructions, set the Disruptor next to the Gate, and put Spanner back into wait state. Glancing at his watch, he saw he had about an hour before Juna's scheduled return. He wanted to be the first person she saw, but with an hour to kill, he decided to go outside to get some air. A little company was always nice, so he headed for the Tech Station first.

"Hey Pom, can I borrow the radio for a second?"

"Sure, go ahead."

Orin selected the frequency for Gigahertz and keyed the mike. "Hey Gig, I'm heading for the ledge. Meet me there if you're not busy."

Back on Cambria, Orin and Gig used to meet regularly on a hill outside The Depot, spending countless hours talking about anything and everything. Here on Earth, they had the ledge.

Orin paused at the back entrance, staring up at a dusky sky. The night's first stars were emerging above the horizon. He climbed over a collection of small boulders, quickly reaching the top, where a large, flat ledge awaited him. After sitting down, he let his legs dangle over the edge, and listened to the surging river below.

Soon, the familiar sound of metal scraping stone announced the arrival of Gigahertz, who emerged through the crevasse and joined him in a single step. Settling down in his favourite spot, Gig's massive metal legs swung out and hung over the edge to match his friend's. He tilted his head back and gazed at the moon.

"A pleasant evening," he observed. "Shall we discuss what is troubling you?"

"How do you always know?"

"I have been your friend since you were a small child. I have learned to sense it."

"I don't know. Testing on Quark went well, and I made progress on the Disruptor today. I should feel great, but I don't."

"And why do you think that is?"

"Maybe it's because I'm taking so long to get the Disruptor working. Every time you guys go through that Gate to fight the clones, I feel like it's my fault."

"You should not feel that way. We know you are doing your best and appreciate your efforts to help. Besides, you made progress today. I do not think the Disruptor is the source of your concern."

Orin remained silent for some time, kicking his feet as they hung over the edge. "I messed up with Juna today," he finally admitted. "After falling into the river, I was too embarrassed to face her. I didn't see her off when she left for Mara."

"That was a mistake, Orin. Juna is your friend. She would not think less of you because you slipped off a rock."

"I know. It's just that... Todd jumped that gap so easily."

"Ah, Todd. So, it is jealousy then. There is nothing good about that emotion, Orin. Do not let it affect your friendship with Juna. It could be a mistake you regret for the rest of your life."

Orin went silent again. Of course, Gig was right. He was being an idiot. Having Juna in his life was something he was thankful for every minute of the day. She deserved a better friend than he'd been lately.

A familiar sound broke him from his trance.

*The alarms.*

Gigahertz moved like lightning. Lifting up on one powerful arm, he pivoted off the ledge and was through the cave's entrance in two steps. Orin leapt to his feet and scurried down the boulders, racing after his friend. He arrived at the central cavern in time to see Spanner, Havoc, Vortex and Geiger step through the Gate to turn back the enemy's attack.

Orin ran to the Tech Station, where Pom was frantically pushing buttons and typing commands. His heart sunk when he looked at the video feed from Geiger's camera. The enemy's Gate was already visible, the swirling images at its centre signalling a portal was imminent. When the process of opening a portal began, a sparkling light show could be seen for some time before the Gate structure appeared. Once that happened, it was too late for his Disruptor to have any effect.

"We got a late start," Pom told him, as if reading his mind. "They changed their landing coordinates. It tock me a minute to adjust for it."

"How's it going?"

Diara approached the station, looking like she'd recently woken from a deep sleep. "Can I help with anything?"

"I'm good," Pom replied. "Just another one of the emperor's pointless attacks on Mara."

Orin scanned the room, surprised by what he saw. There was a time when the alarms would bring every member of the team sprinting to the central cavern. But after countless victories, it seemed the urgency of the response was fading. He saw the General jogging in, but it looked like he and the two Techs would be the only ones joining him to observe this encounter.

Orin returned his attention to the video feed. He watched Spanner place the Disruptor, feeling bad for not warning him to abort the test if the Gate was already visible. As Spanner turned to rejoin his friends, everything went wrong.

The swirling pattern in the centre of the enemy's Gate faded away and, a split second later, a Tortuga clone launched itself through the portal, already at full speed. It slammed into the back of Spanner, severing one of his legs and sending the rest of him flying through the air. Even before he hit the ground, a second Tortuga clone exploded through the Gate, heading straight for the other Mechs.

"Fall back! Fall back!" the General ordered through the mike. "You'll need space to fire your missiles."

One of the Tortuga clones clipped Geiger, sending him spinning away, but the Atomic's hovering ability spared him from any major damage. The wheeled clones continued their assault, slamming into anything that moved. In the middle of all this confusion, two Carnage clones stepped through the enemy's Gate and started launching missiles into the skirmish.

The chaos was spellbinding. Desperate to help, Orin fumed, knowing there was little he could do.

Vortex freed himself from the pack and started launching SIMs at the newly arrived Carnage clones. Geiger got his spinning under control and joined the attack as well. Meanwhile, Havoc grabbed onto one of the Tortugas and ripped the shell right off its body. He appeared shocked when a folded up Rayzor clone popped out to join the fight. A moment later, the other Tortuga threw its hatch open, allowing another Rayzor to join the mix.

Orin couldn't believe it. After months of showing absolutely no creativity in their attacks, the emperor's side had figured out how to get six Mechs into a fight.

To add to the challenge, all the dust being kicked up by the circling Tortugas was making it nearly impossible to see what was going on. Now and then, one of the Rayzors could be seen darting across the screen, but they weren't even shooting at anything. It was the strangest battle he'd ever seen.

Despite the current mess, Orin remained confident their side would prevail. They had one major advantage their adversary could never overcome. The Mechs were intelligent. They could think, analyze their environment, and respond accordingly. The clones were simple, remote-controlled machines. Someone back on Cambria would be watching through a video screen, trying to guide their actions. With the visibility so poor, Orin couldn't imagine how this was even possible. It certainly helped explain why the clones' movements seemed so random and pointless.

Orin checked the video feed from Vortex and saw he and Geiger had destroyed the two Carnage clones, and were now joining the effort to corral the rest of them. Vortex dodged a speeding Tortuga clone, then hit it with three missiles as it passed and blew it to pieces. His gaze shifted to Havoc, who had a grip on one of the Rayzors and, in typical Diesel fashion, was tearing it in half. The dust was now settling as the advantage turned decisively in favour of the Mechs.

All that remained of the invading force was a badly damaged Rayzor and a Tortuga with its shell torn off. Havoc and Geiger released a barrage of missiles, filling the air with the shattered remains of the last of the clones.

"Well, that was exciting," the General said, wiping the sweat from his brow. "It appears the other side has altered their tactics, something we should have expected. We were lucky to win that one." He paused, shaking his head as he stared at the screen. "Pom, open a portal. Let's bring our boys home."

Orin waited anxiously for the portal to open, desperate to find out how Spanner was doing. Watching through the Tech Station monitor, he saw Vortex grab the Disruptor and Spanner's detached leg, while Havoc and Geiger picked up the rest of him. As soon as the portal was open, they all stepped through the Gate. Vortex set down the items he was carrying and assisted the others with Spanner's heavily damaged body. Gigahertz stomped over to check on his friends.

"Get the Wrenches working on Spanner right away," the

General ordered, joining the group at the back of the cavern. "Call the Professor, too. He might be able to help."

"General," Pom called from the Tech Station. "I'm picking up some strange readings—"

A piercing buzz from the Gate drowned out her words.

"TAKE COVER!"

Havoc swept the General to safety while Gigahertz dove for Orin. Vortex sprinted across the room towards the Tech Station.

The blast was deafening.

Gig had thrown himself between Orin and the Gate, so he didn't feel the impact or the heat, but a searing white flash filled the room and stung his eyes. Alarms blared and acrid smoke hung in the air. He couldn't breathe. He couldn't see. The ringing in his ears blurred all the sound together into one dull roar. In the distance, muffled voices echoed in the hallways as the rest of the team rushed to the central cavern to see what had happened.

In an instant, Gig was in motion, leaping to his feet and racing for the Gate. Orin looked over and saw a large gap on the left side of its rim. He watched in horror as the entire structure started tipping, threatening to land right on top of him. Gig reached up, and with all his strength, pushed against the falling mass. Initially, he only slowed its descent, but a moment later, Vortex and Havoc were at his side. Together, they stopped its fall and pushed the massive device back to vertical.

While Orin's attention had been focused on the Gate, the professors and Wrenches arrived, gathering with the General by the Tech Station. Even Todd had joined in. A bolt of fear ripped through Orin when he realized the Tech Station wasn't there anymore.

Dazed and trembling, he moved to join the group sifting through the rubble.

"I've got her!" the General exclaimed. "Pom's here too."

Orin peered over his father's shoulder, dreading what he might see. His heart surged when he noticed Diara moving, wiping blood from a deep gash on her forehead. Pom, however, lay still. She was covered in blood and one of her arms was bent at an impossible angle.

"She's alive," Professor Oletta said. "But she'll need medical attention if she's going to stay that way."

Orin was relieved Pom was alive, but his heart ached for her. She looked so frail lying in that pile of debris. Juna was going to be so upset when she got ba...

And that's when it hit him. His legs went weak, nearly dropping him to the ground when the reality of their situation struck.

*Their Gate was destroyed.*

They had no way to get home... and neither did Juna.

# 8

Juna felt like she was walking on air, but it had nothing to do with the gravity.

*What an amazing day!*

Cold wind whipped past, spraying her with dirty snow, but nothing could dampen her spirits today. Not after such a wonderful first encounter with the people of Mara. She couldn't wait to tell Orin about it. The fact he wasn't there to see her off still bothered her. She certainly hoped it had nothing to do with embarrassment over falling into the river. Boys could be so silly sometimes.

At the end of her meeting with the mayor, he had invited several children to come close and ask questions of their own. As they approached, Juna noticed how much taller and thinner they were than the kids back home. She'd learned the gravity here was about eighty percent of what it was on Cambria, so despite being genetically identical, people here developed differently because of the planet's unique environment.

The children crowded around, getting as close to Juna as they could, settling down on the floor by her feet. Unfortunately, they were impressed with her being a princess and wanted to know everything about that. Surprisingly, many of the other questions revolved around food; what did things taste like and smell like? Juna found these difficult to answer, but she did her best, finding her audience enraptured with every word.

The time flew by so quickly, her four hours were over before she knew it. Apologizing to the kids for not staying longer, she gave them a loving smile and rose to leave. Each one came in for a goodbye hug, then followed her and the mayor as they moved back towards the exit of the Hub. When they reached the bottom of the stairs, someone was waiting there with an extreme weather suit, holding it open so she could step right in.

"But how will I ever get it back to you?" she had protested.

"It is a gift," the mayor replied, showing her his most gracious smile. "You shall wear it each time you come back to us."

Thinking back on it now warmed Juna's heart, despite the frigid conditions. The only stain on an otherwise perfect day was the update she got from Helion upon returning to the surface.

Apparently, a battle between the Mechs and clones had occurred while she met with the Marans. The Mechs were victorious, but shortly after they returned to Earth, Helion lost his link to the Tech Station. Since then, every attempt to get it back had failed.

"Anything yet?"

She and Helion had completed the arduous climb out of the valley and were now awaiting the portal at its designated landing spot.

"No, nothing. I have never experienced a communication blackout of this duration. I am concerned."

Juna had no idea what to do. Her new winter gear was helping with the cold, but she couldn't stay out here all day. As she stood, considering a return to the valley floor, a sense of relief washed over her.

A burst of sparkling lights appeared against the pink Maran sky, like a bright, but tiny fireworks display. She'd never seen the effect before, but was told the earliest stages of a portal opening would look like this. Mentally thanking Orin for that little piece of trivia, she waited patiently for the process to finish.

"I am picking up a vehicle approaching at high speed," Helion warned her. "It appears to be a SCUD, but I detect no armaments."

Juna turned to see the machine, kicking up a cloud of snow as it sped towards them. It was emitting a sound of some kind, but not like one she would have expected. It almost sounded like it was singing. As it drew closer, she finally made out what it was saying.

"You are in danger, you are in danger," it kept repeating over and over with the voice of a young boy. It was unnerving, but she wasn't sure if she should take it seriously. Helion stepped in front of her as the large tracked vehicle screeched to a halt beside them.

"This portal isn't yours," the boy-machine warned. "You gotta get out of here!" A panel popped open on the side of the SCUD, revealing the empty cavity within. "Get in. I'll take you to safety."

Helion reached over and pushed the panel closed.

"She will *not* get in there."

At that moment, the Gate appeared next to them. A chill ran down Juna's spine when she noticed the lights lining its rim.

*Blue and green.*

She knew for a fact the lights on their Gate were orange and red. It was still a mystery who was driving this SCUD, but he was certainly right about them being in danger.

"He's right, Helion. We need to leave."

"Follow me!" the boy-machine urged.

Kicking up a spray of snow, it sped towards the valley's rim. Helion crouched so Juna could climb onto his back, then sprinted after it down the path they'd climbed only minutes ago. When they reached the bottom, Juna saw the SCUD head for the building with the red "1" painted on it. A large door on the side slid open so the machine could enter. Helion caught up to it as it rolled inside.

"Come in. It's safe, but your robot has to stay outside. Have it hide behind the building."

Juna climbed off Helion's back and gave him a nod. "Do what he says, Helion. I'll be fine. Keep a channel open and come help if I need it."

Helion walked around the corner of the building while Juna stepped inside, watching as the large door closed behind her.

"Hi, I'm Kalen."

Juna turned to see a Maran boy, about her age, standing there staring at her. He was tall and thin, with scruffy black hair nearly reaching his shoulders. His blue eyes were friendly, his expression one of concern.

"I hope I didn't scare you," he continued. "I knew you were in danger, but didn't know what else to do."

"I'm Juna. Don't worry about it. You did the right thing," she said, slipping out of her bulky gear. "How'd you know the portal wasn't ours?"

"It's my job. I track all the portals. I can tell whose is whose."

"Thanks for saving us," she said, showing him an appreciative nod. "What's going on out there right now?"

"Come on," he said, waving her to follow. "I'll show you."

She watched him sit down at a desk with two monitors, a couple of joysticks, and a keyboard with large control knobs. Looking over his shoulder, she noticed one monitor showed an image of her looking over Kalen's shoulder. She turned and saw the SCUD pointing right at her. The second monitor showed four Mech clones standing against a dreary Maran sky.

"They stepped through and stayed there," Kalen told her. "Your side didn't show up to fight them."

Something was desperately wrong. This situation was much worse than Helion losing his communication link. She took a moment to update him on the radio.

"I must go stop them," was his immediate response.

"No. That is exactly what you must *not* do. Remember what the General says: don't start a fight you can't win. It's better to plan for one that you can."

Kalen looked over his shoulder with a curious look, obviously confused hearing only half the conversation.

"Helion wants to fight them," she told him. "Why aren't you guys doing something to stop this?"

"I don't think there's anything we *can* do. I called my boss, Mr. Wentz, to let him know. Right now, there's a meeting in the Hub to decide what to do."

"Why don't you send a bunch of SCUDs at them?"

"What's a SCUD?"

Juna pointed to the machine that had guided her here. "One of those, but with guns."

"Oh, a cannonbot. We don't make those anymore."

"Well, we call them SCUDs. Why'd you stop making them?"

"I don't know. I guess we got tired of you guys blowing them up all the time. And I think we have some new plan to get home and don't need them anymore."

"So you have no way to defend yourselves against those things?" she asked, pointing at the screen.

"None I know of."

"Oh boy, this is going to get ugly."

For the next two hours, they sat staring at screens, watching things get very ugly indeed. Every half hour, a portal would open, and four Mech clones would pass through and stomp over to join the ones already there. After the third batch arrived, Juna realized they needed a better place to hide Helion.

Kalen used his camerabot to lead him to a secluded cave near Outpost 1. After squeezing in as far as he could go, Helion dropped into wait state so he wouldn't be picked up by sensors. She felt better knowing he was safe, but with every new arrival, her feeling of dread intensified.

On the last trip, only two clones came through, but they were joined by about a hundred heavily armed royal guardsmen. Juna paced the room, unable to watch the terrifying scene unfold.

"Looks like they're on the move," Kalen reported.

Juna rushed over to the monitor, watching in horror as eighteen Mechs and a hundred soldiers began their march towards the rim of the valley. A jolt of panic hit her when a new thought popped into her head.

"What if they search in here?"

The shocked look on Kalen's face told her he hadn't considered the possibility either. Instantly, they began scrambling around the room, gathering things and hiding them from view.

"Make it look like no one's ever here," Juna ordered. "Hide your jacket and push those chairs under the desk."

They worked frantically, knowing the invaders could arrive at any moment. Kalen turned off his equipment and stood back to survey the room.

"It looks pretty good," he said, sounding a little less confident than she would have liked. "Get in the storage room. I'll go turn off the lights."

Juna opened the door to a small room tucked in the back corner of the building.

"Room? Looks more like a closet if you ask me," she mumbled to herself as she squeezed in next to the three filing cabinets that filled most of the space. Then the lights went out, plunging her into darkness. She heard shuffling in the adjacent room, followed by a dull thud and a couple of colourful curse words. Moments later, Kalen limped into the storage room and closed the door behind him.

It was so cramped, Juna decided to climb on top of the filing cabinets. It gave her more room to move, and the advantage of high ground should it come down to a fight.

Less than a minute later, she heard pounding on the outside door. It stopped after three unanswered attempts, but was soon followed by the thundering crash of a door flying open. Juna held her breath, listening to the soldiers move through the room next door. She fought to reign in her fear, worried her thumping heart might give them away.

"Nobody here," said a muffled voice. "Let's check the big building further down."

For five minutes, neither of them had the nerve to move or speak.

"Do you think it's safe yet?" Kalen finally whispered.

"I guess so. Wow, were we ever lucky." She carefully lowered herself to the ground. "What should we do now?"

"The building doesn't have any windows. Do you think it's safe to turn on the lights?"

Juna pondered the question. It was risky powering everything up again, but it might be worth it to find out what was going on out there.

"Let's see what's left of the door. If we can get it closed, I think we should turn things back on to see what's happening outside."

The door would never lock again, but it sealed well enough to block light from escaping. After turning on the lights, Kalen powered up his equipment to check the status of the camerabots. The one still on the rim showed no activity at all. The other sat right outside the walls of Outpost 1, left there after guiding Helion to his hiding spot.

"I can't see anything from here," Kalen told her. "Can I risk moving it?"

There didn't appear to be anyone in the area, so she gave him a nod. As the machine inched forward and slowly turned the corner, the factory could be seen in the distance. There were several Mech clones standing next to it.

"Can you zoom in?"

Kalen turned a knob on the keyboard and the image of the factory grew until it filled the screen. They could now see a column of people exiting the factory and heading towards the Hub.

"Does this thing have a microphone?"

Kalen flipped a switch and turned another knob to its maximum setting. Juna's blood ran cold. A clone was broadcasting a message on an endless loop through its loudspeaker: "This planet is now the property of Emperor Zoban Volara of the Cambrian Empire. Comply with all orders or you will be executed."

"What? We're someone's property now?" Kalen exclaimed. "Who does this guy think he is?"

"Actually, he's my father," she replied, obviously embarrassed. "He is a horrible person who means what he says. All his threats should be taken seriously."

"Is there any way to stop him?"

"I don't know. Something terrible must have happened to my friends." She paused, trying to think of some way to fix this mess. "Can we find out what's going on in the Hub?"

"I can call my friend," he said, pulling a device from his pocket. Juna noticed it looked a lot like Todd's cell phone. Kalen touched the screen, bringing it to life. After pressing a few buttons, the face of a boy with messy blonde hair filled the screen.

"Kalen! Where are you?"

"Hey Grigo, I'm at work. They searched here, but I hid. Where are you?"

"I lucked out. They pulled me into Spoke 5. I'm here with the mayor and all the other bigwigs."

"The mayor is there?" Juna interrupted. "Can I talk to him?"

"Who's that?" Grigo asked, a huge smile spreading across his face. "You got a girlfriend out there?"

"No! She's from Cambria. I think she's the emperor guy's daughter."

"Oh sure, Princess Juna. I saw her in the Hub today. She's really cute. How'd she end up with you?"

"Well, she was waiting..."

"Would you two stop it," Juna snapped, yanking the device from Kalen's hand. "Let me talk to the mayor."

Moments later, Mayor Cartona's face filled the screen. His anger was obvious. "Juna. Tell me you had nothing to do with this."

"I didn't. I swear. I don't know what happened to my friends on Earth or why they didn't show up this time. I can't reach them. Something's wrong."

"Yes, Juna, something *is* wrong. Our planet has been invaded, and your father is now claiming to own the place."

"And I'll do everything I can to stop him," Juna begged. "But without my friends, I don't know what to do."

"If you think of something, let me know. Until then, I don't have time for this."

The device went dead in her hands. She handed it back to Kalen.

"So, where is Spoke 5?" she asked.

"I have no idea. There are four spokes connected to the Hub. Everybody here lives in one of them. There's always been a rumour about a Spoke 5, some sort of emergency thing, but I was never sure it existed until now."

"Why would your friend be there?"

"Even on a planet full of geniuses, he's super-smart. It's probably because of that."

"He sounds like Orin."

"Who's Orin?"

"My friend from back home. He's a real science geek too."

Thoughts of Orin renewed her concerns about what may have gone wrong back on Earth. Several possibilities ran through her mind, none of which were good. Searching for a distraction, she began wandering, taking in details of the room for the first time. She came to a stop at one of the many drawings tacked to the wall.

"Is this the Starchaser?"

"You know about the Starchaser?" Kalen leapt up to join her at the wall.

"I do, but not many of us know what actually happened to it. We were always told it crashed into the sun and everybody died. Almost no one knows the Marans originally came from Cambria."

"Wow, that is so cool. I'll definitely add *that* piece of information to my archives. The Starchaser mission is my obsession. It's all I think about."

Juna looked at him, seeing how excited he was to be talking about this.

"You must be the guy the mayor was telling me about. He said you could answer questions about the past."

"That would be me. No one else on this planet seems to care how we ended up here."

Juna returned her attention to the artwork on the walls. "Did you draw these? They're really good."

"Thanks. They're mine alright. I even made this cool timeline."

For the next hour, Kalen proudly took Juna for a tour of his archives. He showed her his drawings and pointed out some of the major events in Mara's history on the timeline that wrapped around most of the room.

"This is Operation First Contact," he told her, pointing to an entry on his timeline. "Then, if you want all the details about it..."

He signalled her to follow him to the storage room. "You look it up in here." Opening the "F" drawer on one of the cabinets, he pulled out a file and handed it to her.

Leafing through it, Juna realized this was yet one more event in Cambria's history that had been kept from her people. Long before the First Maran War, the Marans launched a small starship to tell the Cambrians that survivors existed and wanted to come home. The emperor soundly rejected their request, telling them they would kill anyone attempting to return the moment they set foot on Cambrian soil.

"So the next time, they brought a bunch of SCUDs with them," Juna muttered to herself.

"That was Operation Big Stick," Kalen told her.

"We call it the First Maran War."

Juna struggled to contain her anger. This was even worse than she'd thought. The Marans' first attempt to contact Cambria was a peaceful plea to come home, but they were threatened and turned away by her grandfather.

It was so cruel. Lost in her thoughts, she was caught completely off-guard when, without warning, the outside door swung open, blasting her with a gust of cold air.

The royal guardsman stepping into the room seemed as surprised as she was. Neither one moved. No more than ten feet apart, Juna and the soldier stood staring at each other. He was dressed for the cold, so only his eyes were visible above the bulky scarf wrapped around his neck.

There was something strangely familiar about those eyes, but Juna couldn't place where she might have seen them before. As she watched, she noticed his expression change from shock, to recognition, to something almost friendly.

*Was he smiling?*

"All clear!" the soldier yelled as he flipped off the light switch, stepped out of the building, and slammed the door shut behind him.

Juna and Kalen stood in darkness, too shocked to move.

"That was weird," Kalen finally offered.

"Yes, it was," Juna agreed. "I think I know that guy, but I'm not sure. We just got lucky again. I don't think we should count on *that* lasting forever. We need a better place to hide."

They stood quietly for a moment, their faces lit only by the faint glow of the monitors. Juna noticed Kalen's face brighten when the idea came to him.

"Would you like to see the Starchaser?"

# 9

Orin's heart pounded as he clutched the bag tight to his chest. He wasn't looking forward to this at all. Glancing to his right, he saw Todd cradled in Fallout's other powerful arm, an expectant grin plastered on his face.

"This is going to be awesome!"

Orin strongly disagreed. He had hoped the first time he'd done this would be his last. Perched at the top of the towering rock wall, he awaited the death-defying plunge that would soon follow. He and Todd were returning from an emergency trip to Flagstaff to pick up much-needed medical supplies. They'd found everything on the list, so all that remained now was getting it to where it needed to be. Unfortunately, that place was at the bottom of this cliff.

In a heartbeat, he was in motion. He closed his eyes this time, so it was the sound and fury of the rushing air flooding his senses. As violent as it was, it still wasn't enough to drown out Todd whooping it up right next to him. As they neared the bottom, the bone-crushing pressure of the deceleration once again signalled the merciful end to a horrible experience.

Fallout released his grip and lowered his passengers to the ground. Orin stood for a moment, then stepped tentatively, hoping his shaking legs would hold.

"How did that one go?" Todd asked, giving him a gentle pat on the back.

"A little better this time," he replied, not entirely sure if he was lying.

Despite the wobbly legs, Orin sprinted through the cave's back entrance, making his way straight to Pom's bedroom. Inside, Pom was lying on her bed, barely conscious, her breathing laboured. A teary Diara sat on a small stool, holding her hand. Professor Oletta rose from a chair tucked against the back wall.

"Did you find everything?"

Orin handed her the bag he'd been carrying.

"Yes, we got it all."

The explosion had caused unthinkable damage to the central cavern. Vortex had absorbed some of the impact when he dove for the Tech Station, but it wasn't enough to prevent Pom from suffering serious injury. When the Tech Station blew apart, she'd been hit by flying debris, causing three broken ribs, a fractured arm and countless cuts and bruises. Worst of all, one of the ribs had punctured her lung, meaning each passing minute made it harder and harder for her to breathe.

Aeva removed items from the bag and set them on a small table. Among them were tubing, tape, clamps and a large plastic bottle. A worried expression crossed her face as she pulled out the scalpel, the room's only light glinting off its polished metal blade.

"I've never done anything like this before." Her hands trembled. "I hope I spent enough time with that video."

By some miracle, the explosion in the cavern spared the computer the group used for accessing the internet. The massive rim of the Gate's ring had shielded it from damage. Aeva had been on it for hours since the blast, trying to diagnose Pom's condition and learn how to repair her broken body.

After putting water in the bottle, Aeva ran lengths of tubing into it and sealed the top with tape. She took a moment to steady her hands, then used the scalpel to make a small incision in Pom's chest. There was some blood, but not that much.

It was remarkable to see the professor remain so calm during the procedure. Orin was a nervous wreck, observing from the back of the room.

After ten minutes of cutting, sewing and sweating, Aeva removed a clamp from a tube now sticking out of Pom's body. Bubbles started forming in the bottle and, almost immediately, she began to breathe more easily.

Aeva released a sigh and wiped the perspiration from her face.

"I think she'll be OK. We'll need to leave the drain in for a few days, but she's out of danger now."

Diara rushed over, hugging and thanking the reluctant surgeon. Orin bowed his head and slumped against the wall, before bolting over to join in on the embrace. He then slipped out of the room to update the team on Pom's condition.

As he rounded the last corner into the central cavern, he was surprised to see how much work had been done while he and Todd were in Flagstaff. Chains now hung from large anchor bolts drilled into the ceiling and were attached to the top of the Gate to prevent it from tipping. The space, littered with debris the last time he'd seen it, was now swept clean.

Orin called everyone together and told them the good news about Pom, repeating it in English for Todd's benefit.

"That is splendid news," the Professor said as high-fives were exchanged around the room. "A tremendous weight has been lifted from us all."

Knowing Pom was out of danger was a wonderful feeling, but looking at the devastating scene before him, reminded Orin of the perils they still faced.

"Did we figure out what caused all this?" he asked his dad.

"Our best guess is one of those Rayzor clones slipped a bomb into Spanner's detached leg. With all the dust they were kicking up, we never would have seen it happen."

"We wouldn't have had to fight them at all if my Disruptor was working," Orin said, struggling to hold his emotions in check.

"No Orin," the General jumped in. "You can't blame yourself. If anyone was responsible for this, it's me. Their new tactics weren't particularly brilliant. I should have seen something like this happening, and prepared for it."

"Now, now, stop this everyone," the Professor urged. "The only person to blame for this senseless destruction is Emperor Zoban Volara. His greed and disregard for the lives of his people has caused this. We must never forget who the real villain is."

The group remained silent for a moment as they considered the professor's words. Of course, he was right. The emperor's obsession with the conquest of Mara was at the root of this nightmare.

Looking up at the damaged Gate, and knowing there was no way to stop him, Orin put everyone's fears into words.

"Mara is probably swarming with Mech clones right now."

"The portal detector was lost in the explosion," the General said, glancing back at the wreckage behind him. "We can't know for certain, but it's likely Mara has fallen."

"Juna's still there," Orin said, almost too quietly to be heard.

"And we *will* get her back," the General assured him. "But it's not something we can worry about now. Our own survival is priority one. With Pom's condition improving, we can now focus on staying alive on this planet long enough to fix that Gate."

He paused, obviously concerned by the sense of hopelessness filling the room. "Let's take a moment to clear our heads, shall we? We'll meet back here in an hour to figure out what's next."

Orin spent the time sitting on the ledge under a beautiful, cloudless sky. As usual, Gigahertz was there to lend his support.

"Do you think she'll be OK?" Orin asked.

“I do. Juna has proven herself a resourceful girl. Life has thrown her many challenges, and she has overcome each and every one.”

“I think so too,” Orin agreed. “I’m worried about her, but somehow I know she’ll be fine.” He stared down at his feet dangling over the rushing water, thinking of all the other things he had to worry about right now.

“How is Spanner doing?”

“He is recovering well. A new leg has been installed. It is not a perfect match for the one he lost, but he is operational again.”

“I’m sorry he got hurt. If I could have got that Disruptor working earlier—”

“Do not think like that, Orin,” Gig interrupted. “No one is blaming you but yourself. Guilt is an unproductive emotion that serves no purpose. Doing your best is all anyone can ever ask.”

Orin pictured the moment Vortex returned from Mara, setting the Disruptor next to the Gate, along with Spanner’s leg. There was no question it had been vaporized in the explosion.

“I’ll have to start again, but I know I can do it, Gig. I think my last mod was the one to get it working.”

Glancing at his watch, he realized his hour was almost gone. “I better get back,” he said as he picked himself up off the ledge. “Tell Spanner I’ll come visit as soon as I can.”

“I know he will appreciate that.”

“Thanks Gig. I’ll see you later.”

As he reached the central cavern, Orin noticed everyone gathered by the big table, so he strolled over to join them. His dad was writing on the whiteboard. It appeared to be a list of the things they would need to fix the Gate. He was impressed to see it written in English, no doubt so Todd could help with tracking things down. Todd sat alone at the end of the table, so Orin flopped down in the seat next to him.

"Hello Todd. How are you?"

"This is crazy, dude. I still can't believe people are trying to blow you up." He scanned the room while drumming on the table with a pencil. "I'm not so sure I would've signed up for this if I knew *that* was a possibility."

"We can take you home if you wish."

"Nah. I said I was with you guys to the end, so I'll stick it out." He stopped with the drumming and looked Orin in the eye.

"So, how do we get Juna back with a big chunk missing from your ring thingy?"

"The Gate will not work now. We must fix it." He pointed to the list his dad was writing on the whiteboard. "We need those things. Do you know them?"

"Are you kidding me? Half of them I've never even heard of. Iridium. Xenon. Gallium. I mean... are those even real words?"

Orin couldn't help but feel dejected. The list was long, and with the only person from Earth not knowing what things were, the task of collecting it all seemed daunting. To make matters worse, the best scrounger on their team wasn't even here to help.

⚙ ⚙ ⚙

Skeet woke with a start. His brain sifted through a haze of confusion, trying to remember where he was. Squinting against the glare of morning light streaming into his temporary home, it came to him in an instant—a glimpse of amber sky reminding him he was back on Cambria. He'd spent the night in an alley, sleeping in a cardboard box for old times' sake. He stood and rubbed sleep from his eyes, stretching the kinks from his aching muscles. It was a painful reminder of how much he preferred his bed back on Earth.

As he stepped from the box, the toot of a passing tut-tut served as a warning to always stay on your toes when you were in the big city. The tut-tut awakened memories of that first day he met Juna, right here in this alley. It was a day on which the course of his life took such a drastic turn. He dusted himself off and smoothed out a few wrinkles, then set out on the day's quest.

When he'd first arrived, it took him some time to get back into the rhythm of the city. The endless racket and constant motion were so different from their peaceful existence in a remote cave. It had been more than a year since he'd spent much time here, so it felt foreign at first. But once he was walking the streets and chatting with old friends, he soon realized nothing much had changed while he was gone.

His mission on Cambria was simple; find out if the Underground's message was spreading across the city. The most important thing he'd learned so far was the people here loved Juna. The royal family was generally despised on this planet, but when news broke that Juna had been banished from the family for betraying the emperor, she became a legend. This was particularly true among the hods, where she was being hailed as their best chance ever to finally be set free.

She had become a symbol of what might be—a ray of hope in their otherwise dreary lives.

As Skeet walked the bustling sidewalks, he noticed the city particularly energized this morning. Car horns blared and people hung out of windows, shouting and banging pots and pans. It felt like Volara was having a grand celebration. Across the street, he spotted Denzo's shop, an old friend from his days living on the streets. If anybody could tell him what was going on, it would be Denzo. Dodging speeding cars as he went, he zipped to the opposite side, skipped up the stairs and walked through the front door of the shop.

Not much had changed since the last time he'd seen it. A dingy gloom hung in the air, the only light coming from a dirty window near the ceiling. Rows of shelves lined the walls, littered with used and battered items, some of which bore no apparent purpose. Everything was coated with a thin layer of dust. In the centre of the room sat a shabby old desk, and behind that sat a shabby old man. He had greying hair and a beard nearly touching the floor.

"Hey Denzo, what's new?"

"Skeet, my young friend. Where have you been hiding all this time?"

"I spent a year on the coast," he lied. "Near Alderae. What's going on out there today? Sounds like the whole city's having a party."

"What? Have you been living under a rock?"

"More like, in a box."

"We have conquered Mara," the old man told him, a beaming smile on his face. "The emperor has declared an official day of celebration."

The news hit Skeet like a punch to the gut. How could this be? Did the Mechs actually fall to the clones? A thousand other questions crowded his mind.

He said a quick goodbye to Denzo, then dashed out of the shop and turned east, sprinting down the sidewalk towards Lano's. Something must have gone horribly wrong back on Earth. Were his friends OK? And if they weren't, how could he possibly get back to help them?

⚙ ⚙ ⚙

Orin lifted the heavy green orb and eyed it suspiciously. The woman ahead of him had tapped one while holding it close to her ear, so he tried doing that.

"It's a watermelon," Todd informed him from the other side of the bin. "Grab one of those for sure. They're really good."

Orin set the large fruit into the cart and pushed it around to Todd's side. "Do you think we need more?"

Todd glanced at the cart. "We probably have enough for now. You guys only want to try out a few things this time around."

Orin and Todd were back in Flagstaff, sent to pick up ointment and bandages for Pom. The General suggested getting some Earth food while they were here, hoping to find something the Cambrians could eat.

Having lost their access to Lano's, getting food from back home was no longer an option. Under specific orders not to buy meat, they were filling a cart with bread, nuts, fruits and vegetables to take back for the group to sample.

Orin returned to roaming the supermarket's aisles. The selection was almost too much to take in. The store was so much bigger than anything they had back home. It had countless rows of shelves lined with boxes, bags and cans of more things to eat than he ever could have imagined.

Right now, he was holding a bright box with a cartoon animal that appeared to contain colourful rings floating in a white liquid. He shook it vigorously, listening to the small hoops rustle inside. Smelling the box provided no additional information about the product within.

"Never seen a box of cereal before, huh?"

Orin looked up to see that he was blocking the path of a dour-looking woman with strange rolls in her hair.

"No, it is my first one!" he replied enthusiastically, offering a glowing smile that was not returned.

The woman pushed her cart past him, muttering something about foreigners as she sped by.

"We should go." Todd had quietly stepped up behind him. "I

don't know if I have enough money to buy all this stuff."

Orin followed Todd to the front of the store, where a row of clerks waited at fancy machines to record their purchases. Each item passed through a scanner, generating a pleasant beep and adding to the running total shown on the machine's screen. He noticed Todd nervously watching the total, then cross his fingers as he handed over a small piece of plastic. A look of relief passed over his face when the card was returned, and the smiling young woman told him to have a nice day.

Orin wheeled the cart out to the parking lot where Gecko, having transformed back to his bright green colour scheme, was waiting for their return. Gecko had received a few modifications since his first trip to the city. He now had bumpers, front and back, as well as lights he could use to show if he was about to stop or turn. The license plate from Todd's old car had been tacked on as well, at least giving him the appearance of a street-legal Earth vehicle.

"Why are you green again?" Orin asked Gecko after they finished loading.

"I think it's important for people to see me at my best."

"I wish they couldn't see you at all," Todd said as they pulled out of the parking lot. "And don't break any rules. I have no desire to chat with the police anytime soon."

It wasn't long before they were bouncing along the dirt roads on the fringes of Flagstaff, heading for the open desert. Orin stared out the window, hypnotized by the monotony of the passing landscape. Before he realized it, Gecko was slowing down and crawling over the rocks surrounding the clearing at the top of their cliff.

Fallout and Geiger were there, waiting to carry them to the bottom. Orin tried relaxing this time and found the ride much more tolerable, actually starting to see why Todd found the experience so enjoyable. After reaching the bottom, they packed up their stuff and made their way to the central cavern.

The scene awaiting them was not a happy one. The entire group sat in a sullen circle around the big table. Not a single face wore a smile. Every entry on the list his dad had created now included a number next to it. Orin noticed the Earth symbol for money preceded it, so he realized it was the price to purchase each item. At the bottom was the total cost of everything they would need to get the Gate running again.

Orin didn't know much about the local monetary system, but it did seem like a large number. When the General spotted Todd, he tried speaking English for the first time.

"This is big number, yes?" he asked, pointing to the total at the bottom.

"Are you joking? That's over two hundred grand! Yes, that's a very big number. I hope you're not expecting me to cover it. I just spent my life savings on two hats, some medical supplies, and a few groceries."

The room went deathly quiet. Everyone realized how dire their situation was. Getting anything from Cambria was no longer an option. If they were going to get the Gate running again, it would have to be with things they could track down on Earth.

"It's more than the money," the Professor added. "All these things have to be delivered somewhere. We can't ask someone to drop them off at the edge of a canyon."

Another long silence followed that revelation. A feeling of despair filled the room as everyone struggled to come up with a solution to their dilemma.

"We have the Mechs," Orin offered, speaking English so Todd would understand. "They are very strong. People could pay us to use them."

"How do we do that and still keep them hidden?" the General

challenged.

Orin was settling in for the next round of silence when a burst from Diara interrupted his thoughts.

"Follow me, everybody!" she exclaimed, bouncing out of her chair and dashing for the computer. She sat down with a thud and began typing furiously, her eyes flickering across the glow of the screen. The tapping of the keys provided a rhythmic backbeat to her muttering.

"The General has me constantly checking the local news, and I saw something the other day... Ah, here it is," she beamed, spinning the monitor to face the group.

"What if we don't need to keep them hidden?"

# 10

Juna couldn't remember ever being this cold. She nestled in next to Helion's massive chest plate, but his systems were shut down, so *he* certainly wasn't giving off any heat. Moving was likely better than sitting, so she climbed down and started to pace.

She'd spent a lot of time in caves these past two years, and this one was definitely the worst. Frost covered the pitch-black walls, while Mech-sized icicles threatened to fall from the ceiling. It was the middle of the day, but little light reached them here at the back. It was a truly dreadful place.

"Are you cold?" Kalen asked as she stomped around, trying to keep her blood from freezing solid. "Would you like a new battery for your thermapads?"

"How many do we have left?"

"Six."

Juna did some quick math in her head. "No, I think we should save them for tonight." She looked over and watched him sitting comfortably on Helion's foot.

"Aren't you cold at all? I have no idea how you do it."

"I grew up here. I think I'm just used to it." He reached down and picked up his backpack. "Maybe you should eat. Would you like some food?"

Juna's stomach rumbled at the mention of the word food. She'd eaten nothing since leaving Cambria yesterday.

"Yes please. That would be wonderful."

Kalen dug around in the backpack, pulling out a rectangular

wedge made from some sort of milky, gelatinous substance. It wiggled in his hand as he passed it to her.

"What kind of food is this?"

"It's the only thing we eat here, so we just call it food," he explained. "Nothing grows here. That's a synthetic protein we culture in vats from stuff dating back to the Starchaser mission."

All the children's questions about food made sense in an instant. How could they live on nothing but this goop? Sniffing it before taking a tentative bite, she swished it around in her mouth, then chewed a few times and swallowed. It had no smell and little taste. Once you got used to the gooey feeling in your mouth, it wasn't *that* bad. It was certainly a better option than eating a hamburger. Thankful to have anything to fill her empty belly, she devoured the rest of the wedge in four large bites.

"Thanks," she said. "I feel better already."

"No problem. I brought enough to last us a week," he said, slipping off Helion's foot. "We'll figure out a way to get more once we're set up."

Much to Juna's relief, she and Kalen had a plan. By the end of it, they'd be living in the crashed remains of the Starchaser, where they would remain hidden until called upon to help drive the Cambrian forces off the planet. The mayor, along with the rest of the Maran leaders residing in Spoke 5, came up with the scheme.

No one knew exactly how or when the Starchaser base would become useful, but the fact that Helion was with them meant they could bring more firepower to the fight than the rest of the Maran forces combined.

Currently, they were halfway through phase one of the plan, which was getting Helion's batteries charged. It turned out the Professor had been correct about his solar panels being useless over here. When Juna had seen a field full of them, she assumed Helion would be fine, but apparently not all solar panels were created equal.

"I'm not a science guy, but even I knew that," Kalen had told her. "Mara's sun produces a different type of light, so you have to build a solar panel specific to that type."

He threw in a few words like "frequency" and "spectrum," but Juna had stopped listening by that point. All she knew was Helion needed a new source of power. Right now, a Maran solar panel sat outside the entrance of the cave, with a cable tied to Helion's charging system. Once his battery was charged, they'd bring the panel in, strap it to his body, and wait for nightfall.

"What do you think we should do with the camerabot?"

Kalen's question was a good one. She'd been considering the very same issue. When they'd realized Helion required a solar panel, they stripped one off the roof of Outpost 1 and strapped it to the side of a camerabot. Kalen used his controller to drive it to the cave, before the two of them sprinted out here to connect it.

"Let's get it back to Outpost 1," she said. "We might need to use it again."

"Sounds good. I'll talk to Grigo and see if there's a way to operate them from the Starchaser."

At that moment, Helion emitted a gentle ding, signalling his battery was fully charged. Kalen helped Juna drag the panel back into the cave, then used the straps from the camerabot to secure it to Helion's left shin.

"That should do it," Juna said, tightening the last strap. "Helion, you drop into wait state. We'll come back for you tonight."

Juna led the way, racing across the frozen ground back to Outpost 1. She pushed through the damaged door and flopped down into a wheeled chair. Kalen fired up his controller and guided the camerabot to its parking spot next to the building.

"I'll check with Grigo about accessing it from further away."

While Kalen talked to his friend, Juna circled the room, looking at his drawings of the Starchaser. She imagined what it must have been like to be aboard the doomed vessel. Floating in space, knowing your old life drifted further away with each passing second, not sure if you'd ever find a new home. It must have been terrifying.

"Hey." A gentle tap on the shoulder snapped her from her musings.

"Grigo says if we install an amplifier on the antenna, we can control the camerabots from the Starchaser." He held up two small black boxes. "I'll do it for both of them."

Kalen sat down at the control panel and checked the view from the one on the rim.

"I don't see anyone around. I'm going to drive it down here."

Ten minutes later, both of the machines sat idle outside the building.

"I don't want to open the big door, so I'll work outside. It should only take me a few minutes."

After he'd left, Juna continued her circuit of the room, admiring Kalen's handiwork. His timeline of Mara's history was impressive. It had two separate lines for the date, one each for the Cambrian and Maran calendars. She scanned through the historical record, stopping to look at one event in particular.

"Operation Big Stick," she muttered to herself. "Launch of spacecraft."

She moved to her right, tracing Mara's story with the tip of her finger. The next entry referencing the mission was two and a half Cambrian years later. It noted the defeat of their forces in what she knew as the First Maran War. Two and a half years after that, a third entry recorded the spacecraft's return to Mara.

As she moved along the timeline, she noted the same entries included for Operation Bigger Stick and Operation Biggest Stick.

“These Marans sure are bad at naming things,” she chuckled.

Each expedition was a two and a half year journey each way. The only difference being, Operation Biggest Stick specified the launch of three spacecraft, and the final entry was not yet recorded.

“They’re not even home yet,” she whispered, thinking of the three Maran ships that had attacked during the latest war. She considered how much her life had changed since then, finding it sad that the crews of those ships were still floating somewhere in space, waiting to get home.

Returning her gaze to the timeline, another entry caught her eye that stopped her in her tracks. It was right next to the record of the Maran defeat in Operation Biggest Stick.

“Operation Massive Hammer. Launch of ten spacecraft.”

She said the words out loud, but struggled to make sense of them.

*Ten ships!*

If they were headed for Cambria, and already two years into the journey, they’d almost be there by now. That thought sent her mind spinning.

How did Kalen’s system work again?

*The filing cabinets!*

All the details would be in there. As she turned towards the storage room, the door swung open and a blast of cold air swept past her.

“All done,” Kalen announced as he stepped through the door, stomping the snow from his boots. He gave her a curious look. “You OK? You look like you’ve seen a ghost.”

“No, I’m good,” she lied. “Just a little worried about tonight, I guess.”

“It is the riskiest part of the plan, but if we’re careful, I think we’ll be fine.”

Tonight *would* be risky. Phase two of their plan involved stealing solar panels from the big field on the edge of the compound and taking them to the Starchaser.

Kalen glanced at his watch. "Grigo will meet us in an hour. Nothing to do now but wait."

Juna sat quietly, her mind racing, unsure what to do about Operation Massive Hammer.

*What did that name even mean?*

She could simply ask Kalen, but it might be better if he wasn't aware she knew about it. The Marans had been kind to her so far, but was it all for show? Could she really trust them? Ten launched warships told her... maybe not.

Her conversation with Mayor Cartona ran endlessly through her head. What did he say about the money they spent trying to get home? Something about the end not being written yet. And what was it Kalen said when he told her they weren't building SCUDs anymore? They had a new plan to get home and didn't need them anymore. The more she thought about it, the stronger she felt that keeping her knowledge of the operation a secret for now was the smartest thing to do.

"We should go."

Those words snapped her back to the present. Tonight's mission would require her full attention, so any further thoughts about massive hammers would have to wait.

"I'm ready," she said, springing to her feet. "Let's do this."

After slipping into their winter gear and each grabbing a backpack, they exchanged nervous smiles and a thumbs-up. Juna forced the door open while Kalen turned out the lights, and they both stepped silently into the night.

Mara had several moons, but they were all too tiny to give off much light. Flashlights weren't an option, so their progress was slow as they fumbled in the dark. Eventually, they found the entrance to the cave and made their way to the back to wake Helion.

"There are no active sensor sweeps from the clones," Helion told them as they crouched at the cave's entrance. "In fact, it appears sensors were never installed when the clones were built. We should reach our destination undetected."

Because he'd spent so much of his life guarding the royal palace, Helion's sensors were far more advanced than those on any other Mech. They could detect incredible detail up close and extend for miles beyond the range of his friends.

Juna and Kalen clung to his back for the trip to the solar panel field. All his external lights were turned off so he couldn't be seen, and he used sensors rather than visual inputs to move through the darkness. It took him only a few minutes to cover the length of the compound and deliver his passengers safely to the furthest edge of the field.

"Hey, over here," said a soft voice from the dark.

"Hi Grigo," Kalen whispered. "Did you bring the tools?"

"Yeah, I've got them. I brought flashlights too. We're a long way from the Hub, so we can use them out here. Just don't shine them back towards the compound."

Grigo clicked one on and directed the beam at his own face. Juna immediately recognized the boy from Kalen's earlier call.

"I hacked the power system and deleted the last twenty panels from the grid," he added. "We can grab all of them and it won't trip any alarms."

Grigo showed Juna and Kalen how to disconnect the cable from a solar panel and remove the mounting bolts. They scrambled from panel to panel, disconnecting everything while Helion followed behind, grabbing each one and adding it to a growing stack. At one point, Helion's sensors picked up movement near the entrance to the

Hub. Guards began patrolling the compound, so the group lay motionless on the ground for almost an hour while the soldiers completed their rounds and returned to the Hub.

"I don't think I can move," Kalen said as they rose to complete their work.

"I am so cold, I don't think my fingers will *ever* work again," Juna echoed.

By the time they finished, a faint pink glow lit the horizon, signalling their cover of darkness would soon end.

"We gotta go," Grigo said. "We have all twenty. Can your robot carry them all?"

"It will be no problem at all," Helion replied.

"Cooooooool." Grigo said, now directing his words directly at Helion. "I brought a couple of batteries too. It would be great if you could grab those as well."

"It would be my pleasure."

The numbing cold made the walk intolerable. Juna used up the last of her thermapad batteries halfway through the trip. She fought to control her shivering as she marched up a steep incline.

Half the sun was now visible over the horizon, bathing the scene in a pleasant pink glow, but adding no warmth. As she rounded the top of the hill and looked into the valley beyond, she was awestruck by the sight before her.

There it was. The Starchaser.

Her eyes widened as she took it all in. Never in her wildest dreams did she ever expect to lay eyes on this legendary craft. It was fully intact, resting in the shallow trench it carved as it slid to a stop on the Maran surface. It was huge! Getting a sense of scale was difficult from this distance, but it seemed to fill the entire valley.

"Isn't it amazing?" Kalen had approached from behind and now stood beside her, staring at the object of his obsession.

"It really is."

Walking downhill proved quicker than the hike to the top. Before she knew it, she was right next to the hulking vessel, marvelling at how tiny she felt.

"Why don't you and Helion start work on the solar panels," Kalen told Grigo. Then he turned to Juna, his face beaming. "There's a way in over here." He led her to an open hangar near the middle.

Kalen seemed energized by his proximity to the ship, so she struggled to keep up. It was obvious there was nowhere in the galaxy he'd rather be than right here. She followed him through the enormous opening, then tracked the beam of his flashlight as he sped down a series of corridors. Despite the time the ship lay abandoned in this valley, the hallways were white and clean, exactly like a spaceship from one of those Earth movies she enjoyed so much.

At the end of one hallway, Kalen ducked into a small alcove and gestured Juna to follow. It was the bottom of a slender vertical tube with a ladder extending upwards as far as she could see. She directed a sceptical look his way.

"It's worth it. I promise." His eager smile told her he truly believed it.

They began to climb. Hand-over-hand. Foot-over-foot. The cycle was endless. Every so often, they'd pass a landing leading to another level of the ship, but each time, they continued past without slowing. Juna's arms ached, and she was sweating inside her bulky suit. Finally, Kalen stepped off at one of the landings. Juna gratefully joined him.

"Halfway there," he announced, miraculously still smiling.

Juna groaned and recovered a water bottle from her backpack. After a lengthy swig, she offered it to Kalen and watched him take a satisfying gulp.

"Ready?" he asked her.

"Do I have a choice?" She gave him a reluctant nod.

And so the climb resumed. The tedious rhythm continued until, finally, Juna could see the end of the tube. With only a tiny stretch of ladder remaining between them and the top, Kalen stepped off and informed her they had arrived.

After exiting a small alcove, he led her around the corner into a spectacular circular room. Workstations lined the outer rim, but much of their equipment had been removed. An enormous blank screen filled the front wall, and right in the centre sat a large swivel chair with clusters of switches dotting the armrests.

"Just like in the movies," Juna whispered aloud.

Kalen gave her a puzzled look. "What's a movies?"

Juna ignored the question. She moved to the centre of the astonishing space, running a finger over the captain's chair and sweeping her gaze across the room.

"You were right. It *was* worth it."

Kalen beamed. "It's called the bridge. We even have the main screen working." He moved to a workstation on the perimeter. "A lot of it's new. Grigo and I bring stuff over whenever we get a chance."

He flipped a switch on a nearby panel, but nothing happened. "Batteries are dead. I can't wait to get those solar panels working. We should probably go help."

Signalling Juna to join him, he walked off the bridge and back to the alcove with the ladder. He grabbed hold, then scampered up the final stretch, with Juna right on his heels. She emerged into a cramped space featuring a hatch with a metal wheel mounted on the ceiling. Kalen spun the mechanism, then lifted the hatch and climbed through. Juna zipped up after him and found herself outside, standing on top of the massive spacecraft. Twenty feet away, Helion and Grigo were hard at work mounting solar panels.

When Grigo spotted Juna, he leapt over to meet her.

"Your robot is awesome! We'll have this done in no time."

"We call them Mechs and *his* name is Helion."

"That's cool. His artificial intelligence is the most amazing technology I've ever seen. Cambria must be a pretty advanced place."

"You'd be surprised," she replied with a smirk. "How can we help?"

Working together, their little group had all but two of the panels installed in less than an hour. They strapped the remaining ones to Helion, providing him with sufficient power while here on Mara. He stayed on top of the ship, setting his scanners to maximum range, while Juna and her two new friends returned to the bridge.

Grigo sat at a computer terminal, checking system statuses. "We've got enough power to run everything," he said. "You'll even have enough to use the heaters during the day."

That news brought a smile to Juna's lips.

"I brought the codes to the security camera system," he continued. "I've linked it all to the main viewscreen and run the controller through the captain's chair."

He was noticeably excited as he bounced down to the centre of the room. Sitting down in the big chair, he flipped a few switches on the armrest, and the massive screen at the front sprang to life. It showed a grid with dozens of scenes from inside and outside the Hub. He rolled a small ball on the armrest with his thumb, selecting a single image and blowing it up to fill the screen.

"You can move the cameras and zoom in, but try not to do it too often," Grigo warned them. "The guys at the security desk are looking at the same screens, so they'll get suspicious if cameras move by themselves. We have the same setup in Spoke 5, and only move them if we have to."

"Thanks Grigo. This is awesome," Kalen said as he opened up his backpack and started rummaging. "I'm starving. We should eat."

Juna and Grigo joined Kalen, each grabbing a wiggly chunk of food.

"We should find bunks for the night too," Kalen continued. "Do you want to see the crew quarters, Juna?"

"If you don't mind, I think I'll stick around here for a while." She moved to the centre of the room and flopped down in the captain's chair.

"There's somebody I need to find."

# 11

They were airborne again.

Orin floated weightless above his seat, until the violent landing hammered his body, smashing his teeth together with an audible clack. He hoped he didn't chip one.

"We are in no hurry," he begged Gecko. "We should go slow."

Gecko's love of speed was not diminishing and having Todd there to point out every dip and gully that would launch them skyward was not helping one bit. Orin looked to his left and saw his dad in the seat Juna normally occupied, looking like he might be sick. The bright pink "Star Girl" hat sat atop his head.

"That is enough!" the Professor snapped, making no attempt to speak English. "We gave you four wheels for a reason. You will keep them on the ground at all times."

Todd and Gecko both pouted like scolded children, but Orin was pleased his father's warning had the desired effect. He allowed himself to relax now that they were travelling at a more reasonable speed.

The three of them were lined up in Gecko's front seats on a mission to see if Diara's plan was a good one. Everyone in the group was sceptical. The idea seemed completely outrageous, but no one had come up with anything better, so... here they were.

"I think I see it," Todd said, pointing off to his left. "We should probably come at it from the highway."

Gecko slowed his approach, then merged onto the highway. A half mile later, he turned left into the gravel parking lot in front of a small dilapidated building. The faded sign out front read: "Rides on the Rim Amusement Park—Fun for the Whole Family."

Orin had never heard of an amusement park until Diara showed him one on the internet. There was certainly nothing like it on Cambria. It was one more example of how much time and effort humans invested in their own entertainment.

Apparently, this particular park had seen better days. Diara saw an interview with the owner, where he claimed it might close forever because of all the money needed to get it running again. The park had a long history in the area, but that would all come to an end unless, as he had said in the interview, "a miracle dropped from the stars."

Gecko rolled to a stop directly in front of the run-down building, joining a rusty old pickup truck as the only vehicles in the lot. The building appeared abandoned, but Todd walked confidently to the front door and tried pulling it open.

"It's locked," he said before launching three loud knocks on the door. After a few moments of silence, he stepped away and rejoined Orin and the Professor.

"There's a truck here. Someone must be around."

A large wooden fence surrounded the entire complex. They walked over and peered between the gaps. Orin was concerned by what he saw. The amusement park Diara showed him had brightly coloured rides rising high into the air, with colourful signs and flashing lights. What he saw before him now looked like it had the pieces to build a place like that, but everything was faded and in desperate need of repair.

"Whatever it is y'all are sellin', I ain't buyin'," came a gravelly voice from behind.

They turned to see a gruff looking man had joined them under the baking sun. It was decided before they'd set out to let Todd do the talking because of his English skills. He squared his shoulders and approached the man with his hand extended.

"We are not selling anything, sir."

"Everybody's sellin' somethin', kid," he replied, shaking Todd's hand. "We're closed now, and probably for good. What is it I can do for you folks?"

He was a tall, thin man with a narrow, weathered face and deep tan. His hair was red, drifting to grey. His pale eyes were friendly, but not at all trusting. He appeared to be about the same age as the Professor, his years of experience giving him an air of cautiousness.

"Mister McGuiness," Todd began. "We were moved by your story on the local newscast and thought we could help. It's quite possible we are that miracle dropping from the stars you were hoping for."

"This park's been in my family for three generations, so I've pretty much given up on miracles by now, young man."

"Three generations? You must love it here."

"Are you kidding me? I'm sick to death of this place. I'd sell it in a heartbeat if I thought anybody'd give me anythin' for it." He moved his gaze from Todd to the rest of the group, then back again.

"I don't get it. Three guys show up at my place in the craziest lookin' rig I've ever seen, and only one of them talks. This day's off to a pretty weird start, so why don't you tell me about this miracle of yours?"

"How do you like the sound of 'Robots on the Rim'?" Todd had a beaming smile and spread his hands apart as he said it, as if reading the sign as he spoke.

The man looked to the Professor, then Orin and back to Todd, stopping at each momentarily.

"All righty then," he said as he turned to leave. "If you gentlemen would excuse me, I've got a lot to do."

"We can help you," Orin jumped in. "This place can be made great and no money will be cost to you."

Mister McGuiness halted his retreat, then walked back to face Orin. "Your English is a little shaky there, son. You not from around these parts?"

"I am from Austrail—"

"Austria," Todd blurted out. "They're from Austria."

The man spun and gave Todd an annoyed look, then returned his attention to Orin. "So, you say you can help fix this place and it won't cost me a dime?"

"Yes, we can."

"Well, at least you've got my attention. I'll take you for a quick look around to show you what you're up against. If you're still interested after that, I'll listen to what ya' got to say."

Mike led them through the main building and out a side exit, taking them straight into the park. The place was a mess. Stacks of bent and rusty parts were scattered across every square inch of the property. Orin could see in his mind how it all went back together, but every single item appeared to need some sort of attention.

*This was going to be a lot of work.*

"Mister McGuiness, are all the pieces here?"

"Call me Mike. Yeah, everything's here, but I don't have a crew to put it back together. Some of it's busted for good. The motors for the boat ride and Ferris wheel are both shot. I have no idea how I'll ever get those workin' again." He ran his fingers through his hair as he scanned the littered expanse. There was a look of despair in his eyes.

"The season starts in less than a month. I don't see any way to get this park up and runnin' by then."

The Professor signalled Orin and Todd to join him for a private conversation.

"It doesn't look that bad to me," he said. "Getting it back together seems simple enough. Have Todd find out if the man has paint we can use to make it pretty. Then have him negotiate the money."

Orin translated the message for Todd, who immediately walked back to face Mike.

"Do you have any paint?"

"Paint I've got. People to put it on, I don't."

"Well, Mike, why don't you let us worry about that? Here's what we can do for you," he said, sweeping his arms for dramatic effect. Orin couldn't help but think of Lano while he watched Todd transform into a master salesman.

"We will put this place back together and have it looking better than it's ever looked before. You won't have to lift a finger. All we ask in exchange is, at the end of each day, half the profit goes to us."

"You'll do everything?"

"Absolutely."

"You can have the park finished and ready to open in a month?"

"Better than it's ever been."

Orin saw Mike's mind churning as he considered the offer. He ran his fingers through his hair again and swept his gaze across the clutter of broken machinery.

"I guess half of somethin' is better than all of nothin'," he finally said, reaching out to shake Todd's hand. "Let's do it."

With the plan in place, the group climbed back into Gecko for the return trip to the cave. They started out on the highway, but soon made a right turn into the desert.

"It will be hard to get the Mechs there," Orin noted.

"They'll have to travel after dark," the Professor added. "It will take them two nights to walk that distance."

Orin translated for Todd, then looked out over the desolate terrain. "We need to hide in the middle."

As they got closer to the canyon, they saw several rocky outcrops jutting from the desert sands. Gecko altered his course to get a better look.

"This one could work," Todd said as they looked at the backside of one of the enormous stones. There was an indent at the bottom. It was large enough to fit several Mechs, but they would be visible to anyone who passed by on this side.

"They will be here a whole day," Orin said.

"It'll be fine," Todd said, waving the comment away. "There might be a few off-roaders around on the weekends, but I can't imagine anyone being here tomorrow."

Orin looked to his dad to get his opinion. "They could walk to the park from here in three hours. I believe it will work."

It was quiet for the rest of the trip, everyone imagining the Mechs following the route on foot. When Gecko rolled into the clearing at the top of the cliff, Fallout and Geiger stood waiting, ready to take them the rest of the way.

"You might not enjoy this much," Orin said to his dad, trying his best to suppress a smile.

His prediction proved accurate, as both he and Todd had to help the Professor on his short, but shaky walk back to the cave.

"Whatever plans we come up with in the future," the Professor said, still sounding a little woozy. "Make sure they never include me doing *that* again."

The group sat quietly at the big table while Orin walked them through the plan. He would lead a team of Dorel, Annu, Taz and Todd on this mission. The Mechs making the trip would be the Hydros, the Steamers, Tortuga, Armorat and Rayzer.

When darkness fell, the Atomics would drag the Mechs out of the canyon. From there, they would walk to the enormous stone at the halfway point. After waiting there all day, they could complete the journey to the park the following night.

"Pack your tools and welding equipment," Orin told the Wrenches. "There's a lot to do when we get there."

After the meeting, the group dispersed to get ready. The General stepped over to join Orin while he erased the whiteboard.

"That was a good briefing, Orin. You've done well getting the team prepared. I expect this mission will run smoothly."

"I hope you're right." Orin looked down and shuffled his feet, not wanting to meet the General's eye. "It's just that... this seems like such a tiny piece of what we need to do."

"Life is a series of small steps you take every day, Orin. It's when you look back that you see you've actually gone somewhere. We fix the park to make money, then buy what we need to repair the Gate. It's always one step at a time." He placed a reassuring hand on his shoulder.

"Don't worry Orin. We'll have that princess of yours back in no time and then... we'll go deal with her father."

"Thanks General." He looked up and showed him his most confident smile. "Let's go take that first step."

Hours later, Orin stared up at the moon, wishing it wasn't so bright. Those making the trip had been whisked up the side of the cliff and were now assembled in the clearing at the top.

"Anything on sensors, Gig?"

"There is no activity between here and our destination."

"Well then, let's get moving."

Gigahertz led the way as their robotic caravan stepped from the clearing and began the long walk across the desert. The Wrenches were riding inside Armorat near the middle of the procession, while Orin and Todd were in Gecko, right at the back. Orin worried about the moonlight bouncing off the metallic convoy, but Todd assured him there'd be no one within a hundred miles to see it. After four hours of marching, the column slowed, and Gigahertz reported they had reached their destination.

"Alright everyone, we made it," Orin announced over the radio. "Get tucked in as close to the rock as you can, and drop into wait state. Except you, Gig. I'll need you powered up all day with your sensors maxed out. Wake us if anybody gets within ten miles."

Orin thought he'd be too wired to sleep, but surprised himself by waking up to sunlight streaming through Gecko's front window. He was curious to see how well hidden they were, so he ducked outside and walked several paces away. When he turned back, the sight before him was a painful shock. All he could see was a long row of gigantic Mechs standing against a rock, gleaming in the morning sun.

"Nothing we can do about it now," Todd said when briefed on the situation. "Don't sweat it. Nobody's out here, anyway."

The wait for darkness was agonizing. Besides his concerns about being discovered, Orin had to deal with Todd's constant complaining about how bored he was. When the sun finally dipped below the horizon, and the day's light began to fade, the urge to get moving was overpowering. Using all his self-restraint, he waited another hour before setting out.

"External lights off," he ordered. "Let's get this show on the road."

They made good time as the mechanical convoy stomped its way across the desert. The highway was now visible in the distance, but there was little traffic at this time of night. Before long, Gigahertz was stepping over the fence surrounding the park and opening the back gate so the rest of the team could enter.

"Well done, everyone," Orin said, addressing the group. "This will be our new home for a while. All Mechs remember... you are big dumb machines while you're here. Never let anyone see you move and, whatever you do," he pointed directly at Clank for the last part. "Don't talk to anybody. We'll rest until morning, then get to work."

Three short hours later, a call on the radio startled Orin awake.

"A truck has entered the parking lot," Gig warned him.

Orin shot to his feet and rubbed the sleep from his eyes. Giving Todd a nudge on the way, he slipped out of Tortuga's hold and dropped to the ground. Moments later, he saw Mike burst through the park's entrance, his eyes pointing skyward.

"Wha... Wha... What are these things?"

Before he could reply, Orin heard someone running up from behind. He turned to see Todd arriving just in time to do all the talking.

"Good morning Mike. These are the robots we promised you. Remember? 'Robots on the Rim'."

The man appeared too shocked to respond.

"But *how* did they get here?"

"Big trucks, Mike. We had a bunch of big trucks bring them in last night."

"How is that even possible? They're huge!"

"It was a lot of work, Mike. I can tell you that much." Todd rested a hand on his shoulder and directed his attention away from the Mechs.

"But that's not what's important right now. What's important is, they're here and they're awesome." Todd continued to move towards the exit as he spoke, ushering Mike along with him as he went. "We need a few things to get started. I was hoping you could run me into town..."

Orin didn't hear the rest of the conversation as the pair passed through the park's exit. Having quit his job at the restaurant, Todd's new role was keeping Mike as far away from the park as possible. With him here, the Wrenches would have to do everything themselves. If he was gone, the Mechs could do most of the work. Todd was obviously taking his responsibility seriously.

"What's up boss?"

Orin turned to see Dorel's smiling face. Annu and Taz were right behind him.

"I guess we start by finding all the pieces. All that's left after that is putting them together."

The heat was relentless as the group set to work, but they made remarkable progress. Pieces were collected and sorted into piles, while the Mechs assembled them like children playing with a toy construction set. There was little traffic on the road, so the Mechs were free to work almost constantly. Gig monitored his sensors, yelling out "car" whenever one approached. All the Mechs taller than the fence would then freeze in place until it passed.

Eight hours into their work, Gig reported Mike's truck rolling into the driveway. Rayzor was using a sprayer to repaint the fence, so Orin snatched it away and took over. When Mike walked into the park, his mouth dropped open and his eyes looked like they might leap from his head.

"This ain't possible," he kept repeating as he wandered around the park.

Orin went over to greet him. "Hello Mike. We have much done."

"Much done? You can say that again."

Just before Orin could actually say it again, Todd jumped in to take over.

"Here's the team, Mike," he said, waving the Wrenches over.

"This is Dorel, Annu and Taz. Not much for speaking English, but they certainly know their way around a welding torch."

Mike craned his neck to look up at the enormous people. They wore hardhats Todd had scrounged from a shop in the back to cover their ears. "Pleased to meet ya'," was all he could say.

As the Wrenches drifted off to continue their work, Mike turned to face Orin. "I gotta say, I *am* impressed. I would not have believed you could get that much done in one day. You might pull this off after all. Keep up the good work."

And so they did. The team began sleeping during the heat of the day so they could work through the night. It was much cooler that way, and with little traffic on the road, fewer interruptions meant the Mechs could work almost constantly. It also made it easier for Todd to keep Mike away from the park while they worked.

Their progress was incredible. They had already reassembled every ride. The motors for the boat ride and Ferris wheel were beyond repair, so Orin decided to use Mechs to move the rides rather than motors. Everything was repainted, including the new sign out front proclaiming "Robots on the Rim" would be open soon.

Two weeks after their work began, the park was almost ready to go. Mike's eyes sparkled each time he dropped by, unable to hide his excitement.

"Orin, I can't tell you how happy I am. You promised it would look better than it ever did, and you were right. It's amazing. It should be ready right on schedule too, so I'll book the inspection for the end of the week."

"Inspection? What inspection?"

"The state safety inspection, son. We can't open the park without one of those."

# 12

Juna sat in the big chair, silently wishing today would be the day. It had been almost a month since they started calling the Starchaser home, and she was no closer to discovering the identity of her mysterious friend than she was when they got here. The image of those familiar eyes peering over the scarf seared into her memory the moment he'd yelled "all clear," but she couldn't remember who they belonged to.

Life in the Starchaser was comfortable, but frustrating. She'd never felt so useless. Hour after hour spent sitting in a chair, scanning countless images, trying to locate that one face among thousands.

*And for what?*

Would learning the man's identity help her in any way? There was no way to be sure until she knew who it was. So, here she sat, day after day, staring at screens and hoping for a miracle.

Kalen, on the other hand, was over the moons about being here. Access to constant power from the new solar panels allowed him to activate systems he never could before. He spent as much time staring at screens as Juna did, but his displayed logs and data that kept him captivated for hours.

She looked over at him now and smiled. Grigo had been visiting for a couple of days, and the two of them were in an animated discussion about some technical drawing displayed on their monitor.

When she returned her gaze to the huge view screen at the front of the bridge, an image near the bottom caught her eye. She wheeled the cursor, then selected it so it would fill the screen.

Four soldiers gathered in the Hub near the bottom of the exit stairs. What made it unusual was they weren't wearing helmets, making it possible to get a good look at their faces. She adjusted the cameras as infrequently as possible, but zoomed in, deciding this time it was worth the risk.

The moment of recognition hit her like a hammer.

*Sergeant Danto!*

Juna's memory carried her back to when she was a child, looking out her bedroom window, watching young cadets learn to fight. Mustering her courage, she'd gone down and asked to join in, and for one glorious week, trained alongside them. At the end of that week, Sergeant Danto, the very man currently filling her view screen, told her a girl beating up the boys in his squad was destroying their morale, so she was no longer welcome. And now, she realized this man was also her mysterious friend.

"Grigo! Look at the screen. I need you to memorize that face."

Grigo flashed a quick glance. "Oh, sure, I know that guy. I think his name is Danto."

"What! How could you possibly know him?"

"I spend time in Spoke 5, but also run errands and messages," he said. "I've been around all the Cambrian soldiers. Most of them are jerks, but that guy's really nice. He's always bringing treats for the kids."

"Hey Juna, zoom out," Kalen scolded. "The security guys are going to freak out."

Juna quickly adjusted the camera so it wasn't focused solely on Danto. She watched as he talked and pointed, with the others obviously following his instructions. So, he was in charge. That might be helpful.

"I need to talk to him," she whispered to herself.

Walking over to join the boys, she pulled the necklace from

beneath her sweater and showed it to Grigo.

"Could you sneak this onto his body somehow?"

Grigo squinted as he considered the request. "Those suits they wear have about a thousand pockets, and he's always being mobbed by kids. I suppose I could get one of them to do it."

Juna looked at the necklace, made a silent promise to Orin to get it back soon, and handed it over to Grigo.

"Thanks. Give Kalen a call when it's done."

With Grigo back at the Hub, Juna spent every waking moment staring at the viewscreen. On the third day, her hope surged when one camera picked up a scrum of children swarming a soldier. He was handing them things as he walked. She couldn't see if it was Danto, but didn't dare zoom in. Crossing her fingers, she made a silent wish that this was the moment she'd been waiting for. Sure enough, within the hour, Kalen got a call from Grigo.

"It's done," he told her after hanging up the call. "One of the kids put it in a small pocket by his left knee."

"Perfect. I think this plan is finally coming together."

First thing the next morning, Juna and Helion began the trek to the colony. Days of staring at a viewscreen had convinced her that sitting around the Starchaser, waiting to get called into the fight, would never come to anything. Under ideal circumstances, she'd rejoin her friends on Earth, but there was simply no way to make that happen. She could, however, get back to Cambria. Portals opened frequently between the two planets, ferrying people and supplies back and forth. Her hope was Sergeant Danto could help her sneak through one of those.

When they were halfway back to the compound, Helion reported a sensor lock on her necklace.

"OK, let's find a place for you to hide while I wait for my ride to show up." She scanned the hills ahead for any sign of it. "While you're here, I need you to monitor the clone frequencies and figure out how they work."

Minutes later, one of Kalen's camerabots rounded the top of a small hill and rolled up beside them. A hatch on the side popped open to allow her access.

"I never thought I'd ride in a SCUD," she joked.

"It's not a SCUD," came Kalen's annoyed voice through the radio. "I wish you'd stop calling them that."

"They'll always be SCUDs to me," Juna said as she climbed inside. "But I don't care what you call it—just so long as it gets me where I'm going."

The ride was rough. These machines weren't designed to carry a person, so there wasn't a seat, or even a decent handhold for that matter. Juna sat on the floor in total darkness, sliding from one side to the other each time it rolled over a bump. As they neared the compound, the ground became flatter and the ride more tolerable.

"Guards are approaching from the west," Helion reported over the radio.

"Don't worry," Kalen assured them. "I've got this."

*Bang! Bang! Bang!*

The butt of a rifle thumped the side of the SCUD. The resulting sound was so loud, Juna's ears started ringing. "Who's in there?"

"No one is in here," Kalen's tinny voice reported through a small external speaker. "This is a remote-controlled vehicle. I've completed a routine inspection of the solar panel array and I'm returning my bot to its charging station."

"Do you have a permit?" asked the guard. "That sounds like something you should have a permit for."

"I don't need one. It's routine maintenance."

"OK. But... don't let it happen again."

Inside, Juna rolled her eyes, always thankful for the incompetence often displayed by members of the royal guard. She steadied herself as the SCUD lurched back into motion.

"Where is Danto now?" she asked Helion over the radio.

"He is inside the Hub, in a group of five soldiers."

This was the weakest part of Juna's plan. Finding Danto alone, and in a location where she could get at him, would require some luck. She'd been given instructions for accessing Spoke 5, so it might be possible to reach him inside the Hub, but she was saving that as a last resort. Mayor Cartona was already mad at her for wanting to leave, so she didn't feel like bumping into him right now. Ideally, she'd find a way to get to the sergeant outside.

"Kalen, drive me to Outpost 1 for now. We'll wait there and maybe get lucky."

They'd barely started rolling when Helion reported Danto was on the move.

"He and one other soldier have exited the Hub. They are heading for the factory."

At Juna's insistence, Kalen manoeuvred the SCUD to the far side of the factory, around the corner from the main exit. For nearly an hour, she waited anxiously, listening to Helion's constant updates on Danto's movements within the building.

"He is alone, moving towards the exit."

"Pop the hatch," Juna ordered. "I'm getting out." Once outside, she moved to the edge of the building and peered around the corner. The exit was only six feet away.

"He is approaching the door," Helion reported. "It will open in three, two, one..."

As the door swung open, Juna lunged and grabbed the soldier's arm, yanking it towards her and pivoting to gain leverage. Caught off-guard, he offered no resistance. She flipped him over her shoulder, spun back around the corner of the building, and slammed his back to the ground with a resounding thud. As quick as a targacat, she was on top, pinning him, her face only inches from his.

"Why did you help me?"

Shocked at first by this unexpected turn, he appeared surprised upon recognizing his attacker. Rather than answering her question, however, he returned only a beaming smile. Then, without a hint of warning, he slipped his leg out from under her, rolled his hips with more power than she thought possible, and tossed her to the ground. In the blink of an eye, their positions were reversed. Juna stared up into his eyes, unable to move, but was somewhat reassured the smile never left his lips.

"It looks like you could have used another week of training, my dear princess," he teased. "In answer to your question, I helped you because we fight the same enemy."

"You're a member of The Underground."

"Right from the start. I was the first person the General called when he put it together." He smiled down at her. "Just because I work for your father doesn't mean I have to like him."

"Could you let me up, then? You're really heavy."

As they stood, Juna reached down to the pocket near the sergeant's left knee and retrieved her necklace. She gave him an innocent shrug as she slipped it over her head.

"The General did say you were resourceful," he chuckled. "I certainly didn't expect to run into you on Mara."

"Something's gone wrong on Earth, so I couldn't get back. Do you know what happened?"

"No. We suddenly lost contact. Since then... nothing."

"I have to get back, but to do that, I need information. Can you help me get to Cambria?"

"I would, if I could... not sure what I'd do, though."

"It's OK. I have a plan."

⚙ ⚙ ⚙

He needed a plan. Skeet paced the floor of Lano's warehouse like a caged alderbeast. For nearly a month, there'd been no contact with the team on Earth. During that time, he'd stopped in on Lano's occasionally, but was still spending most of his days on the streets, seeking an explanation for what went wrong.

The number one topic of discussion on this planet was the conquest of Mara. It started with a day of celebration, but since then, optimism had faded. The emperor began with promises of amazing inventions the Marans would deliver to the people of Cambria, but they soon realized these wonders would never filter down to them. The consensus was that, as with all things, the Elites would reap the benefits, while their lives would remain unchanged.

Skeet felt like the only person on the planet who knew the truth. Everyone here rejoiced in the victory over an evil race that had attacked them for years. He wanted to scream out to the world that the Marans were their ancestors, exiled and left to die generations ago. But what was the point? No one would believe him, anyway.

And so, he roamed the streets, day after day, hoping to hear one piece of news that might help him learn what had happened to his friends.

"This is a waste of time," he mumbled to himself. He ceased his mindless pacing, then grabbed his backpack and started filling it with supplies.

"If I'm going to find out anything, it will have to be from the big guy himself."

⚙ ⚙ ⚙

Juna hurt everywhere. She'd crammed herself into a space under Helion's chest plate, normally reserved for missile storage. One of his cannons had been removed, along with half his missiles, and left behind at the Starchaser. It was a peace offering to the mayor—an apology for leaving before the fight had even begun.

"I know I can be of more use from Cambria," she had told him. "I promise you, I will come back, and I'll bring enough help to drive my father's forces off your planet."

"Alright Juna," he had replied curtly. "Do *not* disappoint me."

So, after receiving a backpack full of supplies and a nice goodbye hug from Kalen, she stuffed herself into Helion's storage compartment and settled in for the lengthy journey. Kalen showed them a roundabout route for reaching the rim above Outpost 1 without passing through the valley. It turned the normal two-hour walk into a four-hour ordeal, of which Juna felt every bone-jarring step along the way.

The long trip offered an excellent opportunity to reflect on her time here on Mara. She liked Kalen and believed him to be a friend. The mayor, however, was a different matter. In the beginning, she felt he was on her side, but everything changed when the clones showed up. The stress of having his planet invaded could easily explain his new attitude, but he *was* a politician. If he was anything like a Cambrian politician, every word out of his mouth could be a lie. She simply didn't know. The one worry she couldn't shake was Operation Massive Hammer. Her biggest regret was not finding out more about that before she left.

But it was too late now. If her plan worked, she was only moments away from leaving Mara and returning to her home world. She popped open the hatch and sucked in some refreshing Maran air. She listened in as, directly below her, Sergeant Danto yelled into his radio.

"You heard what I said. Some idiot sent a Solar over here!" He paused briefly to hear the response, then resumed his tirade. "I know it's not supposed to happen, but I'm standing here staring at one. So, you tell me how it got here. I want to send it back now before the battery dies, and I'm stuck with it for good."

Juna knew this was the moment her plan may fall apart. Helion had been studying the communications used for controlling the clones. A three-digit identification number had been assigned to each one, with the first digit signifying their power type. There were no Solars on Mara, so they weren't certain, but through the process of elimination, they guessed a Solar's ID would begin with a five.

Soon, they would know for sure.

Juna took a calming breath when she saw the tiny fireworks display that preceded a portal. Minutes later, the Gate appeared, its centre showing a swirling pattern of yellows and ambers. Looking down, she saw Danto resume his conversation.

"It's 505," he said, holding up crossed fingers for Juna to see.

Helion discovered specific commands could be sent to a clone to steer it or move its arm a certain way, but usually it received a set of coordinates and simply moved to that location. That's what they hoped would happen now. After a minute of mesmerizing swirls, the image in the centre of the Gate changed to show the inside of the dome at The Institute on Cambria.

"I have received coordinates for Clone 505," Helion said. "I shall proceed."

Juna waved goodbye to Sergeant Danto, then pulled Helion's hatch shut. His Maran solar panels had already been removed, so he would look like any of the other monstrous machines moving around the facility. She realized the real Clone 505 was likely on the move as well, but that was of no concern. Heading to the designated coordinates was not her intention. All that interested her was finding a place from which they could make a clean escape.

A small vent on Helion's chest plate gave Juna a limited view of her surroundings. As they stepped through the Gate, she noticed two Diesels passing through in the opposite direction. To her right, she noticed the large door on the side of The Institute's dome was open.

"Let's get outside and figure out how this place works."

As Helion stepped through the massive door, a ray of sunshine streamed through Juna's vent. She'd almost forgotten how nice it was to feel the warmth of the sun and look out on a beautiful amber sky.

"It's good to be home," she whispered to herself.

The Institute didn't appear to have organized storage areas like they had at The Depot. Mechs were lined up haphazardly anywhere they would fit.

"Get to the north side and find a spot near the fence, Helion. We'll sneak into the desert when it gets dark."

It was late evening on the planet she'd departed, but appeared to be early morning here. She was far too tired to stay awake for another day. After stuffing her winter gear into the vent, the tiny space fell into darkness.

"Wake me tonight," she told Helion after curling up and resting her head on the backpack. "I feel like I could sleep for a week."

What seemed like a moment later, Helion's voice crackled through her earpiece, informing her it was time to get up.

"We have a problem," he told her. "Motion sensors line the entire facility. I cannot leave undetected."

"If we make a break for it, can you outrun them?"

"I would have a head start, but they have Tortuga and Armorat clones which are far faster than me. I could not evade them for long."

This ruined everything. Her hopes for a quick escape to the desert were now dashed. It was time for a new plan.

"I'll have to leave without you," she told him. "Will you be OK on your own for a while?"

"I will be fine. I am one Mech among many, so I doubt they will notice me. But I dislike the idea of you being on your own."

"Don't worry Helion, I promise to be careful. I'll get to Lano's and find out what went wrong on Earth. In the meantime, you figure out a way to knock out those motion sensors. We'll use the radio to stay in touch."

Helion popped his hatch, allowing Juna to climb out. Using his sensors, he'd plotted a layout of the facility and given her a rough idea on which way to go. She knew darkness would help in covering her escape, so she set off immediately. Less than thirty seconds into her journey, a warning came through the radio.

"Two guards are approaching from the west. You should take cover."

Juna noticed an area to her left filled with tables and chairs, no doubt a place to eat lunch for the people who worked here. It had a roof over it to protect them from the sun and rain. After sprinting to it, she scampered up one of its supports and laid flat on top to wait for the guards to pass. She heard them talking as they approached and then, to her horror, heard the scraping of chair legs as they sat down at one of the tables.

Her heart sunk. This was a setback, but with any luck, they wouldn't stay long.

# 13

“Walter Beck, Compliance Inspector, Arizona Safety Commission,” the humourless man said. “Who’s in charge here?”

His expression was as serious as the tone of his voice. He was of average height, his solid build and perfect posture giving him an undeniable air of authority. His face was red from a recent sunburn, and he had the bushiest eyebrows Orin had ever seen. Wearing a leather jacket over a shirt and tie, he looked like a man with a job to do, and no patience for anyone, or anything, that might stop him from doing it.

Todd stepped forward and shook the man’s hand. “You can speak to me, sir.”

“If you don’t mind me sayin’, son, you look a little young to be runnin’ things.”

“I’m more of a translator, sir.” He turned and pointed to the Professor standing behind him. “This is the man who knows the technical stuff, but he doesn’t speak English, only German.”

“Ah, sprechen sie Deutsch, then?” the man said, directing the question over Todd’s shoulder.

The Professor returned only a blank stare, now involved in a conversation using two languages he had no interest in speaking. He was sporting a new hat for the occasion. On his last trip to the city, Todd had stopped at a thrift store, and picked up an “old man” hat in case the Professor ever needed to speak to a human again. It was black with a shiny silk band and a small feather. Orin recognized the style from a movie he’d seen with bad acting and no colour.

"Just kidding," the inspector chuckled. "That's the only German I know."

Orin wiped the sweat from his forehead and blew out a long breath. He'd asked his dad to come today, so an adult was here to make them look more professional. If Mister Beck had been fluent in German, that decision would have proven a complete disaster.

Getting his dad here had been a challenge. The only way he'd been convinced was by promising to delay their return until after dark, so his descent into the canyon could be done at a leisurely pace.

"My job here today is to ensure every ride at this facility conforms to the safety requirements established by the State of Arizona." Mister Beck read the statement from a small card he withdrew from his jacket pocket. "Shall we begin?"

Orin was proud of how the park turned out, but this inspection did have him concerned. The questionable condition of some of the existing rides had forced him to make a few unorthodox decisions along the way. He hoped none of the unique rides they'd created would fail to meet Mister Beck's standards.

"Let's start with the swinging boat," he offered, looking up at the nearest ride. "What function do the robots at each end serve?"

"This one has no motor," Todd informed him. "The robots provide the motion for the boat."

"What? They push it back and forth by themselves?"

"That is correct."

"How much power can they generate?"

Todd went to the Professor, who whispered the answer in his ear. When Todd relayed the value to the inspector, Orin noticed a look of surprise, but he offered no comment. The man then pulled devices from a case and started taking measurements on the Mechs. It looked to Orin like he was measuring the density and strength of their metal and the power generated by their hydraulic system.

For each reading, he gave a puzzled shake of the head before recording the value and moving on. When he finished with Vortex, he moved to the other end of the boat, repeating the process for Diode. Once done, he stood and looked for the next ride to inspect.

"I see the Ferris wheel has a robot standing next to it as well. I suppose it does all the spinning."

"Yes, he... it does," Todd confirmed.

Mister Beck marched over to Gigahertz, who was manning the Ferris wheel, and repeated his tests. It was the next step in what was looking to be a long day. But the morning passed quickly, with the diligent inspector moving from ride to ride, testing and recording his results. Many were simply repaired versions of the originals, so the inspections on those went smoothly, but Orin cringed, watching the inspector approach the final ride.

"*What* have we got here?"

"We call it the Juggler, sir," Todd replied proudly.

One of the park's original rides was beyond repair, but it included caged spheres with seats inside that could hold four passengers. The new ride they created had the three Steamers standing in a circle, each holding one of the cages. When operating, the Mechs passed the spheres back and forth in an intricate pattern of constant motion. It was incredible to watch, Orin guessing it would become the most popular ride in the park.

"Turn it on," Mister Beck demanded. "I want to see it in action."

Orin hid crossed fingers as he stepped over to a small console and flipped a few switches. The Mechs fired themselves up and began moving the spheres in a spellbinding blur of motion.

"It's very impressive, but what if they drop one?"

"Drop one! How could he possibly accuse—"

The rest of Clank's outburst was drowned out by Todd rushing to the inspector, trying to distract him with a bunch of facts and figures. Fortunately, Clank had used the small speaker on his leg, and not his loudspeaker.

"Wait a minute," the inspector said, pushing Todd aside.

"Who said that?"

"I did," Orin lied. "I thought I would do the prank."

Mister Beck gave Orin a cold stare, but eventually seemed satisfied with the excuse. "Never joke with a safety inspector, young man. Anybody'll tell ya'... we *don't* have a sense of humour."

Finishing up his tests on the Steamers, the inspector grabbed his equipment and started heading for the exit. Todd, Orin and the Professor followed along, with Orin making a point of turning back to scold Clank with a wag of his finger. Mister Beck put his devices away and organized his papers. Orin fidgeted, shifting his weight from foot to foot, while he anxiously awaited the results.

"Well, you have passed the inspection and I will certify the park to open," Mister Beck informed them. "But, I gotta say, there's somethin' mighty peculiar going on around here."

"In what way, sir?" Todd asked innocently.

"These robots of yours are over-engineered by a factor of ten. The metals they're built with are so strong I don't know what half of them are."

"We do take the safety of our riders seriously, sir."

"It's good that you do, son, but this is way over the top. These are the most impressive machines I've seen in my lifetime. And I used to work for the military. To see them standing in an amusement park, pushing kiddie rides around, seems absurd." Taking a folder from his case, he pulled out a colourful piece of paper and signed the bottom.

"Hang this near the door," he told Todd as he handed him the sheet. "Good luck with your opening this weekend." He walked around the group, shaking hands with each of them, then picked up his case and muttered to himself all the way to the exit.

When he was gone, Todd and Orin let out a series of whoops and exchanged a spirited high-five.

"It is good we passed," Orin said, releasing a sigh he'd been holding all day. "Now people can give us the money."

"We're going to have to get them here first," Todd said, flashing him a knowing smile. "Have you ever heard the word 'hype'?"

Fortunately, Todd was a born salesman. He convinced Mike to print flyers, and buy balloons and streamers, to promote the grand opening on Friday night. Then he asked Orin and Taz to decorate Gecko, who loved the idea of touring the local hotspots in his brightest green, attracting people to the big event.

Next, they recruited Rayzor to tag along. He clamped himself onto Gecko's roof, joining the colourful troop as they set off for all the hotels in the area, handing out flyers and telling anyone who would listen how much fun "Robots on the Rim" would be.

Mike kept busy, too. He appeared on local TV and radio shows, drumming up interest in the park and finding dozens of people to work there. Most of the new employees appeared to be about Orin's age. He wanted so much to meet them and ask about growing up on Earth. It was far too risky, of course, so he wisely kept his distance.

All the new faces roaming the park changed life for the Mechs as well. Whenever people were around, which was essentially from sunup to sundown, they weren't allowed to move or talk. For the most part, they spent their days in wait state.

Orin's favourite part of the publicity tour was going to Flagstaff and driving down Main Street. They waved and honked the horn, handing out flyers to everyone who rushed out to see the bright green lizard truck with a robot on the roof.

"Don't look too coordinated," he'd warned Rayzor. "Try to look like a simple robot."

"What's a robot?"

"It's like a Mech, only not as smart."

On the morning of the big day, Orin was up with the sun, too excited to sleep. He lifted himself off the bench inside Tortuga's hold that had served as his bed for the past month. Todd was lying on a similar one on the other side, while Taz stretched out on the floor. Both were snoring away like they didn't have a care in the world.

Orin tip-toed over Taz, grabbed his hat and an orange from a box by the exit, then slipped out into the sunshine. Earth food made up much of their diet now. Some of it was really good. The General loved watermelon, constantly munching it whenever it was around, but oranges were Orin's favourite. With dwindling supplies from Cambria and no way to get more, eating things from this planet became their only means of survival. Unfortunately, buying that food relied on the kindness of Todd and Mike. All Orin's hopes rested on the park becoming successful, so they would finally have money of their own.

As he walked down the centre of the park, or the midway, as Todd called it, Orin was feeling a surge of optimism. It did seem like a place where people would come to have fun. It was so much more than the rides. There was a row of small booths where people could play games, throwing balls or rings, trying to win gigantic furry animals. Some booths sold food or treats, while another featured a sign claiming the person who worked there could read your mind and tell you about the future.

"Are you excited about tonight?"

Orin turned to discover that Mike was also an early riser, and had stepped up to join him. "Yes. I hope many people come. Are you excited?"

"I am, Orin. It's been years since I've felt this good about the park. I can't thank you guys enough for what you've done here. You really are that miracle from the stars I was hopin' for."

"You help us too. It is good for everyone."

"That it is. Say, I gotta go get ready. All the staff will show up soon and I need to show 'em what to do. You and the big fella will be drivin' the dune buggies, isn't that right?"

"Yes. I will get them ready now."

Orin hurried back in the direction he'd come. One of the new attractions at the park would be rides across the desert in Tortuga and Armorat. Because they were both currently serving as bedrooms, he'd need to get them cleaned out. The fact they were intelligent machines had to remain a secret, so Orin and Taz were to sit up front and pretend they were driving.

"You guys up?" Orin called as he rapped on Armorat's hatch.

A groggy Dorel opened it, squinting at the early morning glare. "Yeah, we're up, but I wish we weren't. Yesterday was a long one."

"Shut the door!" Annu yelled from inside the hold. "It's brighter than the sun in here."

"Sorry about that. I'm reminding you to clear out your stuff this morning. Armorat will be open to the public today."

Orin then shifted over to Tortuga, receiving an even less friendly welcome from Todd and Taz. He busied himself cleaning up the hold and piling his things near the hatch. His pulse raced while he worked, excited to finally be moving one step closer to bringing Juna home.

With only an hour to go before the official opening, Orin prowled the midway, unable to sit still. The parking lot was already full and the line of people waiting to get in ran all the way around the fence. He could see eyes peering through the gaps, desperate for a glimpse of all the fun the park had to offer.

At the edge of the midway, Orin saw an oddly dressed woman waving at him to join her. Wearing a long flowing gown with every colour of the rainbow, and a matching scarf wrapped around her head, she looked like a mystic from back on Cambria. When he walked over, she pointed to a chair in the fortune teller booth, inviting him to sit down. As he got closer, he could see she was dressed to look like an old woman, but was really no older than he was.

"I was hoping you might help me, young man," she said, trying to sound like an old woman, too. "Customers will arrive soon and I want to warm up my powers before they get here."

"What do I do?" he asked hesitantly.

"Nothing at all. Just sit quietly, and let me read your mind."

Orin wasn't sure he wanted anybody reading his mind right now. He *was* keeping quite a few secrets these days, but he didn't believe in this stuff, anyway. He sat and signalled her to proceed.

There was a large crystal sphere on the table between them. She began moving her hands over it while humming.

"You have travelled a great distance to be here," she finally said. "Your name begins with an... 'O'—yes, that's it, an 'O'. You are smart, much like your father."

Orin was getting uncomfortable. Maybe on Earth there were people who could do this sort of thing.

"You're thinking of a girl," she continued. "Her name begins with a... 'J'. You love her very much."

Orin sprang from the chair, struck by panic, but before he could sprint out of the booth to get away from this spooky girl, he heard snickering coming from behind a curtain at the back. Drawing it aside, he saw Taz there, his face red from stifling a laugh. When he saw Orin, he cracked up, unable to hold it in any longer.

"Very funny," Orin said, fortunately remembering to speak

English. “It was a good prank.”

A smile still brightened Orin’s face when he left the booth. He’d certainly been worried for a moment there, but had to admit it was a funny joke. As he continued along the midway, he saw Todd walking towards him, eating something in a long skinny bun.

“Hey Orin, have you tried a hot dog yet? They make them pretty good here.”

“Is it made of meat?”

“Sort of. They take all the stuff left over after making meat, grind it up and stick it in a tube.”

“So, it is worse than meat.”

“I guess you could say that.”

“I would not like one then.”

“Suit yourself,” he said, throwing an arm around his alien friend. “Hey, did you see the line-up out there? I think we’re a hit.”

“Yes. It is exciting. I hope the people have fun.”

And they did.

Rayzor was at the front gate, greeting people as they entered. He kept his movements slow and deliberate, so people would assume he was a simple machine, controlled by someone watching on a camera and speaking through a microphone. By joking with everyone and raving about the attractions, he had people in a good mood before they even got in.

Orin was in a good mood, too. He spent most of his time pretending to drive Tortuga, in what turned out to be a popular attraction. The line-up to board one of the enormous machines snaked from the back gate to the Ferris wheel.

To add to the excitement, they set it up as a race between the two vehicles. Tortuga was faster than Armorat, his six rubber tires built more for speed than Armorat’s tracks. To keep the outcome a surprise, Orin made Tortuga lose some races on purpose. He wasn't happy about it, but kept every race close, and allowed Armorat to win *almost* half of them.

Later in the evening, Todd took one of Orin's shifts so he could experience the midway for himself.

*It was amazing!*

The sights, sounds and smells were unlike anything he'd ever experienced. It was dark now, but the lights of the rides lit up the night. The relentless blinking and twirling flashed across clouds, making him dizzy as he tracked them across the sky. Screams from riders filled the night, whether from excitement or terror, he couldn't tell. A smell from something called popcorn floated on the air, making his mouth water. He made a mental note to check with Todd to see if it contained meat.

And music was everywhere! Music was rare on Cambria. There were a few traditional songs, played on simple instruments, but only on special occasions. Here, the music was alive. He could feel it flow through his entire being. Clashing rhythms bombarded him from every direction. He closed his eyes, losing himself in the chaos of sound.

A tap on his shoulder broke the spell. Orin opened his eyes to see Mike, his smile stretching from one ear to the other.

"Ain't it somethin', Orin. This place hasn't felt so alive since I was your age."

"It is fun. I have not been to something like it before."

Mike gave him a puzzled look. "I often wonder where it is you guys really come from. You'll have to tell me about it sometime," he said, slapping Orin's back and continuing down the midway.

"No, I don't think I will," he replied to the now empty space.

Before returning to his duties with Tortuga, Orin checked in on the Mechs. Vortex and Diode lazily tossed their boat back and forth, while Gig spun his wheel, each pausing only long enough to allow riders on and off. The Juggler was the park's most popular ride, the line-up stretching so far, Orin couldn't see the end of it. At least the Steamers had a complicated routine to perform, but even that had to get monotonous after a while. He knew the Mechs were bored, but they were well aware how important this was to the overall mission, so they performed their duties willingly and without complaint.

At the end of the evening, after Tortuga's last race with Armorat, Orin made his way to the front of the park. He drifted along with a stream of boisterous guests, filtering towards the exit. The energy of the crowd had him buzzing as he entered the main building and walked down a narrow hallway to Mike's tiny office at the back. His heart skipped when he saw Mike sitting at a desk, nearly hidden under piles of money. When Orin entered, Mike smiled up at him, spreading his arms wide to highlight the impressive haul.

"Best night we've ever had. By a lot!"

"I am glad. The money will be good for us."

"Of course, there's a lot more on credit cards, too. I've added it up, and taken out enough to pay the staff, but this should be your half here." He handed Orin a huge stack of cash.

"Feel free to check my math."

"No, it is OK. I trust you, Mike," Orin said as he took the money, marvelling at the weight of it.

Inside, his heart surged. He knew this was only the beginning, but it was an important first step. If everything went according to plan, he'd soon be on his way to Mara to bring Juna home.

# 14

This was not how Juna imagined her return to Cambria. Lying flat on a roof, listening to a couple of guards droning endlessly about absolutely nothing, was not her idea of a good time. Why did these guys even get paid? The only things they were keeping safe were the chairs they were sitting on. She remembered the General once saying guards at places like this were lazy, but she never dreamed it could be this bad.

Her heart sunk when they pulled out a Kinco game, the chips clattering as they hit the metal table. She and Pom would often sit, engrossed in the game for hours. It was hard to imagine this ending anytime soon.

The hours ticked by *so* slowly. They were at it all night! The sun was already up! How could she possibly sneak out now?

"The day shift will be rolling in soon. We should get going," one guard said as he stood, cracking his back as he stretched.

"Yup," agreed the other. "That was a long one. I'm glad it's finally over."

Juna rolled her eyes and waited for the guards to slide their chairs under the table and saunter off. When she finally dared to move, she found her body reluctant to do so. She hadn't flexed a muscle all night, knowing the guards, even as inept as they were, would certainly hear her right over their heads. Her entire body ached.

She moved tentatively, rising up to a sitting position before scooching awkwardly to the edge of the roof. After lowering herself over the lip, she slid down the post, releasing a groan when her feet hit the ground.

*So, what now?*

The compound was empty, but she knew that wouldn't last. She keyed the mike on her radio.

"Hey Helion, you see any guards around?"

"Ah, Juna. It is good to hear from you. I have been monitoring your lack of progress all night. Currently, there are no guards in the area, but hundreds of people are now passing through the front gate. I believe the workday has begun."

"Just my luck," she grumbled. "This would have been so much easier in the dark."

She started with a light jog to get some blood flowing, then set off at a run towards the main gate. As she rounded the corner of a large brick building, The Institute's enormous dome came into view. People were streaming in, ready to start their day.

She remembered being in a building just like it once, while rescuing Professor Oletta from her father's clutches. It would have a locker room where she might find a disguise, but it was likely teeming with people at the beginning of a shift. That wasn't going to work. Another long column of people wearing lab coats filed into a building immediately to her right.

*This was a disaster!*

To her left, she spotted a couple of security guards exit a small building and head off in separate directions. One moved for the dome, while the other headed to the back of the facility where Helion was hiding out. Juna smiled as a plan formed in her head. There was no question she'd need a disguise to get out of here, and she now knew where to get one.

"Hey Helion, there's a guard leaving the security building and heading your way. Can you pick him up on sensors?"

"Yes. I've got him."

"Good. Don't lose track. I need to bump into him alone."

After receiving some helpful guidance from Helion, Juna felt ready. She was crouched in a clump of bushes in the shadow of a tall building. Her target would pass by shortly. She was a bit nervous about the upcoming encounter. The last time she'd found herself in a fight, Sergeant Danto had turned the tables on her pretty quickly. Maybe she was getting soft. Through a gap in the bushes, she saw the guard's approach. She'd know soon enough.

She allowed him to pass, then zipped out from behind and tapped him on the shoulder. The moment he turned, she unleashed a sweeping kick to the side of his head. He collapsed instantly, now lying motionless on the sidewalk.

"And I was worried about getting soft," she chuckled to herself as she dragged him by the feet into the bushes. "I don't think so."

Within five minutes, Juna had relieved the guard of his uniform, pulled it on over her own clothes, and was casually strolling around The Institute, pretending to guard something.

Unfortunately, the disguise wasn't perfect. The victim of her theft was quite a bit heavier than her, but slightly shorter. His uniform was a little baggy and didn't quite reach her ankles. She'd also struggled to get all her hair tucked in under his hat. It was passable from a distance, but she'd have to avoid getting too close to anyone.

"Helion, I need a path to the main gate where I won't run into anybody."

The recommended route was effective, but far from direct. Sticking mostly to the perimeter, it took her nearly twenty minutes to get within sight of the exit. There were guards stationed there, so not getting close to anyone would be difficult.

As she stood there pondering her best option, she heard a commotion coming from behind. She turned to see a man, wearing nothing but his underwear, running towards the front gate. He yelled repeatedly about an imposter in their midst.

Coming up with a plan was no longer an option. This moment called for action. Juna bolted for the gate, leaping over a short fence on the way. Two guards stepped in front of her, motioning her to stop. She didn't.

Slamming into the guard on the left, she grabbed his arm and flung him into the one on the right, sending them both tumbling to the ground. She hurdled one more fence to get past the gate, then broke into a sprint.

The wailing of alarms filled the air as she dashed down the grassy embankment ringing The Institute's parking lot. Over her shoulder, she saw the two guards had picked themselves up, and were now joined by a few of their friends.

She raced for the parking lot to disappear into a sea of cars, staying low to avoid being spotted.

"Are you in danger?"

Helion's question actually forced out a laugh.

"Good for now. I'll keep you posted."

She crouched as she moved, darting aimlessly between cars, still having no idea where she was going. Her movements were frantic as she weaved from row to row, struggling to stay a step ahead of her pursuers. When she spotted a tri-racer, her hopes surged. If she could get her hands on one of those, she might stand a chance.

When she reached the open-cockpit vehicle, she kept low and slid her hand over the edge, feeling around for the small compartment between the seats. This is where Juna kept the keys to *her* tri-racer. It was a bad idea, of course, but so handy, she always took the risk. She hoped the owner of this one was equally daring.

After popping the lid, she searched with her fingertips.

*Coins and a tin of breath mints. Ugh!*

"Helion, are you tracking me?"

"Of course."

"Are there any other tri-racers in this lot?"

"There are three, besides the one at your current location."

"Which one's closest?"

Following Helion's instructions, Juna slinked over two rows, quickly finding the bright yellow tri-racer. She flipped the lid open on the centre console and reached in. This one had coins too, but sitting right on top was a set of keys.

*Yes!* A smile crossed her lips when she saw the fob on the keychain was a small replica of Gigahertz.

"Let's get outta here, Gig," she muttered to the keys as she slipped into the car. She twisted her body, wriggling until she sat upright in the driver's seat. There was no helmet, but a pair of sunglasses rested on the dashboard. She slipped them on, hoping they'd at least keep the bugs out of her eyes when she hit top speed.

"Hey, Helion. Any guards close by?"

"There are now fifteen guards patrolling the lot. Based on their search pattern, they will find your location in forty-three seconds."

"Better go then," she said, turning the key to bring the car to life. She hammered the stick into reverse and launched out of the parking spot in a cloud of smoke. The ruckus alerted the guards, all of whom charged towards her.

She shifted into first and tromped on the accelerator, squealing the back tire. When rubber grabbed asphalt, the car lurched forward as if shot from a cannon. A guard jumped into her path with hands raised, but quickly realized she had no intention of stopping. He dove to the side at the last moment, shouting obscenities as she zipped past.

"Which way Helion?"

"Take the first right, then left at the next barrier. You will see the exit from there."

Juna shifted into second and pushed her foot to the floor. She made a sharp right turn, skidding past the corner and filling the air with a haze of burnt rubber. Another drifting turn to the left had her staring down the exit. She shifted into third, pinning the accelerator and aiming the car at the green and white gate arm blocking her way.

The tri-racer was built close to the ground, but not low enough to pass under the gate. Juna didn't slow. She barrelled straight for it, ducking to the side, jamming her head into the passenger seat. The gate arm shattered where her head had been only a split second before. She righted herself and smiled, now clear of The Institute and out onto the streets of Volara.

This felt like home. When Juna had a tri-racer of her own, she spent her days on these roads, learning every twist and turn. Sirens blared as two police cars pulled up behind her, but she felt no panic. No fear. She clenched her teeth and stomped on the accelerator. Leaning into turns, zipping down narrow alleys, blasting through green lights, her pursuers never had a chance. Within two minutes of the chase beginning, it was over. The police had no idea where she was.

The search for her would be relentless, so getting far from the city was her smartest move. Now on Volara's westernmost edge, she turned right onto a gravel road to leave the city behind. A plume of dust followed her as she rocketed down back roads. She thought back to the last time she was here, only a few miles from where the General once owned a farm. Memories of her friends, and all they'd been through since then, made her miss them terribly.

"Juna, you will be out of my sensor range shortly," the squawk on the radio told her, snapping her back to the present.

"Thanks for your help, Helion, but I'll be OK on my own for a while. I'll lie low in the country for a couple of days. Stay safe. I'll let you know when I'm back."

"Please be careful, Juna. I will look forward to your return."

Fifty miles later, the adrenaline of the escape now spent, Juna continued west through the beautiful Cambrian countryside. A glance at the fuel gauge, and a rumble in her stomach, both told her it was time to stop running. Only a mile ahead was a small town where she could catch her breath and contemplate her next move.

After pulling into the town's only fuel station, she parked her bright yellow sports car before climbing out to stretch her tired muscles. She stripped off the guard's uniform and threw it into the passenger seat, then scanned the area for a place to eat. She was kicking herself for leaving the backpack with Helion. Even a hunk of that Maran goop would have gone down pretty well right now. She rifled through the glove box of her stolen car, cheerfully retrieving a wallet with an ample supply of cash.

"Well, I already stole his car. I suppose taking his money doesn't make it *that* much worse," she murmured to herself, before withdrawing a few bills and returning the wallet to the glove box. She made a point of memorizing the owner's name, hoping someday she might repay him for his unintended generosity.

Half an hour later, both the fuel tank and Juna's stomach were full. She leaned against an everwood tree, considering what to do next. A note of concern struck when she noticed a police car turning onto the adjacent street. That quickly turned to panic when a second one rolled in behind it. A town this small wouldn't have two police cars unless they were looking for something. It didn't take a genius to figure out what that was.

She bolted for the tri-racer, throwing herself into the driver's seat and jamming the key into the ignition. By the time she was moving, both police cars were on her. As she turned left, one of them rammed the back of her speeding car, pushing it into a spin. Her head slammed the roll bar, flaring her vision with a burst of stars. In a daze, she turned the wheel to slow the spin, then powered forward, racing down the street with the police hot on her heels.

Her tri-racer wasn't as fast as a police car, but far more manoeuvrable. She spun the wheel hard, drifting into a violent turn to maximize her advantage.

As she swung through the curve, the fender covering her left front tire exploded in a cloud of bright yellow fragments. Looking in her rear-view mirror, she was horrified to see a police officer hanging out the side of his car, pointing a gun at her. Before she could react, the centre console of the tri-racer shattered, showering her with a spray of yellow plastic. A searing pain ripped through her leg.

*She was hit!*

The throbbing of the wound drowned out her thoughts, so she let instinct take over. Her driving became a flurry of motion. Sharp turns, shifting gears, aggressive braking into every corner—the police soon followed only her dust. She plunged the car into a grassy meadow, racing across its slick surface and bursting through a row of hedges on the far side.

A quick glance at the mirror showed no one behind her. Confident she'd lost them, at least for now, she doubled-back, heading in the last direction they'd expect her to go. She replaced constant turns with straightaway speed, knowing that's what she needed now. She pinned the accelerator and never looked back.

Juna found it hard to focus. She had no idea where she was or even how long she'd been driving. Her leg raged while her mind blurred. The knock on her head and loss of blood were taking their toll. She relaxed the pressure on the accelerator and began to slow.

There was a thicket of bushes well off the road, so she steered towards it, and drove straight through its heart. She sat for a moment with branches pushing her into the seat. All she wanted was to sleep. If she had a little rest, everything would be alright.

*No!*

The moment of clarity flashed in her mind. If she went to sleep right here, right now, she was never waking up. Her body felt chilled, so she reached into the passenger seat, untangling the guard's jacket from the branches holding it in place. She pushed aside the large bough trapping her and rolled over the side of the car. The landing sent a jolt through her leg that made her cry out. She clawed at the ground to pull through the underbrush, and finally dragged herself clear.

She felt so cold. The jacket was still clutched in her hand, so she pulled it on and squeezed her arms tight. Still trembling, she looked up to see the tri-racer had vanished into the bushes. At least that was good news. A glance down was not as encouraging. Her leg was a mess. The wound looked deep and blood covered everything. It wasn't flowing now, so there was some room for hope.

She needed help. Instinctively, she reached for the radio in her ear, but it wasn't there, no doubt lost when her head cracked against the side of the car. Helion was out of range anyway, so she'd have to find a way to help herself. Summoning all her strength, she stood tall on shaking legs. She had no idea where to go, but felt an urge to get as far away as possible. Every step sent a fresh wave of pain, but she endured and moved forward.

Through the fog of her own mind, she saw herself at the top of a steep incline leading to a shady valley below. She took a tentative step towards the bank, but her leg buckled, sending her tumbling down the hill. Her world became a blur of grass, trees and sky as she rolled all the way to the bottom.

Her attempts to stand all ended in failure, her leg no longer able to hold. Nearby, a large boulder loomed in the shade. She dragged herself over, then pushed hard with her arms until she sat leaning against it.

She was exhausted. Even keeping her eyes open required more effort than she could give. The coolness of the rock on her back was soothing, but her head felt light, like she wasn't even there. Even the pain in her leg seemed to drift away, as a feeling of tranquility washed over her. She would have a little nap. Everything would be fine when she woke up.

Juna became vaguely aware of rustling near her feet. Straining to open her eyes, she saw a farkee scratching at the ground near her bloody shoe. Farkees were small gentle rodents, often kept by children as pets. She closed her eyes and smiled, despite just discovering how dire her situation truly was.

The bash on the head, the loss of blood, the roll down the hill; it had all been too much. She was delirious. The farkee wasn't there. It was merely a hallucination. She knew this because, unlike a real farkee, this one was wearing a tiny pink hat.

As she sat against her stone, thinking about fake farkees and how nice it would be to go to sleep, she heard a pleasant sing-songy voice wafting through her head.

"Scruffers? Scruffers?" the little voice kept repeating. Juna felt herself floating on air, dancing to the sound of the tiny voice. It stopped abruptly, and she sensed more movement near her feet.

"Are you dead?"

Was the farkee asking questions now? She opened her eyes for a moment, seeing the nonexistent rodent with the pink hat was now being held by a small girl, the "H" on her tunic telling the world she was a hod. Juna didn't know of any rules against conversing with a hallucination, so she decided to join in.

"I don't think I'm dead," she replied, her voice hushed. "What's your name, sweetie?"

"Tru."

"That's a pretty name."

"Are you a soldier? Were you in a war or something?"

"No, I'm not a soldier. I stole this uniform. Don't tell anyone, but I'm actually a princess." With what little strength remained, she raised her hand and extended one finger over her lips to show it was a secret.

"Are you Princess Juna?" asked the make-believe girl.

"And how would you know about me?"

"My ma told me all about you. She says you're trying to help us."

"I really am sweetie," Juna whispered. "But I'm too tired right now. If I get some rest, I can try again later."

"That's OK, you look too sleepy anyway. Maybe I should help you instead."

Juna thought that sounded like a great idea, but didn't have the strength to respond. She used the last of her energy to open her eyes, but the imaginary girl was gone. What a shame. It had been nice talking to her.

Without the strength to sit upright, the coolness of the rock slowly slid across her back as she began to tip. And just like that, her whole world went sideways.

Then it went dark.

# 15

Orin's knuckles glowed white from his grip on the armrests, bracing himself as Tortuga drifted around the far pylon. The crowd in the back screamed as they watched the race unfold on the huge internal view screen. Off to the left, Armorat approached the final pylon as well, but was slowly falling behind.

Tortuga had allowed his friend to win several races this day, but he always enjoyed showing off his best stuff on the last run of the night. As he streaked down the final stretch, it was apparent to the raucous group onboard that victory was well in hand. The exuberant chorus of whoops as they crossed the finish line put a smile on Orin's face, despite having seen the same result a hundred times before.

For over a month now, it seemed Orin existed only inside the cramped confines of Tortuga's hold. During the days and evenings, it was racing across the desert with a load full of guests. Often, that was followed by a journey back to the cave, delivering parts dropped off at the park that day. And then, after it was all over, he would curl up on one of Tortuga's benches, and sleep through the morning, just so he could get up and do it all over again.

"Good race, Tee." Orin stood to go help his passengers off-load. "Why don't you go fuel up? I saw a delivery truck come in today, so we'll be making a run to the cave tonight."

The supply of Cambrian bio-fuel had run out weeks ago, but fortunately, the Wrenches made a few modifications to the Bios' engines that allowed them to run on an Earth substance called gasoline.

"Will do, Orin," Tortuga replied. "I'm feeling quick tonight, so I'll have you there in no time."

Once the last of the riders had departed, Orin followed the pack towards the park's main gate. As with most days this summer, the night was hot and sticky, with hardly a breath of wind. Sweat streamed down his face as he strolled along the midway, listening to screaming customers finishing up their final ride of the evening. The flashing lights brought the sky to life, and the smell of popcorn drifted through the night air.

Despite the monotony of life at the park, he still enjoyed it here, and the way it kicked all his senses into overdrive. As he reached the main building, he saw Todd approaching from the other side.

"Hey Orin, another big day at 'Robots on the Rim'." He threw an arm around his friend, squeezing him in tight. "You guys are clearing over ten grand a day. You'll have that Gate fixed in no time."

"It's been great alright," Orin replied, returning the squeeze. "We have everything ordered and most of it's here already. I think we're only a week away from trying it out."

"Awesome news, dude! I can't wait to see Juna again."

"Neither can I."

They stepped into the main building together and tromped down the hallway to Mike's office. As usual, he was sitting behind his desk, sorting large stacks of cash.

"There they are," Mike said, serving up a welcoming smile. "Come on in, boys. It's been another incredible night."

"I'm glad the park's been so successful," Orin agreed. "It's great all our hard work paid off."

Mike leaned back in his chair and gave Orin an admiring look.

"You know, Orin, it is amazin' how much better your English has gotten since we first met. It sounds like you grew up right here in the ole U S of A."

"Todd's been a big help, and it's easier when you use it all day. Sometimes it feels like I've never spoken German."

"You should be proud of yourself, that's for sure." He reached across the desk and handed Orin a big wad of bills. "Here's your share of the loot for today. Don't go spendin' it all in one place."

"No, I'm sure we will spend it in many places."

Mike laughed at that. "Say, another delivery came in today. You guys surely do buy some strange stuff. I hope I'm not gonna get in trouble some day for signing off on it all."

"The robots do require many different materials to operate, but I don't think you should worry."

"Well, that's good to hear." He leaned back in his chair. "Say, did you happen to run into that tall guy with the straight back? He was in here earlier, askin' about the robots. I told him to go lookin' for you on the midway."

"No, I've been driving a dune buggy all night." He hoped the concern he felt didn't show on his face. "I didn't talk to anyone."

"You might want to check outside and see if he's still pokin' around."

Orin felt uneasy as he and Todd left Mike's office. A couple of things in that conversation had him worried.

"Todd, would you or Mike get in trouble if someone found out about us?"

"I'm not sure. I don't think so. Mike doesn't even know you're aliens, and I'd probably lie and say I didn't either."

"It would make me sad if anything bad happened. You have both been such good friends."

They stepped into the warmth of the night and breathed in popcorn-scented air. The park was nearly deserted now, with staff members shooing away the last of the night's stragglers.

"There's the guy with the straight back," Todd said, pointing to a man staring at the boat ride. "Maybe he wants to be your friend, too. Why don't you go say hi while I shut things down?"

Before Todd left, Orin handed him the stack of money. To buy everything needed for repairs, the team required an Earth invention called a credit card. Unfortunately, this was not something made available to citizens of Cambria.

Todd had convinced his mother to get him one by promising to pay it off every month. At the end of each day, all the money they earned went straight into Todd's account, which was then used to purchase what they needed. The system worked, but Orin realized it was one more reason to fear for Todd should their presence on this planet be discovered.

*One worry at a time.*

A feeling of dread gripped him as he approached the mysterious man with the robot questions. Something about the way he carried himself reminded Orin of the General. As he drew closer, he called out to get the man's attention.

"Hello, I'm Orin. Mike told me you had questions about the robots."

He was a tall man with perfect posture and a focused stare. Dressed casually, with a leather jacket and rugged boots, he had short hair, dark eyes and a crooked nose that had probably been broken more than once. There was a certain calmness about him, but even from ten feet away, Orin found him intimidating.

"Pleased to meet you, Orin," the man said. His hand was extended and his smile warm. "Major Tom Buchanan, US Army. I used to work with a gentleman named Walter Beck. I believe you two met when he inspected this place. He's been telling me about the amazing machines you've got out here, so I thought I'd come have a look for myself."

Orin reached out to shake the man's hand. "Do you like robots?"

"I can't say I've seen that many of them," he chuckled. "But Walter gets a bit paranoid sometimes, and he's worried these ones might pose some sort of threat."

"What do you think?"

"Well, they're mighty impressive, that's for sure. As long as they're only pushing a few rides around, I don't find them particularly scary."

"I'm glad. That's all we use them for."

"Now, that's the part that doesn't make sense," he said, reaching out and placing a hand on Orin's shoulder. "Walter's right about one thing—it seems they could be used for so much more." He paused a moment to let that one sink in.

"Listen, the park's closed now, so I best be on my way, but you should expect to see me again, Orin. Something tells me I'll be spending quite a bit of time out here." He patted Orin twice on the shoulder and walked toward the exit.

"See you soon," he called back without turning.

Orin thought he was going to be sick. It was obvious Major Buchanan's presence here would complicate their lives considerably. He was glad they were making a delivery to the cave tonight. He needed to talk to the General about this.

Orin, Todd and Taz were loading Tortuga for the trip back to the canyon. There were only three of them now. Dorel and Annu had moved back to the cave to begin work on the Gate. When loading was complete, Taz drew in a deep breath and stepped into Tortuga's hold. Orin followed him up the ladder, but turned before entering.

"Are you sure you won't come with us?"

"Nah," Todd replied. "My folks don't much care what I do, but I should probably drop in once in a while to let them know I'm still alive."

Todd had his own car running now. On one of his many trips to the city, he took Dorel with him, who got it working in ten minutes. "By the way," he added, "I threw a surprise in there for the Wrenches."

"What is it?"

"It's called duct tape."

"What is it used for?"

"That's the beauty of it—there's nothing it can't do. It's a well-known fact; if you've got something to fix, you can never have enough duct tape."

Orin found it hard to believe anything could be *that* useful, but it certainly had him intrigued.

"Thanks. I'll make sure they get it."

"I bet they'll love it!" he said with a wave. "I'll close up when you're gone. Tell the gang I say hi."

"Thanks Todd. See you tomorrow."

During the trip back, Orin reflected on his encounter with the major, their conversation running through his head in an endless loop. Lost in thought, the trip was over before he knew it. The load tonight included a lot of large boxes, so Geiger and Fallout chained themselves to Tortuga's front tow hooks and lowered him down the side of the cliff. This was always Orin's favourite method to make the descent—nice and slow, with no bone-crunching stop at the end.

It had been five days since his last visit, so Orin noticed big changes. The chains holding the Gate to the ceiling had been removed, with the ring now stable enough to hold itself up. Sparks flew as both Dorel and Annu attacked the structure with welding torches, putting the finishing touches on the repair. After delivering Todd's gift, he noticed his dad and Aeva wiring a cable harness on the opposite side of the ring. He slid over to say hi.

"Hey Dad, how's it going?"

"Good, son. We're putting together the last cable. We got lucky. If the explosion had taken out this side of the ring, where all the control equipment is, we would've been stuck on this planet for years. Maybe forever. As it is, we should have it running in a day or two."

"Great news, Dad. It can't happen soon enough for me."

Seeing the progress put a spring in Orin's step. The end of the project was finally feeling within reach. Today's delivery consisted mostly of computer and radio equipment, so he wandered over to the big table, where Diara and Pom sat chatting.

"You look great, Pom. It's nice to see you up and about," Orin said. Her arm was still in a sling, but that was the only visible reminder of the horrific injuries she'd suffered last month.

"Feeling stronger every day," she said, the playfulness returning to her piercing blue eyes. "I should be scaling mountains again in no time."

"Well, that's good news, because you two have a lot of work to do. The computers and radio gear showed up today. It's being offloaded as we speak."

"That's great!" Diara said with a pump of her fist. "It'll take time to figure out how this Earth stuff works, but it sure will be nice to have a Tech Station again. It gets us one step closer to home."

"One step closer," Orin echoed, allowing himself a hopeful smile.

"There he is." The General's voice boomed as he sauntered up to join them. As was often the case these days, he was munching on a piece of watermelon. "We haven't seen you for a while, Orin. I was starting to worry."

"The radio equipment showed up today, so we should have communications between here and the park soon."

"I *will* look forward to that. You know how much I hate not knowing what's going on." He sat down in a chair and signalled Orin to do the same. "Tell me what I've missed."

Orin filled the General in on all that had happened since their last meeting. It was mostly business as usual until he came to the part about meeting Major Buchanan. The General agreed this was a concerning development.

"You'll find a military man is like a daggit with a bone when he latches onto something like this," the General warned. He took a bite of watermelon, spitting the seeds into the small tin he always carried.

"Try not to add to his suspicions. Answer his questions as best you can without appearing to hide anything. He'll keep digging until he gets what he wants."

Orin thought about the General's words all the way back to the park. He was supposed to answer the major's questions without actually telling him anything, or adding to his suspicions.

*How was he supposed to do that?*

The General assured him he'd do great, but Orin wasn't so sure. One thing was certain; he did *not* look forward to his next confrontation with Major Tom Buchanan.

When they arrived at the park, Rayzor was waiting for them at the back gate. Taz was already sprawled out on Tortuga's floor, his snoring making more noise than the engine. Orin was jealous, knowing he had no hope of falling asleep with all the things running through his mind. With the entire park to himself, he decided to go for a tour to check in on the Mechs.

Rayzor reported having a wonderful time greeting people at the main entrance. He wanted this assignment to go on forever. The Steamers, however, were bored, constantly juggling spheres full of screaming people.

"Why can't I tell them stories during the ride?" Clank protested. "I'm sure it would be much more fun for everyone if I did that."

Orin drifted off to see the Hydros while Spanner explained to Clank why his idea was a bad one. Vortex and Diode had the worst job in the park, endlessly pushing the big boat back and forth. They would do whatever it took to complete the mission, but hoped to progress to the next phase soon.

Gigahertz already knew Orin was coming before he arrived. Fortunately, the Mechs could speak with each other over their radios without making a sound. They spent much of the time chatting, trying to break up the monotony of the day.

"Ah Orin, I heard you were making the rounds this morning. It is nice of you to visit, but you should be sleeping. The sun will be up soon."

"Hey Gig. Couldn't sleep. Too much to worry about right now."

"What is troubling you, my friend?"

Orin explained his fears about Major Buchanan's recent visit. Gig agreed the news was concerning and offered to help keep track of the man's movements while he was in the park. As was often the case, Orin felt better after his chat with Gig. He made his way back to Tortuga, climbed into the hold, and curled up on a bench to rest up for a day that would arrive far too soon.

The following day got off to a great start, but took a turn after the second last race of the night. As Orin was helping his passengers off the ride, Todd arrived at a sprint.

"Orin, the army dude's back. He's over looking at Gig."

Todd offered to take over for the final race, so Orin scrambled down and dashed off towards the centre of the park. The major was standing outside the small fence surrounding the Ferris wheel. Today, he was dressed like a soldier, with a green camouflaged uniform and matching hat. The label sewn to his chest said "Buchanan."

"Orin!" the man exclaimed when he saw him, a pleasant smile spreading across his face. "I was hoping I might run into you this evening."

"It is good to see you again, Major Buchanan," Orin lied. "Is there something I can help you with?"

"Please, call me Tom. I do have a few questions if that's OK."

"Of course, Major Tom. Ask me anything you'd like."

"Walter showed me some numbers the other day, and I hoped you might confirm them for me." He pulled a folded sheet of paper from his jacket pocket and handed it over.

Orin studied the figures on the page. They were results from Mister Beck's tests on Gigahertz, mostly relating to the strength of his metal and the power of his hydraulic system.

"These look about right," Orin said, handing the paper back.

"So, that means the machine right here," he said, pointing in Gig's direction, "could provide a downward force in his foot eight times more powerful than those machines that can crush a car flatter than a pancake."

"As long as he doesn't step on any cars, I don't see the problem."

"Maybe you're right, Orin. Maybe you're right. Say, I never did catch your last name."

"It's Umbra."

"And you're from Austria?"

"Yes. That's right."

Orin knew this would be a problem. If the major went looking for a person named Orin Umbra in Austria, he probably wouldn't find one. As he was trying to think of a way to explain this, a heavy hand dropped onto his shoulder.

"Hey Orin," Taz beamed. "Armorat finally won the last race of the night. It must be your driving that makes the difference."

"That's great, Taz," Orin replied as his friend shuffled off.

The major's mouth hung open while he watched Taz retreat. "That might be the largest person I've ever seen. His accent is a lot like yours. Is he from Austria too?"

"I'm not sure. We just met a couple of weeks ago," Orin said through clenched teeth, struggling to hide his irritation.

"So you say. Listen Orin, you seem upset. Let's call it a night." The major headed for the exit. "Maybe I'll see you again tomorrow."

And he did. And then again every evening after that. His questions were endless. How did the Mechs get here? What was Taz's last name? What's with the hats? Orin couldn't take it anymore.

On the fifth night, he found the major inside the fence surrounding the Ferris wheel, running his hand over Gig's shin plate.

"You shouldn't be in there."

"Orin! Good to see you, son. I apologize, but I noticed someone had carved something into your robot, and I wanted to see what it was."

"I've never seen that before."

"It looks like a kid with a crush carved his initials into it. But, look at this." He pointed at the engraving Orin had made as a child. "They aren't letters. It's some sort of squiggly thing that isn't a letter. That's not Austrian, is it?"

"No, it's not Austrian," Orin snapped.

"You seem a little tense tonight, Orin. Are you OK?"

Orin stood up straight and looked the man in the eyes.

"I guess I'm getting tired of all your questions."

"Just one more for tonight, OK?" The major raised his eyebrows, his way of asking permission. When Orin nodded, he continued.

"What's in it for you, Orin? You seem like one of those kids who graduated from college when they were eight. Why are you and these machines here?"

Orin allowed his gaze to drift back to Gig's shin. "I'm trying to help someone."

"Ah, I've seen that look before. Girlfriend?"

"It's not like that. She's just my friend."

"That's what I thought. Girlfriend." The major smiled, knowing he'd caught Orin in a lie.

"We've chatted enough for now, but let's pick things up there when I drop by tomorrow."

Orin allowed himself a brief smile as he watched the man leave. Once again, he found the encounter terrifying, but he definitely wouldn't be seeing the major tomorrow. He ran his hand softly over the engraving on Gig's shin. If everything went according to plan, tomorrow he'd be going to Mara to bring Juna home.

# 16

"Twenty-eight... Twenty-nine... Thirty!"

Tru squealed with delight as she counted off the last rep in Juna's set. The two had been constant companions while Juna healed from her injuries. Not only was Juna getting stronger, but Tru's counting was improving, now using numbers she didn't even know a month ago.

"That was awesome!" Tru exclaimed, sitting on her tiny bed petting Scruffers. "What's next?"

"Why don't I take a little break?" Juna replied, releasing her grip on the shack's central beam and wiping the sweat from her eyes. "You've been working me pretty hard this morning."

Tru clapped her hands and let out a shriek that sent Scruffers skittering to the other side of the bed.

"I know! I want you to be the strongest princess ever!"

"Now Tru, what did I tell you about using the 'P' word?" Juna said, playfully wagging her finger.

"Sorry Juna." Tru's shoulders sagged. "I forgot."

"That's OK, I forgive you."

Juna stretched her tired muscles, being careful not to bump her head on the beam holding up the shack's roof. Looking around the tiny space that had been her home for the past month, she wondered if calling it a shack wasn't being a bit generous. It was nothing more than a rectangular hole cut into the ground, with a large timber beam running along its length to support a pitched roof and two leaky windows.

The walls were dirt and the floor was covered with a thin layer of round pebbles. There were two small beds, one for Tru and one for her mother, with a lumpy mattress on the ground for Juna. The whole building wasn't much bigger than Juna's quiet place in the dormer window of her old bedroom.

Juna awoke in this room two days after her harrowing escape from The Institute. Tru's mother, Reyn, had removed the bullet from her leg with a kitchen knife, and sewn the wound closed with a needle and thread. Then, for the next two days, she would rouse Juna every hour to give her water or broth, until she finally regained consciousness. Sharing what little they had, Juna's saviours nursed her back to health, a debt she could never fully repay.

When she could walk again, Juna had suggested she and Tru go on an adventure.

"Take me to the rock where you found me. We'll start there."

Juna had to shield her eyes from the sun when she first ducked her head through the tiny door to get outside. The cool morning air felt so good, she stood for a moment to drink it in. By keeping a leisurely pace, they soon found themselves facing the large stone.

"This is where we met," Juna said, reaching down to run her fingers through Tru's hair. She looked up to see the hill she'd rolled down to get here.

"Do you think you can climb that?" she asked, pointing to the top.

"I've never tried, but if you're with me, I can do it."

It was much slower going up than it had been coming down, but they eventually pulled themselves over the rim of the valley and lay panting in a grassy field at the top.

"That was hard, but fun," Tru said after taking a drink from Juna's water bottle. "Is our adventure over?"

Juna scanned the horizon, spotting a familiar thicket of shrubs in the distance.

"There's one more place I'd like to go."

The walk dragged on as the sun crept higher in the sky, but the two travellers pushed forward, until they sat wearily in the shade of the thicket, enjoying another gulp of water.

"There's something in here I want to show you."

They crawled on their bellies to get under the low branches, emerging in the centre where the bright yellow tri-racer remained concealed.

"Wow! Is this yours?"

"Sort of. It's a bit complicated." Juna was reluctant to reveal herself as a thief to her biggest fan. "Let's just say, for right now, it's mine."

Scooching up beside the machine, Juna leaned in and removed the keys from the ignition before sliding them into a pocket. She reached into the small compartment between the seats to collect the coins, then opened the glove box to retrieve the cash from the owner's wallet. Tru's eyes were as big as saucers, and her mouth hung open as she watched Juna gathering up the bounty.

"I didn't know there was that much money in the whole world."

"That's because the people who run the world don't want you to have anything. And it's so wrong, Tru. You should have so much more than this." Juna tucked her spoils into a pocket and began inching her way out of the bushes.

"Come on, let's go home."

"Ma, Ma, we're rich! Richer than the emperor himself!" Tru screamed as she burst into the shack.

Reyn cried when she saw the money on the table, her hand shaking as she reached out to touch it. "I can't take this," she whispered.

"It's not for you, it's for us," Juna said, taking Reyn's hands in hers. "I need to heal, and then get strong. I'll need food for that, lots of it, and maybe other things too. This money could help every hod on the planet if I can get my strength back."

And so, Juna began to train. It was discouraging at first, only doing a fraction of what she could before. But by working hard, more of her power returned every day. She spent hours doing pull-ups, sit-ups and push-ups, often with Tru sitting on her back or hanging off her arms. After that, she'd go outside and lift rocks until her muscles ached, or run for miles through the valley.

When she wasn't training, she would sit on Tru's bed and talk endlessly about her life. Tru hung on every word, but was always most interested in stories that included Pom. These were always Juna's favourite moments of the day.

"Come sit."

Juna snapped back to the present to see Tru patting her bed, signalling an end to the workout and the beginning of story time.

"I still can't believe the princess's best friend is a hod," Tru began. "And now she's helping the Mechs fight the emperor! When I grow up, I want to be just like her."

"I hope you can grow up to be anything you want." Juna took a moment to give Scruffers a scratch behind the ears, careful not to knock off his little yellow hat.

"I think this farkee has more hats than my sister."

That made Tru giggle. "My ma is a seamstress, so whenever she has a tiny piece of cloth left over, she makes Scruffers a new hat."

"Well, Scruffers is a very lucky farkee, and you are a very lucky girl," Juna said, passing the wriggling animal back to Tru. "Your mother is a talented seamstress."

"Why is she making you those black clothes?"

"It's to replace my shadow suit. I told you about that."

"But why do you need one? You never have to sneak around in the rafters again."

"Oh, but I do. I need to go back and talk to my father."

"What are you going to talk about?"

"I'm going to tell him about you. And your ma. And everyone else who lives in the valley."

"You're going to talk to the emperor about me?" Tru's eyes filled with pride. "What are you going to tell him?"

"How beautiful you are," she said, reaching out with a loving tap on the nose. "And how much you deserve a better life."

"Do you think he'll listen?"

"I don't know. I hope so. But I promise I'll never stop trying until I get someone to listen."

Tru sat quietly, her feet dangling off the bed. "It sounds kinda scary. Maybe you should stay here with us. Forever."

"I would love that, sweetie, but I can't," Juna said, reaching out to pull Tru into a hug. "What I need to do is important. I *will* come see you again when I'm done. I promise."

At that moment, the space filled with light as the door to the shack swung open. Reyn stepped in, carrying a small package.

"I brought what you asked for," she told Juna, handing over a roll of cloth. "Are you sure about this?"

Juna took the package, peeling away a corner of the fabric, careful to shield it from Tru's prying eyes. The sun glinted off the steel wrapped inside.

"Yeah, I'm sure."

The time to leave had come. Moving on with her quest had Juna excited, but she would miss this place. The eight small shacks in the valley, each housed a hod family, with a mother and between one and three children. All the fathers were miners in The Wash.

Cambria's moons created an enormous tide. As they moved away from Mount Volara, the oceans receded, exposing hundreds of thousands of square miles of land often hidden underwater. The area cycling from wet to dry with the tides was called The Wash, and most of the planet's natural resources lay beneath it. Mining there was the most dangerous work on the planet. Hods did all of it, many of whom lost their lives each year.

The women here would often go more than a year without seeing their husbands, never knowing if they were dead or alive. Tru could only remember seeing her Da on three occasions, and each visit had lasted less than a week. It was cruel, and Juna vowed to put an end to it. The mission to do so began today.

Everyone in the valley set out on the adventure. Carrying ropes and planks, the eight women and seventeen children marched across the grassy meadow, past Juna's rock and up the hill to the rim of the valley. It was early in the evening, so most of the day's heat had drifted away. The sun was a sliver on the horizon, but the moons hung high in the dark orange sky, providing all the light they would need.

When they reached the thicket, Juna crawled inside, fastened the rope to the back axle of the tri-racer, and placed a plank behind each wheel. Twenty-six sets of hands, some strong, some tiny, gripped the rope and tore the machine from its lair.

"It's seen better days, but it'll get me where I'm going," Juna said confidently as she stood back to survey the damage.

It was full of branches, the fenders were gone, and a few new bumps had joined the bullet hole in the centre console. But the wheels looked straight, and it had fuel in the tank.

The sun was down by the time the debris was cleared and Juna felt ready to go. Everyone gave her a hug and wished her well. The looks on the women's faces showed fear, but there was hope there, too. They couldn't know if they would ever see this young girl again, but if they did, it was possible their lives might be forever changed.

"You take care of yourself," a teary Reyn whispered in her ear as she squeezed her tight. "We'll be rooting for you, but even if you fail, we'll never forget that you tried."

Juna returned the embrace, then knelt to look Tru in the eyes. "You mind your Ma. When I get back, I don't want to hear you've been misbehaving."

Tru threw her arms around Juna's neck. "I love you."

"I love you too, sweetie." Juna kissed the top of her head and stood to leave.

After wiping away a tear, she threw the rope and the package from Reyn into the cockpit. She sat down in the jet-black driver's seat, nearly disappearing in her new shadow suit. She turned the key to spark the car to life, then gave a final wave and sped off towards the road. Tears blurred her vision as she watched the beautiful families disappear in the rear-view mirror.

She had planned the trip at night to reduce the odds of her bullet-ridden, bright yellow sports car being spotted by police, but kept to back roads just to be safe. Even using a less direct route, she was within walking distance of the royal palace in three hours.

The tri-racer rumbled to a stop in a copse of trees near the base of Mount Volaris. Juna snapped up the items from the passenger seat before beginning the long climb to the palace. She was winded when she reached the fence surrounding the grounds. Throwing her stuff to the other side, she scowled at the moons for being so bright, then carefully slipped over the top.

After grabbing her gear, she sprinted for the palace and the base of the drainpipe she knew so well. She scaled the wall quickly, then pried the window open before sliding silently into her quiet place.

It felt so good to be here again. She stood for a moment, soaking up the beauty of the night sky through the dormer's massive window. Nandoo and Aradoo, Cambria's spectacular moons, filled her view from one edge of the frame to the other.

"Hey Princess."

Juna spun and locked into her fighting stance. She was about to strike, before recognizing the face illuminated in the moonlight.

"Skeet! You almost gave me a heart attack. You're lucky I didn't punch you in the face."

"It's good to see you, too."

"Oh, it really is good to see you," she said, throwing her arms around him, squeezing so hard he let out a squeak. "What are you doing here?"

"I basically live here now. It's very fancy. No wonder you turned out so soft."

That comment earned him a punch on the shoulder. Juna looked around her old quiet place, noticing it now featured a mattress, complete with pillows and blankets. There was also a spooled pile of knotted rope tied off to a rafter.

"So, *you* live in the royal palace?" she asked sceptically. "How do you not get caught?"

"The key is to look like you belong. I wander the halls, stand in the food line, carry stuff around. I've even handed something right to Mister Stotz, and he didn't bat an eye. I'm pretty sure he thinks I work here."

"Only you could get away with something like that."

"I also spend a lot of time in the rafters above your father's office, trying to find out what's going on."

"What have you learned?"

"Your brother's a real jerk, Colonel Pavic, too. I think they're even worse than your dad. Mara's been conquered. Lots of their scientists have been brought over and your dad's trying to get them to help with stuff. I think he might be hurting them." He looked down to stare at his own shoes. "It's really bad."

Juna turned her gaze to the window, both enraged and terrified by the news. "The Marans have a portal detector like ours. I hope my father doesn't get his hands on one of those."

"Do we even have a Gate anymore?" Skeet asked. "How'd you get here? Does this mean everything's fine on Earth again?"

"No. I came in from Mara. Have you heard *anything* about what happened on Earth?"

"Not really, but I know it's not good. They mentioned a bomb and think it might have wiped out our whole team. They're worried about keeping the Gate working, because they think Professor Oletta is dead."

"What if they're right?" Juna whispered, touching fingers to her lips.

"I'm not letting myself believe it yet," he replied, watching as she knelt to grab a roll of fabric. "So, why *did* you come back?"

Juna stood and unwrapped the cloth to reveal a sheathed dagger with an eight-inch blade. She removed the weapon, holding it up to let the moonlight reflect off its polished surface.

"I've come to talk to Daddy."

The walk through the rafters felt familiar, but Juna knew this trip would end much differently. The coil of rope was slung over her shoulder and the dagger tucked securely into her waistband. Skeet made the trip with her, offering to stay up top, to come help if she needed it.

The sun was nearly up when they arrived over her father's office. Juna uncoiled the rope until it hung a foot off the ground. After tying it off, she pulled the loose end back up and sat down to wait.

She knew it wouldn't be long. Her father was a creature of habit, always sitting at his desk, preparing for a day of treachery, soon after the sun peeked over the horizon. His henchmen were not so diligent, so he often began his day alone. She felt good about her decision to come. Her days of sneaking around in the rafters, hoping to pick up some useful tidbit, were over. It was time to take a more direct approach.

Her heart skipped when the small door behind her father's desk swung open. Emperor Zoban Volara stepped through and sat down. Juna took a deep breath to calm her nerves and steady her hands. She gave Skeet a quick wave, before tossing the rope to the floor and nimbly sliding down. As soon as her feet hit the ground, she reached for the main door, throwing the bolt to lock it from the inside.

She turned to face her father.

The emperor was an expert at hiding his emotions, but appeared to struggle with it now. He was definitely surprised, and there was a touch of fear as well. Juna thought she saw something else, too.

*Relief, maybe?*

In an instant, she was in motion. Pulling the dagger from its sheath, she sprinted for her father's desk. All the emotions, with the exception of fear, drained from his face. As she approached the desk, she leapt up, placed one foot on top and vaulted to the other side, with the dagger raised high over her head. As she landed, she thrust her arm forward, burying the dagger halfway to the hilt into the jamb of the door behind the desk, pinning it closed.

"That's better. Now we won't be interrupted," Juna said, turning to smile at her father. "If you'd installed a bolt on that door, we could have saved ourselves a lot of drama."

The emperor regained his composure quickly, his unreadable mask returning in an instant.

"Juna, it's good to see you. I've been worried."

"Somehow, I find that hard to believe." She looped back to the other side and took a seat, propping her feet up on his desk.

"There's no time for chitchat, anyway. I have questions. I expect answers."

The emperor shuffled some papers on his desk, then looked her in the eye. "Very well. If you wish to be unfriendly, we'll do it your way. What are your questions?"

"Why can't the Marans come home?"

"Simple. They were troublemakers when they left, and stewing for a few generations on a horrible planet won't make them any more agreeable. People like that will never serve an emperor. Not by choice, anyway. Next."

"Why did you want to blow up the palace?"

He paused, obviously surprised she knew about that.

"It hurt when you betrayed me, you know."

"Don't care. Answer."

"It was meant to be a symbol," he said. "With all the Gates and spaceships floating around these days, the Marans *will* end up here eventually. The Cambrian people may accept them willingly, but if they were blamed for blowing up the royal palace, they'd be traitors until the end of time. Besides, with their amazing grasp of technology, they can easily build me a better one."

Juna couldn't accuse him of not thinking things through. Some of what she'd learned studying Earth's history confirmed he might be right about some of this. But there was still one question desperately needing an answer: was he simply a calculating politician or a truly evil man?

She sat forward in her chair.

"Things are going to change, Daddy. You can't stop it forever. The world we've built here is wrong. I've met the Marans. And hod families, too. They're so beautiful. There's this little girl—"

The emperor held up his hand to stop her speech mid-sentence. "We need the hods to do the work—"

"No!" she shouted, springing from her chair and pounding the desk. "It's not right what we do. If you met them, if you had any heart at all, you would see that."

Her father stared back, but something softened in his gaze, and he had to look away.

"Things *will* change, and you have to decide how history will remember you," Juna pleaded. "Do you want to be the last emperor, torn from his throne by an angry mob, or the man who used his power to make things right?"

When he turned back to face her, the mask had returned. "Change is hard," he replied softly.

At that moment, the door behind the desk shook. "Emperor, are you alright?" the muffled voice asked.

The knife holding the door jiggled, but held.

*At least for now.*

"Gotta go!"

Juna grabbed her chair and launched it at the picture window, sending it, and a hail of shattered glass, hurtling into the garden. Before leaping through the new opening, she turned back with a final plea.

"It's time to do the right thing, Daddy."

And with that, she was gone.

# 17

Orin wasn't so sure this was a good idea. He'd worked hard to convince everyone it was, but now that the moment had arrived, he was much less certain.

Before him stood the Gate, the familiar dancing swirls telling him a portal would open soon. Looking to his left, he saw Gigahertz, all his weapon systems attached, ready to join him on this journey. Several preliminary tests had been done on the Gate. It performed well, but this was the first time since the explosion that someone would travel somewhere from which an emergency exit may be required.

Their destination was Mara, which explained the ridiculous outfit he was wearing. Todd took part in a sport called snowboarding and offered to bring in his gear when he heard Orin might visit a cold weather planet. He certainly appreciated the bulky suit, heavy gloves, helmet and goggles to protect him from Mara's harsh environment, but what was with all the fluorescent colours? He was trying to be sneaky here. The only place he had any hope of blending in would be a mystic convention.

The hostile climate was one thing, but his biggest concern was the condition of the Gate. The look of the repairs did *not* inspire a great deal of confidence. Parts welded in to replace the missing section did not fit perfectly, and some bits and pieces were being held on with duct tape.

Todd had felt immensely proud when Dorel confirmed his theory that duct tape was the single greatest invention of all time.

Right now, about to step onto a distant planet, Orin would have preferred something that looked a little sturdier.

"It's the best we could do with all these Earth parts," Dorel had told him. "Their stuff just doesn't work the same as ours."

Professor Oletta had warned that the Gate would never be the same. It was slower, its maximum capacity was reduced, and it was far less reliable. She said having a month to work on it back in her lab might have got it close to where it was, but in a cave on an alien world... this was as good as it was going to get.

The Tech Station was a bit shaky, too. Diara often screamed in frustration when the display on her Earth-built computer showed nothing but a blue screen. She'd have to turn it off, then flip it back on, to get it running again.

"Are you ready for this?"

The General had dropped a hand onto Orin's shoulder. The Professor stood next to him, with obvious concern.

"The Gate has not received adequate testing," his father urged. "What if you need to get back in a hurry? It's impossible to rely on this device in its current condition."

"Aeva told us there's nothing we can do to make it better," the General countered. "At some point, we'll have to trust it."

"It's OK, Dad. We're not doing anything crazy. We'll go through, Gig will do some scans, and we'll come right back. The portal will never even close."

Just as the Professor opened his mouth to continue the argument, the scene at the centre of the Gate changed to show a dreary Maran landscape under a dull pink sky.

"I have to know if she's OK," Orin said as he stepped toward the open portal. "I'll be right back."

Gigahertz joined him at the portal's glistening surface, and together, they stepped through to the other side. The instant they passed the barrier, the Gate disappeared behind them.

"Great. That's just what we needed," Orin groaned as he looked back, seeing nothing but pink sky where the Gate should have been. "What's the status of the comm link?"

"The communications portal is down," Gig replied. "I pick up intermittent chatter, but it is currently inactive."

A shiver ran down Orin's spine; from fear or temperature, he wasn't sure. The cold seeped through even Todd's neon suit. He wouldn't survive long out here, but getting a portal back was beyond his control. All he could do was hope and stay busy.

"I'm sure it'll be fixed soon," he said confidently. "Let's do what we came to do, so we can leave as soon as it's back."

They had chosen a location close to their normal landing spot, but in a rockier area. That would provide some cover while they peered over the rim. Orin had stayed up all night installing upgrades to Gig's sensors. They still wouldn't be as powerful as Helion's, but he hoped they'd be good enough for a detailed scan of the Maran colony and to get a lock on Juna's necklace.

Orin led them into a gap between two enormous boulders. Staying low as he crept, he peeked over the ridge into the valley below, with Gig crouched at his side. There wasn't much to see. The Marans had rebuilt the factory, but the smokestacks lay dormant. He saw several Mech clones standing around, but no sign they were turned on.

"You picking up anything?" he asked Gigahertz

"I detect no activity on the surface, and all clones are powered down. There is a large underground complex housing thousands of people, but my sensors read little detail on the structure itself."

"Any sign of Juna's necklace?"

"No."

"Would you pick it up if it was in there?"

"Likely, but there is no way to be sure. She could be very deep or inside a metal enclosure of some kind."

Orin didn't even want to consider that possibility.

"I am picking up a SCUD moving rapidly in this direction," Gig told him. "It does not appear to be armed."

Orin could hear the engine as it approached. "What's it doing?"

"Unknown. It slowed near the spot we landed, and is now heading in our direction. What should I do?"

"I'd rather not use missiles right now. See if you can crush it with a rock."

Grabbing a boulder, Gig stood and slid out of their hiding spot. As the SCUD rounded the corner, he jumped out, smashing it with the rock as he landed.

"It was unarmed," Gig reported after returning through the gap. "It contained only a camera."

"Probably a scout drone," Orin guessed. "We better stay on our toes. They might know we're here."

"Communications with Earth were re-established momentarily, but I lost the link almost immediately," Gig said. "The only thing I heard clearly was a reference to something being on fire."

More bad news. This trip was quickly turning into a complete disaster. No sign of Juna, no way to get home, and the relentless cold was becoming unbearable. Orin fought off a feeling of panic. He had limited options and none were good.

"I am picking up another unarmed SCUD coming out of the valley," Gig informed him. "What should I do with this one?"

Orin wasn't sure how to respond. Someone knew they were here. Feeling his toes turn to ice, he wondered if getting captured might be his best option at this point. At least he might find Juna that way. He heard the rumble of the SCUD's engine, but another sound floated along with it.

“Is it singing?”

“It is broadcasting a message on loop,” Gig replied. “It continuously repeats the phrase ‘I am a friend’.”

Orin didn’t know what to make of that. As far as he knew, he didn’t have any friends on Mara.

*Except Juna, of course!*

But if it was Juna, wouldn’t she be more specific?

“Let’s not crush this one,” Orin said. “First, we’ll see what it has to say… keep a rock handy, just in case.”

As Orin stepped from the gap, Gig provided him with some much-needed good news.

“I have regained communications with Earth,” he said. “The Gate was on fire, but it has now been extinguished. The damage will take several hours to fix. They are suggesting we find a place to hide until repairs are complete.”

Orin looked around, shuddering at the thought of spending several hours on this barren wasteland. In the distance, he saw the SCUD rolling towards them, kicking up a trail of icy dust as it moved. Its tinny speaker continued to remind them how friendly it was. He really wanted to believe it.

“My name is Kalen,” was the SCUD’s new message as it pulled up beside them. “Something was wrong with your Gate. The power levels were fluctuating and the transmission frequencies were different. Is it broken?”

Orin was confused. How did this SCUD, or whoever was driving it, know so much about their Gate? He was reluctant to provide too much information to a stranger.

“It’s not working now, but should be fixed in a few hours.”

“A few hours? You’ll freeze to death.” At that moment, an access panel on the SCUD popped open. “Hop in. I’ll take you someplace warm and safe.”

Warm and safe. Orin liked the sound of those two words, but had no idea who he was talking to.

"You want me to climb *inside* a SCUD?"

"It's a camerabot! My last one, thanks to you guys. I wish you people would stop calling them SCUDs."

"You people? Who else called it a SCUD?"

"Juna."

Orin's spirit surged at the sound of her name.

"You know Juna! Is she with you?"

"She was here, but she's gone."

"Gone!" Orin's heart sunk at the news. "Where did she go?"

"Back to Cambria. She's been there about a month."

"How did she get there?" Orin's mind spun, thinking of the possibilities. "Was she taken by the emperor's men?"

"No. She snuck back on her own. She took Helion with her."

Juna was on Cambria. Orin took a moment to let that sink in. All his efforts convincing people to send him here, and she'd been on Cambria all along. And now, *he* was stuck on Mara without a way to get home. One thing was clear, though; Juna had trusted Kalen. Maybe he could too.

"If I get in this thing, where will you take me?"

"It's a place about eight miles to the west. It'll take four hours to get there."

"Gig, tell the team back on Earth where we're going," Orin said as he climbed into the SCUD. "Looks like we're going on a road trip."

It wasn't long before Orin realized calling this journey a road trip had been a touch optimistic. Whatever it was they were travelling on certainly wasn't a road. On the plus side, he was finally warm again. The machine's engine was putting out enough heat to keep the enclosure at a reasonable temperature, but that's where the comfort ended. There was no seat and nothing to grab onto, so he was being tossed around like the riders on the Juggler.

"At least *they* have seat belts," Orin mumbled to himself.

"Sorry. No seatbelts," Kalen replied, thinking the remark had been aimed at him.

By far, the best part of the journey was getting to know Kalen. They chatted about their adventures and discussed the differences between life on their respective planets. It was obvious Kalen had been helpful in keeping Juna safe after the clones showed up, so Orin was thankful for that. The only thing concerning him was how secretive his new friend was being about his current destination.

"You'll see when you get here," Kalen kept telling him.

Orin's conversations weren't limited only to Kalen. Through his earpiece, he kept in touch with Gigahertz, too. The team on Earth adjusted the position of the comm portal as the trek across the Maran surface progressed, so the radio link stayed open. Repairs on the Gate moved slowly, so it would still be hours before a return to Earth was possible.

Orin didn't even want to think about that right now. All he wanted was for this trip to end, so he didn't have to bounce around inside this SCUD any longer.

At one point, he felt the machine climbing a steep hill, pinning him to the back of the hold. As they rounded the top, the machine rolled to a stop.

"Tell me this trip is finally over," Orin begged.

"Not yet," Kalen replied. "But I thought you might want to get out and see where you're going." The hatch on the side of the SCUD popped open.

"I want to get this over with. So, if you don't mind, let's keep moving and—"

"You should see this," Gigahertz interrupted.

Orin murmured under his breath as he closed up his jacket and donned the goggles. As he stepped out of the SCUD, he saw Gig staring into the valley below. Orin followed his gaze, stunned into silence by the sight before him.

"Wow," he finally managed. "I didn't think it would still be in one piece."

"Awesome, isn't it?" Kalen's excitement was obvious, even through the tinny speaker. "I've seen it dozens of times and it still blows me away. Get back in and I'll bring you the rest of the way. It's even cooler inside!"

His glimpse of the Starchaser had Orin energized. Now he couldn't wait for this trip to end for a completely different reason. He leapt back into the SCUD, struggling to contain his anticipation of getting a closer look.

When the SCUD jerked to a stop, twenty minutes later, he burst through the hatch as soon as the door swung open. Standing next to the massive vessel, he ran his hand over the dull metal surface. He knew it would be cold, but he took his glove off anyway, so there was nothing between him and this incredible ship.

"You can climb to the top from this side," Kalen's voice informed him. "Your Mech can help on a couple of tricky parts. Head for the front by the solar panels. I'll meet you there."

The Starchaser had dug a trench as it slid to a stop on the Maran surface. It was tilted a bit, so scaling the enormous machine from this side was challenging, but certainly possible. The surface was not completely smooth, with countless grooves and ledges where you could get a grip or stick in a toe. On a couple of steeper sections, Gig latched on tight, while Orin scaled his back, like he'd done a thousand times before.

Orin's chest heaved, and his arms and legs burned as he pulled himself over the final lip and stood on the very top. The view from up here was amazing, and the scale of the ship overwhelming. Orin spotted a cluster of solar panels not far from where they stood, so he started off towards them.

As they neared the array, the lid of a hatch tipped up, and a boy about his age popped his head out. He wasn't dressed for the cold, so he waved frantically, encouraging them to move faster.

"Hey Orin, I'm Kalen. Come on in, it's freezing. Sorry, but your Mech will have to stay outside."

Orin said goodbye to Gig, then slipped through the small opening. After following Kalen down a short ladder, he stepped into the alcove at its base.

"You can take off that wacky outfit. I have the heaters running," Kalen said, giving Orin an odd look. "They must like bright colours on Cambria."

"This actually comes from Earth." Orin shrugged off the bulky suit. "Now, that's one crazy place."

"I'd like to hear about it sometime," Kalen said, bouncing from foot to foot. "But first, you gotta see this."

Stepping around the corner, they emerged onto the Starchaser's bridge. Orin was speechless as he took it all in.

"Pretty cool, huh? Juna told me you were a science geek, so I knew you'd like it."

On Cambria, people rarely mentioned the Starchaser—other than the crashing into the sun part, at least. There were no pictures or descriptions of the legendary craft, but somehow this is exactly what he expected it to look like.

"It's amazing." He walked down to the large swivel chair in the middle, running his fingers over the buttons on the armrest.

"Juna spent hours in that chair," Kalen told him. "You can control the view screen from there." Kalen jumped down to join him, flicking a switch that brought the massive display to life.

"She was looking for some guy named Danto. He helped her get back to Cambria."

"Never heard of him," Orin mumbled, his eyes wide as they tracked across the screen. "Wow, you can see everything from here. Who's the guy in the fancy robe?" he asked, pointing to an image in the bottom corner.

"That's the fake mayor. The real one is hiding out, so that guy's pretending to run the place, but acting like a total idiot all the time. I think our strategy is to frustrate the Cambrians into leaving."

"I don't think it'll work. The emperor's heart seems set on conquering this place."

"Yeah, Juna thought so too."

Orin walked back up to the perimeter of the bridge. Drawings of the Starchaser hung on every wall. There was also a chart stretching halfway around that looked to be a record of every event that had ever happened on Mara.

"Did you make all these?"

"Yup."

"They're really good. How long have you lived here?"

"Just a couple of months. I drew these earlier at the place where I worked. I didn't want anybody else to have them, so I went back and brought them here. I stole the portal detector, too. That's how I knew you'd arrived."

"I'm glad you did. I'd be pretty cold right now if I was still on the rim." Orin was about to ask more about this portal detector, when Gigahertz called in on the radio.

"Professor Oletta believes the Gate has been sufficiently repaired. They have our current coordinates and will open a portal shortly."

Orin relayed the news to Kalen before slipping back into his winter gear.

"Thanks for your help, Kalen. I hope we meet again sometime."

"Me too." He offered a friendly wave. "When you see Juna, tell her I say hi."

Orin scampered up the ladder and scooted out through the hatch. From there, he rejoined Gig for the precarious trip down the side of the hull. Somehow, the weather had gotten even worse while he was inside, the wind now so strong it threatened to peel him off the ship. By the time he reached the bottom, Orin was colder than he'd ever been in his life.

"The portal's starting over there," he said, pointing at a cloud of tiny coloured sparks. "Let's go."

It took longer than usual, but the light show eventually gave way to the appearance of the Gate. At one time, Orin considered it the most impressive structure he'd ever seen. Now, standing next to the Starchaser, it looked minuscule. After an excruciating wait, the amber swirls at the ring's centre were finally replaced by a view of their home in Earth's canyon. He and Gigahertz leapt through immediately, just in case it decided to disappear again.

"Juna's on Cambria!" Orin blurted out as soon as he arrived.

"Good to see you too," the General joked. "How do you know that?"

"I met someone who was with her. Apparently, some guy named Danto helped her."

The General gave a nod, acknowledging this made sense.

"Well then, the next portal goes to Lano's."

Toes were tapping, and hands were wringing as the team waited for the portal to open. It had been nearly two months since their last contact with The Underground, and they knew how desperate the emperor was to find them. It was possible they could be walking into a trap. Happily, the group waiting to greet them included Lano and Skeet, rather than a troop of royal guardsmen.

Everyone wanted to catch up and exchange news, but Orin's sole focus was on finding Juna.

"Gig, can you get a lock on her necklace?"

"Yes, I have it." There was a brief pause as he completed his scan. "She is near The Institute. I have also established communications with Helion. He is inside the facility, but has had no contact with Juna in over a month. He is currently monitoring her progress outside the fence."

"What? She's trying to break in?"

"That is how it appears."

"She doesn't have any of my gear, and isn't in radio contact with Helion?" Orin bounced the situation around in his head for a moment.

"So, how's she supposed to get in?"

# 18

*This was going to be tricky.*

Hiding in a clump of bushes on the edge of The Institute's parking lot, Juna watched the main entrance, trying to devise a way in. Oh, how she wished she hadn't lost the radio during her escape last month. A little advice from Helion would have been so handy right now. Even having a couple of Orin's gizmos would have been nice, but for now, she was on her own.

Unfortunately, she wasn't entirely focused on the task at hand. Two hours ago, she'd been sitting in her father's office, trying to talk some sense into him, and that conversation replayed over and over in her mind.

Was there something else she could have said? One little thing that would have opened his eyes? Or maybe he was just evil, and the whole effort had been a waste of time.

She knew another opportunity to make her case was unlikely. Her father's blaming skills were legendary, so those in charge of security at the royal palace would be hearing a few harsh words. The number of guards roaming the halls would increase, and the odds of them looking up into the rafters more frequently were high. She hoped her little visit with Daddy didn't put an end to Skeet's cushy new lifestyle.

The question was: had it all been worth it? Perhaps she'd never know for sure, but didn't regret trying. It may have been a waste of time, but there was a look in her father's eyes, right at the end, that told her some part of her message got through.

What was a waste of time, however, was worrying about it now.

"Time to get your head in the game, Juna," she scolded herself. "Let's do what we came here to do."

She had debated whether or not returning to The Institute to check in with Helion was the smartest thing to do. Ultimately, she decided it was. If he'd figured out some way to disable the motion sensors surrounding the facility, they could slip out at night and find a decent place to hide. If not, she'd stick around for a few days. There was certainly enough of that Maran goop in her backpack to keep her alive for a while.

The guards here were a joke, so if she avoided the outside lunch area, she'd be free to roam around at night, picking up useful information for the General. After all she'd been through this month, the idea of staying off the grid and hiding out with Helion, definitely had some appeal. The immediate challenge was getting inside.

A sudden burst of activity drew her attention to the main gate. A swarm of people streamed out, heading for their cars. It was lunchtime, so they were likely on their way to a local restaurant to get a bite to eat. This might be the opportunity she'd hoped for. Every employee sported an identification badge clipped to their clothing. If she could get her hands on one of those, she could use it to scan herself in.

After slipping out of the bushes, she zigzagged through the parking lot towards the main gate. As she got closer, she noticed each ID badge included a photograph. Ideally, she'd nab one from somebody who looked at least somewhat like her. Up ahead, a knot of people emerged from a series of turnstiles, so she plunged straight for its centre.

"Excuse me. Sorry. My fault. So clumsy," Juna muttered as she jostled among the group, keeping her eyes low, looking for an ID card to grab. It was chaotic in the scrum, so being selective was impossible. She clutched the first one she could, emerging from the cluster with a confident step towards the entrance. A glance down at the badge in her hand revealed a picture of a heavy-set man with a bushy beard staring back at her.

*Ugh!*

Too late to do anything about it now. Hopefully, it wouldn't be an issue.

When she reached the automatic gate, she slipped the card in, breathing a sigh of relief as it swung open in front of her. With three forceful strides, she burst into the complex with her head held high.

"Just look like you belong," she murmured to herself, repeating Skeet's advice as she moved forward, hoping not to be noticed.

Despite being a member of the royal family, Juna had little fear of being recognized. She imagined how different it would be if she lived on Earth. With television and the internet, it's likely she would have been a celebrity there, her picture spread from one end of the planet to the other. Cambria didn't have celebrities. Unless you made a point of putting your face on a poster and plastering it all over the city, like her father or Lano, it was unlikely someone would know what you looked like unless you'd met them in person.

That thought brought a sudden jolt of panic. What if she had met some of these people? Did any of the Professor's old team from The Depot work here? After a parade celebrating the victory in the Third Maran War, she'd met them all. Could they be here right now? She recalled wearing a disguise during the Great Mech Heist for this very reason.

Looking down at her clothes, she realized how poorly she blended in with the people around her. After the meeting with her father, she'd snuck back to the tri-racer to recover the outfit she'd brought with her. It was a baggy sweater and a pair of loose-fitting pants, which she'd pulled on over her shadow suit. No one here was wearing anything like this. It now felt like she carried a large flashing sign proclaiming: "I do not belong here."

Now on alert, Juna moved cautiously, glancing back and forth, scanning the area for trouble.

*Well, this was even worse!*

Not only did she look like she didn't belong, now she was acting like she didn't belong. As she stood, pondering how best to alter her behaviour, a shrill sound ripped through the air. She looked back over her shoulder to see a guard, only twenty feet away, blowing his whistle and pointing at her. When their eyes met, he pulled the whistle from his mouth and smiled.

"Hey Princess. Long time, no see."

"Hello Gimbal," she called back. "Not long enough for my liking."

Turning quickly on her heels, she raced in the opposite direction.

*Gimbal! What were the odds of meeting him here?*

Gimbal had served as Juna's personal servant for a year and they never did get along. The last time she saw him, she'd knocked him unconscious with a kick to the head, and left him tied up in a closet. She certainly hoped he wasn't the type to hold a grudge.

Gimbal's whistle had attracted a lot more guards to the area. She made a silent plea that they were slow and lazy, then sprinted for the rear of the complex. If she could somehow get to Helion, perhaps escaping this mess was still a possibility.

The footfalls and yells of her pursuers gave her a burst of adrenaline she very much needed. She ducked down a sidewalk between two low buildings and began to pull away.

Halfway to the end of the narrow corridor, she stopped in her tracks. Four guards had turned the corner at the other end and were headed straight for her. A glance over her shoulder showed the six guards chasing her had now entered the passage. To her left, she saw a drainpipe strapped to one of the buildings blocking her in.

"I guess it's up, then," she said to herself, running over to grip the pipe and begin her ascent. A brick gave way, causing her to slip, but she quickly regained her footing and started up again. As she neared the top, a hand latched onto one of her ankles. She tried to pull free, but a vicious tug on the other ankle tore her free from the wall.

Held between two powerful guards, Juna fought and squirmed, but knew it was in vain. Unable to move, the reality of her predicament hit home when she saw the smile on Gimbal's face.

"Juna, Juna, Juna. I cannot tell you how often I have dreamed of this moment."

"That's funny. I haven't thought about you once," she replied with a sneer.

"That's probably because I didn't ruin your career using a dirty trick in an unfair fight." He pointed an accusatory finger in her face.

"Is that what you've been telling yourself all this time? Would you like to try again right now? I'm sure your friends could watch to make sure I don't run away."

Gimbal appeared to consider the possibility, but soon thought better of it.

"You're not tricking me again, Juna. Catching you might be exactly what I need to get my life back on track. Guard duty at The Institute isn't exactly a prestigious position, but when my boss hears I single-handedly captured the mighty Princess Juna, I could earn myself a nice promotion."

Juna noticed the other guards rolling their eyes at the "single-handed" comment, but there was one part of Gimbal's rant that was undeniable; she *was* captured.

"Let's take her back to the security building, boys," Gimbal said to the assembled group. "I've got a call to make. I believe Jakol might want to come out and have a chat with his long-lost sister."

Juna's muscles tensed at the mention of her brother's name. This was not a reunion she looked forward to. As the gaggle of guards hauled her back to the front of the compound, she saw their destination. It was a small single-story building with no windows and a flat roof. It probably wasn't even as big as her bedroom back in the royal palace. She scrunched up her nose as they dragged her inside, the foul smell, an unpleasant combination of sweaty men and spoiled food. It was dark and dusty, without a single item adorning the dull grey walls.

A wooden chair was placed in the middle of the room, where Juna was instructed to sit. Nine guards formed a circle around her, foiling any chance of escape. She noticed one of them leering at her, with hate in his eyes. Looking closer, she realized it was his uniform she stole on her last visit here. She offered an apologetic smile, but he remained unmoved. A moment later, Gimbal returned from the phone, joining the others in the circle.

"Jakol was pleased to hear you've come back. He's on his way. Says he can't wait to see you."

"Yeah, me too," she replied, her voice dripping with sarcasm. "It'll be great."

The wait was agonizing. No one said a word to Juna the whole time. She sat there, staring at the floor, not daring to look up and see Gimbal's gloating face. Everyone squinted when the door swung open, flooding the dreary space with a sudden blast of sunlight. Then Jakol stepped through, wearing a long purple robe and a taunting smile. Juna noticed he was using a cane, and there was a slight limp in his step.

"I hope that's not because of me," she said, pointing to his cane.

The last time she'd seen her brother, they were in a brutal fight, and Juna had landed a crushing blow to the side of his knee.

"You know, sister," he said, moving closer so he could tower over her in the chair. "I'm glad about this. Now, with every step I take, I am reminded how important it is to deal with things as they arise, not let them fester to become even bigger problems in the future."

"I'm happy to be of service," she replied, smiling up at him. "You're welcome."

Jakol slowly shook his head and wagged a finger in her face. "You shouldn't taunt me, sister. I hold your life in my hands right now." He raised his cane and rubbed it softly across her cheek.

Juna swept it away and attempted to stand, but two guards leapt forward and rammed her back into the chair.

"You always were the troublemaker, but that ends today. As I already told you, I learn from my mistakes." He spread his arms wide and spun in a circle. "Enjoy this beautiful room, Juna, because it's the nicest one you'll ever see. I will stick you in a dungeon so deep, no one will ever find you." He shot her a mocking glare. "Unless, of course, you want to tell me about The Underground?"

"I'm not telling you anything!"

"I am so glad you said that," he spat, a look of pure evil crossing his face. "I will have so much fun changing your mind."

Juna felt defeated. She had managed some clever escapes in the past, but there was simply no way out of this one. Fear gripped her, realizing she was about to experience every inch of her brother's cruelty.

"Why can't you see this world is wrong?" she said, looking straight into his eyes. "The Elites have everything handed to them, while everyone else has to work so hard. How is that fair? If you would get out there and meet—"

"No! Don't you try that with me!" he bellowed, crashing his cane down on a table. "It's bad enough you've got Father babbling like a fool. You're poisoning his mind with talk like that, but it won't work on me."

Juna couldn't believe what she'd heard. Her father had listened. She smiled up at Jakol.

"Father is starting to see. Others *will* follow. It's only a matter of time, Jakol."

"A moment of weakness is all it was. When you're not around anymore, I'll get him straightened out." He moved to the back of the room, shrugged off his robe, then turned to face her with a hideous grin.

"I don't wish to discuss this further. We have so much fun ahead of us. So... tell me about The Underground."

Before Juna could utter a word, the room exploded with the shriek of twisting metal and a blinding flash of light. Juna looked up to see the roof of the building was gone. Helion peered in over the walls and reached in with his massive hand.

"Get her!" Jakol screamed.

Unfortunately for him, his fearless guards had already dived for cover.

Juna stepped onto Helion's outstretched palm, then turned back to face her brother. He continued to call for action from the guards, while cowering in the corner himself.

"Sorry brother, gotta go," she said with a wave goodbye. "But maybe we'll have time to talk again soon."

Helion lifted her high into the air, then reached around so she could grab hold of his back. Once she had a firm grip, her gigantic friend turned and thundered across the compound. Juna climbed higher, so she could see over his shoulder. He was heading for the back where the Mech clones were stored. None of them had moved yet, but she did notice the eyes of a Diesel come to life. Helion fired a single missile, blowing it into a thousand pieces. Without breaking stride, he passed the clones, hurdled the fence and headed for the heart of the desert.

"Thanks Helion," she yelled over the rushing wind. "You showed up just in time. How'd you know I was here?"

"I have been tracking you since you arrived at The Institute's parking lot," he replied, continuing his sprint across the sand.

"What! Why did you wait so long to come get me?"

"You did not appear to be in imminent danger."

Juna decided at the next available opportunity, she and Helion would have a long discussion about what imminent danger looked like.

"Besides," he continued. "I had to wait for a viable means of escape."

Juna looked ahead and saw it: a large metal ring in the distance, its centre swirling with colour. A sense of relief consumed her when she realized, in only moments, she would see her friends again. Helion was running as fast as she'd ever seen, the distance to the Gate closing with each mighty stride. She took a moment to glance over her shoulder. Her smile widened when she saw they were now closer to the Gate than they were to The Institute, and there still wasn't a single clone giving chase.

As the Gate drew closer, Juna noticed it had changed. One section near the bottom looked like it had been removed and replaced with mismatched spare parts. The once continuous arc of glistening metal etched in ornate symbols, now had gaps, and extra pieces jutting out at awkward angles. The look of it was a bit unnerving. She hoped it still worked as well as it used to.

"What happened to the Gate?" she asked Helion.

"An explosion caused significant damage. It took them some time to make repairs."

That explained why the team on Earth had failed to pick her up from Mara on schedule. At least it was working now. As they approached the giant ring, she wondered if that was, in fact, the case. The view of the swirly things seemed to be lasting much longer than usual.

"Is something wrong? Shouldn't the portal be open by now?"

"The Gate has been unpredictable," Helion told her as he slowed to a stop in front of it. "I have been told to remain patient."

Patient? Juna wasn't good at patient. When she looked back over her shoulder, she saw several clones stepping over The Institute's fence to begin their pursuit. Fortunately, she didn't see any Tortuga or Armorat clones yet. She returned her attention to the Gate, crossing her fingers and wishing for it to open. Then, in a heartbeat, it was gone. The enormous metal ring that had been standing right in front of her simply blinked out of existence.

"I still have comms," Helion reported. "They will re-establish the portal ten miles further north."

Helion resumed his sprint across the desert, with Juna making frequent checks for pursuers. Five minutes in, she looked back in horror to see plumes of dust following the two Armorat clones that had joined the chase. Only moments ago, she'd been so certain of reuniting with her friends, and now it seemed like a hopeless dream.

"Juna, I do not wish to alarm you, but I must activate my shields," Helion warned her. "You may feel a tingling sensation."

She heard a faint sizzle, and her hair stood on end. It felt like her skin was trying to crawl off her body. She looked back to see several missiles arcing towards them. Helion weaved to avoid the projectiles, while sand exploded all around them. One missile hit the shield directly. The resulting flash made her feel like she was inside the sun.

Juna poked her head over Helion's shoulder and saw the Gate looming in the distance. As it drew closer, she saw the familiar image of Earth's red rock cave at its centre. Another barrage of incoming missiles swept over them, resulting in more flying sand and the blinding flash of another direct hit.

Through it all, Helion's powerful legs kept churning relentlessly towards the open portal. Over her shoulder, she saw another flight of missiles in the air, and wondered if the shields would survive another assault. Straight ahead, she saw how close they were to the Gate and realized, with an immense sense of relief, the missiles would not reach them in time.

As they passed through the Gate, and the portal closed behind them, Juna's eyes found the Tech Station where Pom stood, her arm in a sling, and Orin bounced in triumph. At that moment, she realized, she may have just left the planet of her birth, but only now was she truly home.

# 19

*Life was good.*

Orin's face hurt from smiling, watching from across the cavern as Pom filled Juna in on the adventures she'd missed. Her one good arm swung wildly as she told the tale, no doubt describing the terrifying moment of the explosion. When Pom raised her shirt to show the surgery scar, Juna's eyes went wide, and she held a hand over her open mouth, listening to the grisly details.

"Nice to have her back, huh?"

Orin turned to see Skeet had joined him.

"I'll say." He reached out to tousle his young friend's hair. "And it's nice having you back, too. When we opened that portal to Lano's, and you were there, I was over the moons."

"I had nowhere else to be. They tripled security at the palace, so I had to clear out in a hurry."

"And now you're stuck here," Orin added, shifting his attention to the Gate, and the lingering cloud of smoke surrounding it.

The moment Helion had charged through with Juna, it burst into flames again. It seemed the only guarantee that came with the Gate these days was that, at some point, it would end up on fire. He noticed the professors and Wrenches huddled together, trying to figure out what went wrong this time.

"Hey you."

Orin spun at the sound of Juna's voice, finding himself staring into her eyes. It was so good to see her again. Her hair was longer, nearly to her waist, and her green eyes shone brighter.

"I'm sorry I wasn't there when you left for Mara," he blurted out.

"You should be," she said, wrapping her arms around him. "Don't let it happen again."

"Never," he whispered in her ear.

Orin felt at peace as they embraced. He could have stayed like that forever.

"OK, you two... break it up," Skeet said, pushing between them and taking their hands so he could lead them across the cave. "You know how much I hate that mushy stuff. Besides, the General wants to hear all about the mission to Mara."

Tucked in a recess of red rock walls, under the glare of a string of bulbs, the group sat riveted by Juna's story. Orin had already told them about the Starchaser, but Juna had lived there for a month, so she shared far more detail about the ship. She also told them about the Maran portal detector, their special solar panels, and how bad they were at naming things.

Her description of the Hub shocked everyone. So far, all they'd seen of Mara was a dreary planet with horrific weather. To think a whole other world existed underground, with technologies to rival Earth's, seemed inconceivable.

"Maybe they don't need our help as much as we thought," Orin offered. "I mean, the place sounds really nice."

Juna smiled, reached into her backpack and offered everyone a piece of Maran food to sample.

"Nope, I was wrong," Orin joked, squishing the tasteless goo around in his mouth. "We definitely have to help these people."

That got the table laughing. It felt so good to have the team back together. Orin's eyes swept the table, catching Juna's and sharing a smile. Ah, life *was* good. He felt bad that Taz and Todd were missing out on all the fun, but they were stuck at the park, keeping the rides running. With the Gate still broken, more parts would be required, so the flow of Earth money remained critical.

The General rapped on the table to refocus the group. He wanted to know everything about the meeting with Mayor Cartona, believing that relationship would be crucial to their victory.

"We need to stop thinking in terms of helping the Marans, and start thinking about working together," he said. "After all, our goals are the same."

"I want to believe we can trust them, but there's something I haven't told you yet," Juna said tentatively. "You see, there's this thing called Operation Massive Hammer."

The group sat silently as Juna told them about Kalen's timeline, and secretly learning of the mysterious mission with the ominous name. She knew little about it, but what she did terrified everyone.

"Ten ships!" the Professor exclaimed. "How can we possibly deal with that?"

The news hit them hard. Orin thought the General might be sick, and both professors turned white as ghosts. Everyone sat quietly, horrified by the prospect of repelling ten warships. It was Juna who finally broke the silence.

"Maybe we won't have to fight them at all." A note of optimism brightened her voice. "Everything would be fine if my father *allowed* the Marans to come home."

"I'm not holding my breath for that," the General scoffed.

"There might be a chance." Juna's eyes sparkled as she told them about the meeting with her father. She described the scene as two people having a friendly chat, but Skeet jumped in to tell them how exciting it had been.

"You should have seen her," Skeet said, re-enacting her leap across the desk to plunge the knife into the door. "I thought the old man was going to drop dead of a heart attack right then and there."

Juna laughed off Skeet's performance, but it was obvious she'd taken a huge risk to see her father. Her story captivated the group. Orin almost stood up and cheered, picturing the chair flying through the window, and Juna diving after it to make her escape.

"Is there a chance he listened?" Pom asked quietly at the end. "Could he really set the hods free?"

"I don't know, but I think some of my message got through. There was something in his eyes... for the briefest moment. I think it was when I mentioned Tru."

"Who's Tru?" Orin asked.

Juna spoke softly, telling them of her harrowing escape from The Institute, and how Tru and her mom had saved her life. She told them about the other women and children in the valley, and the fathers that rarely saw their families. This was the hardest part for Orin to hear.

*Juna had been shot! She almost died!*

He had never met Tru or her mom, but they had become as important to him as they were to Juna. At the end of the tale, she looked as fierce and determined as he'd ever seen her.

"I will *not* rest until I've done everything I can to help those people get the life they deserve."

The General walked over and wrapped an arm around her. "And we'll be with you every step of the way," he promised. He then turned to address the team.

"This is a good reminder to us all why we're here," he said, clapping his hands together to dismiss the group. "So, get back to work. Except you Orin... we need to talk."

Everyone shuffled off, leaving Orin alone with the General. "Orin, I'd like you to drop everything you're doing and get back to work on your Disruptor. Having the superior Gate was always our biggest advantage, but that's gone forever. If we go toe-to-toe with the emperor right now, we *will* lose. That invention of yours might be our only hope."

Orin spent so much time at the park these days, he'd let things slide on his other projects. "OK General, I've got a prototype started that I can probably have running in a couple of hours."

"That's the spirit." The General patted his shoulder as he stood to leave. "Let me know the moment it's done."

Orin set off immediately for the maintenance shop, but the excited calls of his friends brought his trip to an abrupt halt.

"Orin! Pom showed us a video of the park," Juna exclaimed, grabbing his arm to spin him around. "We have to go!"

"It looks totally awesome!" Skeet agreed. "When do we leave?"

"Sorry guys, I can't today. I have something to do for the General. Besides, there's a creepy army guy hanging around that I'm trying to avoid."

Orin offered up a big smile to hide his disappointment. "But you guys should definitely go. It *is* fun, and I know Todd and Taz would love to see you both."

"OK, but next time, you come too," Juna said, clasping Skeet's hand and yanking him back towards the main cavern. "Thanks Orin. See you later."

Orin's smile widened as he watched them disappear around the corner, pleasantly surprised he didn't feel that familiar pang of jealousy about Juna rushing off to see Todd. Todd was a great person and had proven himself a wonderful friend to them both. He was glad they could spend some time together.

Orin resumed his trip to the shop with a bounce in his step, eager to finish up his project while his friends had fun at the park.

*Things could not have turned out any better.*

Juna burst into the central cavern, with Skeet at her side, then raced for the Tech Station. It was disappointing Orin couldn't come, but she was so looking forward to this. How long had it been since she could simply forget the troubles of the world and do something fun? Approaching the Tech Station from behind, she rested her hands on Pom's shoulders.

"Hey Pom, Orin can't go to the park today, but Skeet and I still want to see it. Are you sure you guys can't join us?"

"I don't feel up to it quite yet," she replied, placing her hand on Juna's. "I hope to go soon."

"How about you, Diara?"

"No, I think I'll stay too," she said, reaching out to squeeze Pom's hand. "We'll get there eventually."

"Well, I'm definitely going," Skeet jumped in. "So, how do we get there?"

Diara leaned over and grabbed the radio. "We'll get Isotope to scoot you up the cliff and then Gecko—."

"Wait, did I hear someone say they're going to the park?" Dorel walked over to join them at the Tech Station. "The Gate is ready for another test. Maybe you guys could help us out."

Half an hour later, Juna sat with Skeet, strapped into Gecko's front seats. Isotope had lowered him into the canyon, where he now sat facing the Gate. Juna's pink "Star Girl" hat rested comfortably on her head, while Skeet wore Orin's red cap with the angry bird.

"Do you think it's safe?" Juna asked.

"Sure. Dorel says it never blows up until after something goes through it."

The spinning amber pattern at the Gate's centre vanished, replaced by the close-up view of a towering stone wall. For this test, their destination was the backside of a rocky outcrop less than a mile from the park. It was safely tucked behind cover, to hide the Gate from prying human eyes.

"Here we go," Gecko announced as he rolled slowly over the portal's threshold. As soon as they passed through the Gate's ring, it disappeared behind them. Juna was pretty sure that wasn't supposed to happen. She keyed the mike on Gecko's dashboard.

"We made it Dorel. Everything OK back there?"

"Lots of sparks and a few flames," he reported. "I'm afraid it's back to the drawing board at this end. It'll take us a few hours to fix this mess, so you'll have to come back the old-fashioned way."

"Will do, Dorel. Good luck." Turning to Skeet, she let her concerns about the broken Gate drift away. "That doesn't mean we can't have some fun." She raised her hand for a high-five. "Let's get to that park, Gecko!"

After a two-minute drive over bumpy terrain, they pulled into a nearly empty parking lot. Juna giggled, watching Skeet fidget. As soon as they rolled to a stop, he shot out of the hold like a bullet. Juna followed, getting hit with a wave of heat that almost sent her scurrying back inside. She caught up to Skeet at an entrance booth, where a smiling young girl awaited them.

"Welcome to Robots on the Rim," she said in a sing-songy voice. "Admission is ten dollars. You can buy tickets for the rides here, or at any of the booths inside the park."

Juna looked at Skeet and shrugged. This was not something she'd anticipated. Neither of them had any Earth money, nor had they spoken any English recently. Skeet was about to explain their situation when a familiar metallic voice stepped in to save the day.

"Not to worry, Mandy. These are friends of the owner. I think we can let them in for free."

"Thanks Rayzor," Juna whispered as she stepped through the turnstile. "It's good to see you again."

"I am pleased to see both of you as well. Enjoy the park. I shall radio Taz to let him know you are here."

Juna followed Skeet in and immediately sought out a shady place to wait. There weren't many guests, but an occasional scream echoed through the park from one of the few rides spinning. The air felt heavy from the heat, and an odd scent floated on what little breeze there was.

After a short wait, she saw an immense figure, wearing blue overalls and a white hardhat, jogging towards her. His arms were spread wide to match the smile on his face.

"There they are!" Taz's voice boomed as he pulled Juna into a bone-crushing hug.

"I've missed you guys so much." After releasing Juna, he latched onto Skeet and squeezed so hard it looked like his eyes might pop out of his head.

"Let's get you guys to the office. There's this stuff called sunscreen here. If you don't use it, you'll be redder than a barcaberry by the end of the day."

"It's not as busy as I thought it would be," Juna said as they walked down a hallway and slipped into an office halfway down.

"It's too hot," Taz told her. "On the warmest days, people don't show up until it cools off. Wait till later. This place will be hoppin' tonight."

"Hey, what's with all the German talk?"

A large man with a red-checked shirt and friendly smile swept into the room. "You boys know I don't git a word of it."

"Oh, hello Mike," Taz said, quickly switching over to English. "This is Juna and Skeet. They are friends from, ah... back home."

Mike reached out and shook hands. "Pleased t'meetcha. Any friend of the big fella here is a friend of mine. What brings y'all to these parts?"

"They have come to see the park," Taz answered for them. "Right now, I will give them sunscreen."

"Good idea. Sun's hot enough to roast a gopher on a spit out there today." He grabbed a ledger from the desk. "Just popped in t'git this. Y'all have fun."

Juna watched Mike walk down the hallway to an office at the far end. "Can you understand anything he says?" she asked Taz in a hushed voice.

"Some of it." He grabbed a blue bottle off a shelf and squeezed a blob of white lotion into his hand. "Orin talks to him a lot, so I think he gets more of it." After passing the bottle to Juna, he gave a brief demonstration on how to apply it.

"So, he has no idea where we're from?" she asked.

"No idea."

"What about the Mechs? He must wonder where they come from." She took a squirt of sunscreen and passed the bottle to Skeet.

"They're not allowed to speak or move when humans are around."

"What about Rayzor? He was talking in front of that girl."

Taz gave a little chuckle. "Mike thinks that's a friend of Todd's who's connected over the internet. Writes him a cheque every week. I guess Todd just throws them in the garbage."

"OK, that's hilarious and all," Skeet said, stepping over to Taz. He grabbed him by the front of his overalls and pulled him in close. "But when do we go on the rides?"

"What? Did you guys forget how to speak English already?"

Everyone turned to see Todd entering the office, the smile on his face a mile wide. He reached out to give Skeet a high-five, then stepped in for a hug with Juna.

"You certainly are a sight for sore eyes," he told her. "I've been so worried about you."

"It is good to see you, Todd," she replied. "I am sorry to make your eyes sore."

Todd laughed at that, pulling her in for another hug. "Boy, have I missed you. Come on, let me show you around."

*It was so much fun.*

Juna asked to start with the rides powered by Mechs, so she and Skeet could say hi. After that, the morning became a blur of spinning, screaming and wobbling to the next electrifying ride.

Skeet's favourites were the fast ones that spun in every direction at once, but she preferred the Ferris wheel. No one else was on it, so Gigahertz spun them right to the top, leaving them there and raising his enormous hand to provide some shade.

The three of them stayed up there for an hour, laughing and joking as they exchanged stories and caught up on their recent adventures. It was perfect. This was exactly what she needed to wash away the stress of the past two months.

At one point, Skeet grew restless and wanted to get back to the action, so Gig spun them to the bottom. Skeet dashed for the Juggler for at least his tenth spin of the day. Juna and Todd followed slowly, deciding to sit this one out.

"Thank you, Todd. It is a wonderful day," Juna said, showing him her brightest smile.

"It has been my pleasure," he replied, presenting her with a modest bow. "I am happy—"

Todd stopped mid-sentence, distracted by someone clearing their throat behind him.

"Sorry to interrupt," Major Tom said. "It's Todd, isn't it? Say, I haven't seen Orin for a while. Any chance he'll be here today?"

"Orin is not here. Can I help you?" Juna stepped in.

The major paused, looking her over from top to bottom.

"Same age. Same accent. And you wear your hat the same goofy way he does. You must be the girlfriend."

"And you must be the creepy army guy."

"I'm not creepy," the officer said, feigning offense. "I'm curious, that's all. There are so many questions I have about these wonderful machines of yours."

"Like what?"

"Here's one. Who's the guy doing the voice for the robot at the entrance? He's a scream. I'd like to meet him."

"You can't," Todd snapped. "He connects over the internet. I think he's up in Canada somewhere."

"You know, it's those types of answers that make me so curious."

It looked like he was about to continue, but got distracted by something in the distance.

"Strange time of day for fireworks. You have a license for those?" He pointed over the fence bordering the back of the property.

Juna was shocked. A burst of light signalling an impending portal was flashing over the desert sands only a few hundred feet from the park.

*What was Dorel thinking?*

A moment later, the Gate flashed into existence.

The major's mouth dropped open. "What the..."

Juna didn't hear the rest. She started running for the radio in the office the second she saw the Gate appear, the blue and green lights lining its rim heralding the terrifying truth.

That wasn't their Gate.

# 20

The cave was already buzzing when Juna's radio call came through. Diara had picked up the enemy portal on the new Tech Station's detector.

Orin's pulsed raced, desperate to act, but he knew there was nothing he could do with the Gate out of commission. Diara's announcement that the portal would open on Earth shocked everyone.

"Are you sure?" the General asked.

His expression was one of disbelief. Once the location was confirmed, he paused a moment to collect his thoughts. This was obviously a scenario he'd never envisioned.

"Protecting the humans is our highest priority," he finally ordered. "Diara, get Tortuga to the main entrance. Tell Juna to get every guest and employee onboard, then drive them into the desert as far from trouble as possible." He paced while Diara relayed his instructions. Orin thought he looked like a man who had simply run out of ideas.

"How could this happen?" he demanded, glowering at the Tech Station monitor. "I thought we came to Earth so we could *never* be found."

"Juna did say the Marans had a portal detector," Orin said. "And Skeet told us the emperor was bringing Maran scientists to Cambria. They must have built him one." Orin shook his head as he pieced the puzzle together. "The last time we opened a portal, it *was* close to the park."

"How they did it is irrelevant. Stopping them is the new challenge." The General's pacing brought him directly in front of the Gate. "What's the status of this thing?"

"It's down, sir," Dorel reported, shutting off a welding torch and lifting his visor. "We're doing what we can, but it'll be at least an hour before we can test it."

"There won't be anything left in an hour," the General growled, turning back to the Tech Station. "Orin! Have you got that Disruptor working?"

Orin held up the device in his hand. It was about twice as big as a lunchbox with a small radio dish sticking out the front. There was a knob on the side for adjusting the frequency.

"I think it's ready, sir, but I'll have to test it on an active portal to be sure."

"Not that it matters," the General mumbled, turning to give the Gate an angry glare. "We can't get it there, anyway."

Orin glanced at the staging area next to the Gate and saw Carnage, Havoc and Mayhem, their weapons attached, standing in a tight circle. They were eager to get to the park to fight with their friends, but there was no way to get *them* there either.

Orin decided to pace, too. It didn't appear to be doing the General any good, but he was willing to try anything at this point. The situation seemed hopeless. There were plenty of Mechs at the park, but none had weapons, or even a single missile onboard. If he couldn't get the Disruptor or the Diesels to the park, defeat was a certainty. He fought to keep images of Gigahertz blown to bits, or the Steamers reduced to piles of scrap metal, from flooding his mind.

Orin realized the arrival of the enemy Gate changed everything. Helping the hods or getting the Marans home were now issues for a distant future. All that mattered now was repelling the emperor's invasion of Earth, and making sure it could never happen again.

“The clones are coming through, sir,” Diara announced.

Orin raced for the Tech Station, arriving only a step behind the General. Gigahertz had abandoned his post at the Ferris wheel, and now stood facing the back side of the park. The view from his camera filled the Tech Station’s monitor. It showed the ring of a Gate, surrounded by desert sand, with two Helion clones stepping out to join the two Solitaires that had already arrived. Each had their cannons installed, no doubt loaded to the max with SIMs. As soon as the second Helion passed through, the Gate vanished behind it.

“We have a half an hour before they can send more,” the General said, clearly struggling to dream up some way to survive that long. He snatched the radio from Diara.

“Split up,” he ordered. “Get behind them to draw their fire away from the park. Stay alert. Dodge everything they shoot. Remember, every miss is a victory for us. When they stop to reload, attack. If we get them fighting hand-to-hand, the advantage is ours.”

Armorat was the first to move, racing out into the desert to get behind the enemy. The two Helion clones tracked him and fired, but his speed made him a difficult target. Most of the shots were misses, but a few SIMs latched onto his shield, draining it of power.

Inside the park, the Steamers went right while Vortex and Diode went left. Gig, however, stood his ground in the middle, well aware Tortuga had not yet left with his hold full of humans. He tore the Ferris wheel from the earth to use as a shield.

The two Solitaire clones began launching missiles at the park. The Steamers moved away from the entrance, so misses would pose no danger to the humans. Their plan was to dodge everything they could. Gig used the Ferris wheel to knock missiles from the air, but with each explosion, it became a less effective shield. He started pulling other rides from the ground, using anything he could get his hands on to deflect the enemy missiles.

Orin saw one get through, exploding right next to the park's main building. He so hoped Juna would climb aboard Tortuga and escape with the others, but he knew deep down it would never happen. Taz, Skeet and maybe even Todd would likely stay as well. His heart sunk as he watched another missile strike close by, starting a storage shed on fire.

He knew Juna was a capable warrior, but it was hard not to fear for her safety. He could only imagine what she must be going through right now.

⚙ ⚙ ⚙

The room shook, another missile landing far too close for comfort. Juna stood on a covered porch at the main entrance, watching the last of the humans pile into Tortuga's hold. Todd stood to one side, with Mike on the other, shaking his head as he watched the family business reduced to rubble.

"We are sorry, Mike. We did not think this could happen," she told him. "Go with them." She pointed to Tortuga's open hatch. "We will make everyone safe."

He turned to her, looking like he had a thousand questions, but shook his head again, silently following the last person into the safety of the hold.

"You should go too," she said, turning to Todd.

"Not a chance, Juna." He showed her a brave smile. "Right to the end, just like I promised."

Juna gave Tortuga a quick wave, so he snapped his hatch shut and took off in a cloud of dust. Skeet and Taz walked up to join her on the step.

"That's everyone," Skeet said. "What do we do now?"

"The Gate's still broken and likely to stay that way for the next hour. The General's trying to figure out a way to hold off the clones until it's fixed."

"What do we do until then?"

"I guess we try to—"

Without warning, a powerful hand slammed onto her shoulder and spun her around. It was the creepy army guy.

"That's not German you're speaking," he shouted as he flipped Juna's hat off her head, pulling her hair back to reveal her Cambrian ears.

"Who are you people?"

Taz stepped forward and pushed him away. The major reached for the gun holstered at his side, but Taz snatched it away like it was a toy.

"Have a little respect," he told the fuming officer. "She's a princess."

At that moment, a massive explosion rocked the building, starting a collapse. A large beam supporting the roof over the porch sunk towards them. Taz reached up to slow its descent, but it was too much weight, even for him. In a flash, Rayzor appeared out of nowhere, latching onto the beam and lifting it easily.

"The building is coming down," he warned in English. "Get out now!"

The group scurried out from under the collapsing structure. When they were safely away, Rayzor released the beam, then zipped out before the roof crashed to the ground, sending a plume of debris high into the air.

Juna watched the cloud drift away on a desert breeze, wondering how such a beautiful day had gone so wrong, so fast. Major Tom's shouting broke through her thoughts.

"Who are you and why are those machines out there?" he bellowed.

Before she could respond, a desperate call came over the radio.

"Juna, are you OK? The main building just came down."

Juna held up a finger in the major's face before turning to speak on the radio.

"We're fine Orin. We got out in time."

"I heard you say Orin!" the major yelled. "Is that Orin? I want to speak to him!"

Juna keyed the mike. "Your creepy army guy is here. He wants to talk."

"Put him on."

Juna handed the radio to the major, who began screaming the moment he hit the talk button.

"Orin, you will tell me who you are and what you are doing here. Right now!"

"Someday, there will be time for that," Orin replied calmly. "But not now. What I can tell you is we are your friends and mean you no harm. The same cannot be said for the four robots that stepped through that ring."

"Friends?" the major scoffed. "You've been lying to me for weeks."

"And I'm sorry about that, but right now I'm trying to help. Do you have helicopters close by that can lift ten tons?"

"Ten tons? I suppose a couple of Chinooks could do it. I have six of them at Camp Navajo. Why?"

"If you get them to coordinates 35.92 North by 111.54 West, I can send something to help with the attacking robots."

"What? I'm not worried about them. I called in an airstrike the second they showed up." The major glanced at his watch. "In about thirty seconds, every robot within ten miles of here is going to get torn in half."

"I doubt that, sir. Those machines have shields you have never encountered. Your weapons will be useless against them."

"We'll see about that," the major said, pointing at the horizon as a confident smile spread across his face.

Even over the sound of the battle, the shriek of the jets' engines was deafening. Two of them approached from the south. The major turned to Juna, a smug expression on his face.

"A-10's. Biggest gun to ever fly."

Juna had no idea what he was talking about, but she doubted that smile would last long. As the jets approached, massive guns in the nose began to fire, the onslaught of bullets so powerful, it appeared to slow the planes down.

Unfortunately for the major, all those bullets bounced harmlessly off the shields, causing nothing more than a spray of sparks. The streaking planes banked into an aggressive turn, then lined up for another pass. This time, large missiles flew from the wings of each plane. Huge fireballs flared when they hit a shield, but the machines within remained unscathed.

Without turning his gaze from the battle, Major Tom held out his hand, palm up with flexing fingers, signalling Juna to hand him something. Struggling to keep the grin off her face, Juna passed him the radio.

"Orin," he said, walking away to find a more private place to talk. "Would you mind sending those coordinates again?"

The encounter with the Earth jets had no effect on the ongoing battle. Juna watched the retreating planes disappear over the horizon, then returned her attention to the clone assault.

It was difficult for her to think of the two machines that looked like Helion as enemies, but she realized, other than their appearance, they shared nothing with the friend she loved so dearly. The Helion clones were tough to see now anyway, drawn far out into the desert to deal with Armorat and the Steamers.

A wave from Gigahertz caught Juna's eye. He signalled her to move to the far corner of the park. She rallied the others, ushering them away from the heat of the battle. Rayzor served as their escort, now staying with the group to keep them safe from stray missiles.

Gigahertz was now the only other Mech still inside the park. Vortex and Diode had moved to flanking positions, drawing missile fire from the two Solitaires, and dodging the ones that came their way.

It was a risky strategy, and not an entirely successful one. SIMs hung from all three Hydros. Their shields held, but Juna had no idea how many more hits they could take before failing.

She noticed the Solitaire clone closest to Gigahertz had lowered its arm, reaching for a cartridge attached to its leg. It appeared to be reloading.

In a blur of blue-trimmed titanium, Gig was in motion. He grabbed the enormous boat from the boat ride and charged at the doomed machine. Juna knew the clones couldn't think. They were remote-controlled drones, operated through a radio by someone on Cambria.

By the time this Solitaire's operator directed its camera towards Gig's attack, it was already too late. The boat struck it like a battering ram, sending it sprawling to the ground. Gig pounced on top and swung his massive fists, crashing them into the toppled clone. Sparks flew as shield met shield, but damage was done with each powerful blow. Soon flames spewed from the downed machine, and its attempts to fight back were over.

Gig looked up to see the second Solitaire clone sprinting towards him, cannons raised to fire. But before it got off a single shot, a diving Vortex tripped it up, sending it skidding through the sand. It continued to slide, coming to a stop right next to a waiting Gigahertz. He reached back to retrieve the boat and used it as a club, smashing the clone until it was flat.

Juna realized they were machines, but somehow, the Hydros looked exhausted. Rising slowly to their feet, they dropped their shields for a moment, so the spent SIMS could drop to the ground. They looked to the south, watching their friends trudge back towards the park, away from two piles of debris that had once been Helion clones.

While the Hydros had wrestled with the Solitaires, a similar battle must have unfolded, further out in the desert, between the Steamers and the Helion clones. Juna was glad she didn't have to witness the demise of her friend's twins.

The Mechs assembled near the site of the battle. Rayzor and Gecko went out to join them, the two smallest Mechs dwarfed by their exhausted friends. Gigahertz tore a leg off one of the downed Solitaire clones. He swung it like a club, checking its weight and balance to see if it might be a useful weapon when the next batch of clones showed up.

Juna's body froze, horrified by that thought. She didn't know exactly how much time had passed since the last portal opened, but it must have been close to half an hour. It was hard to believe that in the next few minutes, a Gate would appear, and four fully armed clones would step through to start the process all over. Judging from the condition of the Mechs standing before her, another victory appeared doubtful.

"When am I going to get some answers?"

Juna glanced to her right, seeing Major Tom now stood beside her, holding out the radio.

After grabbing the device, she turned back to face the scrum of Mechs.

"I am not best to ask," she said awkwardly. "My English is bad and I have been here not long."

"Where have you been?"

Juna paused a moment, still focusing her gaze on the Mechs.

"Elsewhere."

"Another planet?"

She paused again, knowing full well their secret was out. Nothing could explain away what this man had seen.

"Yes."

The major had clearly expected the answer, but it still seemed to rattle him. He moved away from her, walking in circles while muttering to himself. When he appeared composed enough to resume the conversation, he returned, only to find Todd blocking his path.

"Why don't you leave them alone? They don't want to hurt anyone."

The major looked right, then left, gesturing towards the debris riddled field.

"I'm looking at a lot of damage here, son. Are you telling me someone couldn't have been hurt during this?"

"It's not their fault. Her dad's the evil one."

"The princess's evil father? So, what are we talking about here? Some diabolical space king?" He stomped in a circle, then poked his finger in Todd's face. "That's what we're mixed up in now?"

"I guess, sort of."

"I'm assuming you're from around here, young man. That means you're already in a heap of trouble. You knew a bunch of aliens were roaming around this planet, and—"

"Stop!"

Juna stepped in front of Todd and stared directly into the major's eyes. "Todd is good. He did no wrong." She jabbed a finger into the man's chest to emphasize the point. "No bad must come to him." She took a deep breath to calm her nerves.

"I will answer your questions."

The major stepped back, partly due to tensions getting high, but also because Taz had moved to Juna's side.

"Listen, I don't want to be a jerk here. If this is a first-ever interstellar meeting of some kind, I don't want you thinking Earth people are hard to deal with, but I need to know where we stand." The officer paused a moment to collect his thoughts. Taking off his cap, he rubbed the sweat from his brow before returning it to his head.

"Did I just witness some monumental climactic battle?" he asked. "Is this thing over?"

"No."

"So, they'll send more of those things?" He pointed at the circle of Mechs.

"Yes."

"When?"

Juna directed her gaze to where the Gate first appeared.

"Very soon."

"Are you going to win again?"

Juna turned to face him, failing to hold back a look of despair.

"I don't know."

"Look!" Todd pointed to a cloud of colourful sparks hovering in the desert. "They're coming back!"

Juna looked to the group of Mechs, standing perfectly still, no doubt pouring all their resources into charging their shields. When the Gate appeared, they moved towards it, taking positions off to the side, so they could attack from behind when the clones stepped through.

Juna gasped when the swirls disappeared, the image at the Gate's centre now revealing a terrifying sight. Four Gigahertz clones, equipped with cannons, were ready to step out onto the desert sand. Juna's shoulders sagged, the feeling of hopelessness too much to bear.

Just then, her attention was drawn to a strange sound in the distance. The *whup-whup-whup* grew steadily louder until it filled the air in every direction. She turned to her left to see six huge flying machines, each with two spinning rotors on top.

They flew in pairs. Between each set, cables hung, forming a "V" shape below them. Something large dangled at the bottom of each. As they drew closer, Juna recognized the familiar outline of the objects they carried.

The corners of her mouth drifted slowly upward.

*Perhaps all hope was not lost after all.*

The Diesels were coming.

# 21

Orin had never been more terrified. A hundred plunges down the side of a cliff in the arms of an Atomic, would have been far less scary than doing this just once.

Held between Carnage's massive fingers, his feet dangled a thousand feet above the ground. Looking down made him queasy, so he directed his gaze skyward. Unfortunately, things didn't look much better up there.

Carnage was suspended between two huge helicopters by cables that seemed far too thin for the job. The flying machines were so large, it seemed impossible they could lift themselves off the ground, let alone do it with a ten ton Mech hanging between them. Looking to his left, he saw Havoc and Mayhem, similarly hung between helicopters of their own. It seemed a miracle the whole procession wasn't a smouldering heap in the desert sands below.

To add to the horror, the assault on his senses was unlike anything he'd ever endured. Four massive rotors, two on each chopper, created a noise that hurt, and a blistering wind that tested even a Mech's powerful grip. But Carnage held tight, Orin in his right hand, and the Disruptor in his left. Ten minutes into the flight, they pushed hard for the scene of the battle.

As they drew near, Orin could see the brawl underway. The combatants looked so tiny from this height, sparks flying with each blow as the mighty machines clashed. He was encouraged to see them fighting hand-to-hand. If the Mechs stayed close, it would help negate the clones' advantage of having missiles onboard.

More of the battle came into detail as the helicopters began their descent. Orin now saw all four enemy machines were clones of Gigahertz. Spotting the real one was easy enough. It wasn't because he knew the fine details of his friend so well, but because four of them had cannons, while the fifth swung a Solitaire leg like a madman.

As they swept down over the battlefield, Orin's heart sunk, seeing the Steamers engaged with two of the clones. Torque had a grip on one of them, but the other had separated from its foes and launched a torrent of missiles. Spanner staggered, his shields littered with SIMs, while Clank was already down, cut in half and lying in a heap in the sand.

Then, a blinding flash set Orin's world on fire, the heat so close, he felt his skin tingle. Stunned by the sound and fury, it took him a moment to realize what had happened.

Carnage's shoulder-mounted cannons had fired a barrage of missiles at the clone fighting Spanner, and they had streaked right over Orin's head on the way to their target. Looking to his left, he saw Havoc and Mayhem had done the same. It took only seconds for the clone to succumb to the assault and shatter into a thousand pieces. Orin let out a whoop when the clone disintegrated, but he feared for the fate of Clank and Spanner.

The wash from the rotors surged, and the thunderous sound grew louder as Carnage's feet touched the ground. A massive metal hand placed Orin gingerly on the sand, while the other passed him the Disruptor.

"Thanks for the ride, Carnage," Orin yelled over the pounding rotors. "I'm sure glad you have a good grip."

"My pleasure. But if you will excuse me, I have damage to do." He reached down to unclip the large hooks attaching him to the cables, then charged towards Torque. He released a savage war cry as he ran.

Torque grappled with his opponent, meaning Carnage couldn't use missiles for fear of hitting his friend. The chopper had dropped him close to the action, so he joined the fray after only a few strides.

Torque already had a grip on the upper half of the clone, allowing Carnage to reach down and lift its feet off the ground, suspending it in the air, unable to move.

They began a mighty tug-of-war that soon saw the clone's legs ripped from its body. The bottom of its torso dropped to the ground with a thud. Carnage flung the legs aside, then grabbed one of the clone's arms, while Torque took the other. The two Mechs tugged again, quickly removing the last of the clone's limbs, then used them to pound their opponent flat.

They celebrated the victory with a clanging high-five before looking around for something else to pulverize. It was when Orin heard the two friends' hands clank together that he realized the helicopters were gone. They had delivered their payloads to the battlefield, then retreated beyond the horizon. Havoc and Mayhem were gone too, having dashed off to help the Hydros deal with the other two clones.

Orin was so focused on the battle, he failed to notice Gecko skidding to a stop until he was hit with a spray of gravel.

"Hey Orin, can I give you a lift?"

"Absolutely," Orin said, grabbing the Disruptor and climbing into Gecko's front seat. "I have to find Gig."

As soon as the hatch closed, Gecko was off, sending a geyser of sand high into the air. Orin scanned the area through the windshield, hoping to catch sight of the action. There was a scrum to his left, so he directed Gecko to head over for a look.

They arrived in time to see Vortex, Diode, Havoc and Mayhem mobbing a Gigahertz clone, tearing its cannons off in a shower of sparks. The clone was now defenceless in a hand-to-hand battle with four highly motivated Mechs. The encounter lasted only seconds, as Havoc and Mayhem gripped the enemy machine, tore it in half and stomped the pieces into the ground.

"There's only one left!" Orin's cheer echoed through Gecko's hold. "Go find Gig."

"Do not worry. I will have you there shortly."

Gecko took off like a shot, arriving quickly at the site of Gig's one-on-one fight with his twin. The clone was trying to get away so it could make use of its missiles, but Gig's pursuit was relentless, swinging the Solitaire leg like a broadsword. The clone's operator decided to retreat, trying to increase the space between them. As soon as it turned, Gig used his weapon to sweep the legs out from under it, sending the towering machine sprawling.

When it hit the ground, Gig lunged and grabbed it by the feet. With his grip secured, he began to spin, so fast Orin got dizzy just watching. When he gained enough speed, Gig let go, launching the machine in a sweeping arc through the sky. By this point, all three Diesels had made their way to the site of the final battle, and were there waiting when the doomed machine landed. Ripping and tearing, it took only seconds to reduce the last of the invaders to a pile of scrap.

Relieved the last of the clones was down, Orin wanted nothing more than to congratulate Gig and the Diesels on the victory, but his thoughts returned to Clank and Spanner.

He wrapped on Gecko's dashboard. "Find the Steamers and take me there!" he ordered.

By the time they arrived, a crowd had gathered. Orin was delighted to see Juna, Skeet, Taz and Todd were there, but was far less happy to see Major Tom with them. As he climbed down from Gecko's hold, his friends rushed to greet him. He received a wonderful hug from Juna and a slap on the back from Todd.

“Whoa man, you got here just in time. We were getting our butts kicked until you showed up with those choppers.”

“I wish it could have been sooner.” Orin felt numb, seeing what the battle had done to the Steamers. Clank was in two pieces, and Spanner’s right leg was bent at such a severe angle, Torque had to hold him up.

“Will Clank be OK?”

“I think so,” Juna replied. “Let’s go say hi.”

Clank was already chatting by the time they arrived.

“Ah, Orin, maybe you can help with this. I am having some difficulty moving my legs. I issue the appropriate commands, and I can see them right over there,” he said, pointing to the other half of his body twenty feet away. “But for some reason, I can’t get them to move.”

“I think I see the problem, Clank.” Orin chuckled, now realizing his mechanical friend would be fine. “And I’m pretty sure it’s something we can fix once we get you back to the shop.”

“Great news, Orin. I knew you were the right man for the job.”

“And what job might that be?” Major Tom had walked up to join the group. “What are you planning now?”

“We’re not planning anything,” Orin snapped. “All we want is to keep people safe. I wish you could see that.”

“What I *can* see, young man, is a bunch of talking robots, shooting missiles and blowing stuff up.” He extended his arms to highlight the devastation. “There’s no traffic out here now, but what if someone saw this? What if a video turns up on the internet?”

Orin did feel bad for the man. He was just doing his job, after all. By coming to Earth, the Cambrians had inadvertently put this planet in grave danger, and that certainly wasn’t the major’s fault. Orin tried to think up a decent apology, but was interrupted by a squawk on the radio.

"The detector picked up another portal opening," Diara's voice warned. "Same spot as the last one."

"Let's see if I can stop it," Orin said, clapping his hands together.

As he started off towards Gecko, a heavy hand dropped onto his shoulder, spinning him around.

"You're not going anywhere until I get some answers," Major Tom said, wagging a finger in Orin's face.

"Listen, Major. I might be able to stop these attacks from ever happening again. You can come if you want, but I *am* leaving."

At that moment, Taz stepped forward, directing a menacing glare at the officer.

"What he said."

The major returned the glare, but released his grip on Orin's shoulder. Orin raced to Gecko, then zipped through his open hatch with Juna right on his heels. The major approached as well, but not quickly enough for Orin's liking.

"If you're coming, hurry up. We don't have much time."

As soon as they were aboard, Gecko slammed his hatch shut and bolted for the portal. The burst of coloured sparks was right where they'd expected. Orin picked up his Disruptor, pointed the dish out Gecko's window and brought his invention to life.

Nothing happened. The device was set to its lowest frequency, so he slowly turned the knob on the side of the unit. As it passed the halfway point, he started to worry. When it neared its maximum, he began to panic, knowing at any second, the Gate could appear and it would be too late.

Then the scene out the window changed. The flashes of light flared more brilliantly, the air appearing to catch fire. But each explosion of colour winked out of existence as it burst. Soon the sparkly display that preceded the arrival of a Gate, vanished before their eyes.

"It works!" Orin exclaimed, jumping so high he hit his head on the ceiling. It was a bit embarrassing, particularly with Juna there to see, but he didn't care.

*His invention worked!*

It could put an end to any future battles with the clones. Turning, he saw Juna's smile was as wide as his own. He wrapped her up in a hug.

"I don't get it. What happened here?" the major demanded, completely ruining their moment. "What does this mean?"

"It means… we can keep your people safe."

⚙ ⚙ ⚙

"I'm sorry about your park, Mike."

Orin stood next to his human friend, in what was once the "Robots on the Rim" amusement park. "We didn't think this could ever happen."

Three days had passed since the epic battle took place on this site. Clank was again in one piece, still as chatty as ever, happily recounting his ordeal with anyone who would listen. Spanner was walking again too, now sporting a mismatched leg taken from one of the defeated Gigahertz clones. Here on Earth, however, little progress had been made on cleaning up the mess.

"It's all good, Orin. All good," Mike replied, looping an arm around Orin's shoulder. "The government owns this place now. Paid top dollar, too. They were even nice enough to let me drop by today to pick up any stuff I left behind." He swept his gaze across the ruined park. "But it's all flatter than a worn nickel, so I don't expect to find much."

"They let us come today, too. So we could say goodbye."

"Goin' back to your own planet, huh?" Mike laughed and shook his head. "If that don't beat all. Actual aliens. The government's payin' me a pretty penny to keep that a secret, too. I always knew there was somethin' funny about y'all, but I never woulda guessed that."

"I'm sorry we had to lie. You were a good friend to us, so you deserved better. I am pleased you will be OK."

"OK? I'm gonna be doin' a whole lot better than OK. What with the best summer we ever had, sellin' this place for more than it's worth, and all that alien hush money, I am sittin' pretty. I'll be spendin' my days fishin' crystal clear waters, with sand in my toes, and slurpin' fruity drinks with little umbrellas in 'em."

Orin was never completely sure what Mike was talking about, but he was glad things turned out well for his friend. He shook the man's hand, then pulled him in for a hug.

"Thanks for everything, Mike. I will miss you."

"I'll miss you too, Orin," he said as he turned to leave. "And don't fret about the park. I can't picture how things coulda turned out any better."

Orin felt good as he watched Mike walk away. Coming today, he had worried Mike would be angry about his park getting squashed. It was a pleasant surprise to hear he was actually happy about it.

"Is that it, or is there something else you wanted to do here today?"

Orin turned to see Major Tom, his constant companion for the past three days, had stepped up to replace Mike by his side.

"I need to say goodbye to Todd. Then we can go."

Fortunately, no video of the battle ever turned up on the internet. Major Tom still didn't like the idea of aliens running around on his planet, so he was keeping them on a short leash.

Originally, he'd planned to round them up and take them to a secret facility in New Mexico, but Orin had seen enough movies to know what a bad idea that was. The major didn't take the refusal well, but when Gig dropped by to explain what would happen to anyone trying to take his friends away, he saw the light and abandoned the idea.

What he did do was shut down the highway, cordon off a ten square mile area around the park with stories of a chemical spill, and keep the Cambrians tucked away in their cave until he was sure they were gone and never coming back.

That's when the negotiations began. The major wanted them gone, but he also wanted to hold on to as much of their technology as he could. Orin, the Cambrians' chief negotiator, agreed to leave the planet as soon as possible, taking into account the unpredictable nature of the Gate. In exchange for keeping them safe and secluded in the meantime, the major got to keep the abandoned bodies of the eight clones destroyed during the battle.

"And I want that thing," he had said, pointing to the Disruptor. "I'm pretty sure we'll need it to keep the evil space king away after you leave."

Much to the Professor's dismay, Orin had agreed. The Professor argued that leaving the Disruptor behind would give the humans a hundred year head start on figuring out how to build a Gate of their own.

"I don't see the problem," the General had said. "They seem like nice enough folks. What's the harm in them popping around the galaxy a little earlier than expected?"

Orin suppressed a laugh, thinking about the look on his dad's face after that comment. Fortunately, the Disruptor hadn't been required since the day of the battle. The emperor had tried three more times to open a portal after the fight with the Gigahertz clones, but Orin shut them all down before they got started. Since then, further attempts had not been made.

The Disruptor currently sat in one of the US Army's fastest

helicopters, right outside the park's fence, waiting for word a portal was imminent. Orin doubted there would ever be another attempt. The emperor surely realized there was nothing to gain by bringing another planet into their conflict, particularly one with the military firepower of Earth.

"Well, go find your friend then," the major said, snapping Orin out of his daydream. "I have this contained for now, but I don't like it when any of you are away from that cave."

Orin spotted Todd and Juna sitting at a picnic table that had miraculously survived the battle. Walking over, he sat down on the bench next to Todd.

"Hey, Orin. I was telling Juna how it makes way more sense for you guys to stay here." It appeared Todd hadn't slept much in the last couple of days and his eyes looked teary. "I mean, Juna's dad sounds like a total psycho. Why would you want to mess with him? On Earth, you'd be the biggest celebrities we've ever had. You could have an amazing life here."

Orin smiled at his friend, resting a hand on his shoulder. "I will miss you, Todd. Thank you for all your help. We could not have survived here without you."

"This whole thing started with you guys saving my life, so I guess we're even."

"So, what will you do now that the park is gone?"

"There's still a ton of money in our bank account, so I suppose I'm rich now. I'll find some way to have fun with it."

"I hope you do," Orin said as he stood to leave. "Have a wonderful life, my friend."

"I can't believe I'm never going to see you guys again." Todd's voice cracked, struggling to hold in his emotions. "I'm definitely going to need something to remember you by," he said, reaching into his pocket to pull out his cell phone.

"OK, bring it in."

The three of them squeezed together until they all appeared on the tiny screen. "And lose the hats. I want a good look at those ears."

They all smiled as Todd took the photo. When it was done, they shared a group hug and Orin turned to go.

"Hey Orin," Todd said, reaching out to grab his arm. "You know about this crazy 'Owangatuu' thing, where Juna thinks she needs to fix the whole world by herself." He looked at Orin, his eyes pleading. "Promise me you'll help her enjoy her life, too."

Orin looked into Juna's eyes, and they exchanged a smile.

"I promise."

Orin walked away, so Todd and Juna could say their goodbyes. As he stood back watching, his thoughts drifted to what lay ahead. He had enjoyed his time on Earth, and felt confident the humans were now safe from the emperor, so it was time to get back to the original mission. The hods still needed help, as did the Marans. Not knowing exactly what Operation Massive Hammer was all about certainly complicated the issue, but they would deal with that when the time came. He had no idea what the future held, but he knew it wouldn't be boring.

He watched as Juna kissed Todd goodbye—the civilized way, twice on each cheek like normal people do—then walk slowly towards him. She grabbed both his hands and rested her forehead on his. Orin felt at peace, thinking about all they had been through together, and all that was yet to come. As he stood there, wishing the moment could last forever, Juna gave his hands a squeeze, released a long sigh, and uttered those three little words he had waited to hear for so long.

"Let's go home."

# Acknowledgements

First up, I'd like to thank my son, Jason, for starting me on this path with his question: "Does your game need a back story?" and for his amazing artwork on the covers. To my wife, Martelle, thank you for help in ways too numerous to count, including love, support, reassurance, and being my chief alpha, beta and even gamma (assuming that's a thing) reader.

I would never have reached the conclusion of my Mech Trilogy journey without some help along the way. From the beta readers who stuck with me to the end, providing much-needed advice and criticism, to those who offered assistance or encouragement just when I needed it most. I would like to express my endless gratitude to Acacia Scabar, Rae-Lynne Byerley, Johann Preller, Taija Morgan, Yuri Duraan, Brett Salter, Bob and Kathryn Worthingham, Richard Jones and Dawn Mecaj.

# About The Author

Ken Deeprose is a retired engineer, board game designer and author of the critically acclaimed *Mech Trilogy*. As a lifelong fan of science fiction, he's enjoying the opportunity to launch the next generation of young readers down the same path. He lives in Calgary, Alberta with his amazing wife, teenage son, a cat, a dog and a pond full of fish.

# Want More MECH?

Follow Ken Deeprose on:

GOODREADS.COM

Or Visit:

MECHtheBook.com

→ News and Updates

→ Blurbs and Reviews
(You can even leave your own!)

→ MECH Artwork

Manufactured by Amazon.ca
Acheson, AB

13329488R00146